S0-BXB-679

THE AESTHETICS OF
PIANOFORTE-PLAYING

Da Capo Press Music Reprint Series

GENERAL EDITOR

FREDERICK FREEDMAN

VASSAR COLLEGE

THE AESTHETICS OF
PIANOFORTE-PLAYING

By Adolph Kullak

Translated by Theodore Baker

DA CAPO PRESS • NEW YORK • 1972

Library of Congress Cataloging in Publication Data

Kullak, Adolf, 1823-1862.
   The aesthetics of pianoforte-playing.

   (Da Capo Press music reprint series)
   Reprint of the 1893 ed.
   Translation of Die Asthetik des Klavierspiels.
   1. Piano music—Interpretation (Phrasing, dynamics,
etc.) I. Title.
MT235.K842 1972   786.3   69-16652
ISBN 0-306-71095-1

This Da Capo Press edition of *The Aesthetics of
Pianoforte-Playing* is an unabridged republication
of the 1893 translation, published in New York,
of the 1889 third German edition edited by Hans Bischoff.

Published by Da Capo Press, Inc.
A Subsidiary of Plenum Publishing Corporation
227 West 17th Street, New York, New York 10011

All Rights Reserved

Manufactured in the United States of America

THE AESTHETICS OF
PIANOFORTE-PLAYING

AUGUSTANA LIBRARY
UNIVERSITY OF ALBERTA

THE
ÆSTHETICS OF PIANOFORTE-PLAYING

BY

Dr. ADOLPH KULLAK.

TRANSLATED BY

Dr. TH. BAKER

ROM THE THIRD GERMAN EDITION, REVISED AND EDITED BY

Dr. HANS BISCHOFF.

NEW YORK: G. SCHIRMER
35 UNION SQUARE.

COPYRIGHT, 1893, BY G. SCHIRMER.

PREFACE TO THE SECOND EDITION.

It has afforded me the liveliest satisfaction, that my deceased brother's work, The Æsthetics of Pianoforte-playing, a monument of a mind earnest and fruitful in art and science alike, should have proved its vitality so decisively, that a new edition has become necessary. Unhappily, my already almost overwhelming duties awakened the doubt in my mind, that I should hardly be able to undertake the editing of the same with undivided energies; for it was evident that the needful additions and a possible remodelling of the work would require no inconsiderable amount of labor. I therefore entrusted the revision to my pupil, Mr. Hans Bischoff, whose abilities as an artist, supported by his special course of academic study, rendered him competent to carry it out. This work being for me, however, not only an eminent scientifico-artistic product, but also a dear personal inheritance, I have at least been in regular communication with Dr. Bischoff concerning the way in which the revision should be carried out, and have thus gained the conviction, that the newly-added articles are in close touch with the spirit of the work as a whole, and further, that occasional deviations from the original form probably increase the value of the book. May the work in its new shape continually win new friends, and through its stimulating influence on pianoforte-playing and instruction preserve the memory of a musician, too early snatched from art, among the rising generation.

BERLIN, 1876.

Theodor Kullak.

EDITOR'S PREFACE TO THE SECOND EDITION.

Pianoforte-playing now stands on the summit of a completed evolution. Its technical possibilities are exhausted. Thanks to a method developed with ever-increasing thoroughness, brilliant execution has become quite common even in dilettante circles. The reproductive genius of a Liszt, a Bülow, a Rubinstein, and a Tausig, have constrained the coy instrument to divulge all the secrets of its musical capacity. And as regards pianoforte literature, its latest augmentations are not calculated to impede our view over the field to be surveyed. The main current of musical development is at present setting strongly towards a point on or beyond the circumscribed bounds of pianoforte-playing. All the freer, however, is the development allowed by the present epoch to scientific method and æsthetic criticism; for these chiefly require a survey, undisturbed by the stress and striving of the present, over the material ready to hand.

It is the aim of "The Æsthetics of Pianoforte-playing" to treat of our art exhaustively both from a philosophical and pedagogical point of view. It does not behoove me to comment, in this place, either on the happiness of the idea or on the success attending its execution. The work may speak for itself; it has already stood the ordeal of fire. Only one point I will emphasize, herein anticipating the reader's judgment, in order to set in the proper light the principles which guided me in the revision of the work. Its essential quality is far more that of an ingenious method for pianoforte-playing than of pure philosophical reflection. Had it been merely the author's intention, taking a limited province of art as his point of departure, to reach definitions of the Beautiful unattainable through abstract deduction, so careful an examination of technical details would have been superfluous. Moreover, a scientific settlement of the most important question in musical æsthetics — concerning any psychic factors observable in musical art — has not been attempted here at all. Consequently certain portions of the Part on Rendering make the impression of suggestive aphorisms, rather than of members of a firmly-knit system.

I have therefore regarded this work, on the whole, as a text-book. Its originality lies in shifting the point of view in such a way, that it does not aim at increasing the mechanical skill through examples for practice, but endeavors to supply an intellectual basis for the player's productive art by equally comprehending technique and interpretation, while continually referring to the laws forming the foundation in part of the universal science of art, and of the philosophy of music in particular.

I shall therefore not be accused of arbitrary self-assertion because I strove, in the new edition, to avoid philosophical disquisitions having no direct bearing on the subject, and also to reduce the necessary æsthetic explanations to narrower limits. The most popular style possible is indispensable in such a text-book.

Other alterations which the work has undergone are in part changes in form, in part additions of new matter. With regard to the first, the need of more exact expression and more definite arrangement occasioned abbreviations and re-modellings of greater or less importance. The discriminating reader who compares the two editions, will perceive the reason for the same and, as I trust, find them justifiable. Various chapters, particularly those relating to the rendering, have thus taken on an essentially new physiognomy. The selection of examples in notes given therein is also partially altered.

My own independent work in the "Æsthetics of Pianoforte-playing" is found partly in the continuation of the two historical chapters (Chap. 2 and 3), and is partly connected with technical specialties, which, though practiced at the author's time, were then not ripe for systematization. To these belong the legato with hand and arm (Chapter 7), and yet another branch of arm-technique discussed in Chapter 9. I have rewritten the method for octave-playing, for the sake of systematization, in agreement with the teachings of Th. Kullak. Further, the eleventh chapter and, with the exception of the closing remarks on improvisation, the first, are entirely my work. The influence of Ad. Kullak on these sections is of an indirect nature.

I am well aware, that I have assumed a weighty responsibility in offering to the public a work of proved quality in an essentially new form. I am encouraged to do so only by the consciousness, that I have been guided in all work relating to the same by sincere respect for the thoroughly solid inner worth of a treatise, to which I owe many most happy suggestions. Nothing could afford me greater pleasure than to have succeeded in contributing slightly to its most far-reaching efficiency.

To Prof. Th. Kullak, my revered teacher, my warmest thanks are due for the friendly counsels with which he has assisted me during the revision of this edition.

May, 1876.

Hans Bischoff.

PREFACE TO THE THIRD EDITION.

In the present edition the "Æsthetics of Pianoforte-playing" again appears in somewhat altered guise. The revised form in which I published the second edition has been, it is true, retained on the whole. But numerous additions were needed. Several new literary publications demanded notice, even if nothing more than a slight sketch. In pianoforte technique or interpretation many remarkable attempts required to be briefly summed up. Some few points which I formerly held to be important no longer appeared sufficiently so to retain their place in this work, in consideration of the tendency of the same. An excuse is perhaps necessary for my non-continuation of the history of pianoforte virtuosity. But I could not feel it to be appropriate, that a work, whose permanent value it was my endeavor to increase, should occupy itself with questions of the day and of fashions which to-morrow may be without interest. Far rather would I have given room, in the second chapter, to modern pianoforte literature, with its many characteristic phenomena. But it was repugnant to me to pass final judgment, as it were, upon authors still in the full tide of creative enjoyment.

In passing I observe, that numerous changes in style have been made, and that the first chapter, which was essentially from my pen, has been partially revised.

April, 1889.

Hans Bischoff.

ADDITIONS AND CORRECTIONS.

Full translations follow of German titles on

p. 36, fourth line from below: "Method for Clavier-players, explaining Bach's Fingering, the Graces, and the Rendering".

p. 37. line 14: "Essay on the true Method of playing the Clavier".

p. 40, line 8: "Method for Clavier-playing, devised in accordance with the elegant Practice of the present Time".

p. 40, line 8 from below: "Clavier Method, or Instruction in Clavier-playing".

p. 60, line 8 from below: "Clavier Method".

p. 61, line 20: "Detailed theoretico-practical Instruction in Pianoforte-playing, from the first Elementary Teaching to the most complete Development".

On page 49, No. 10, the term *Bebung* should be rendered by *balancement,* not *vibrato.* — The effect described by the Author *can be obtained* on modern pianofortes having a sensitive Erard action, and the sustained, singing tone thus produced is extremely effective in many situations. The vibration of the key must be very short and rapid, the finger never leaving the key, nor letting the same rise to its usual level. Perfect looseness and delicacy of touch cannot be more strikingly displayed than in this effect.

TABLE OF CONTENTS.

PART I.

The Idea in General.

CHAPTER I.

Importance and peculiarities of the Pianoforte.

The artistic value of an instrument, and the limits within which it can satisfy musical requirements, depend upon its tone and the manner of its treatment. To present exhaustively the entire realm of the beautiful in music is within the power neither of song nor of any single instrument. True, the former is the original source of all musical conception and emotion to such a degree, that instrumental music, too, is essentially based upon it. But the artistic imagination, were it to renounce all agencies of outward manifestation but the human voice, would feel constrained. It demands more in compass, volume, and celerity than the voice can give. Above all, it demands greater variety of timbre.

Thus there is a double necessity for extending the boundary of musical art beyond the domain of vocal music. First, instruments must supply what the voice lacks in range, volume, and variety of figuration. Second, each instrument must make its individual timbre felt in a characteristic manner.

Although this latter condition opens a perspective of endless variety in beautiful effects, precisely those organs, which by reason of their manifold nuances in tone most completely satisfy the craving of a soul striving for musical ex-

1

pression, labor under one serious deficiency; the principle by which their tones are formed renders it impossible for the single artist to produce, without assistance from others, an artistic performance complete in itself.

It is this last circumstance which, despite all imperfections in the tone of keyed instruments, insures their decided predominance. Among these latter the pianoforte is that best adapted to satisfy the artistic sense within wider limits. For the dedication of the organ to religious worship impresses upon its whole literature the stamp of religious consecration, and it therefore appeals to but one side of the emotional life. Neither does the imagination find full gratification in the heaviness of nuance proper to the organ-tone. The pianoforte at least permits of a swell and decrease in successions of tones. Further, there is not the slightest reason for binding pianoforte literature to any exclusive style.

The pianoforte owes its cosmopolitan popularity above all to the convenient operation of its mechanism. The handy arrangement of the key-board enables the player to add an harmonic basis to the melody, and to reproduce the polyphonic interweaving of the parts unassisted. It consequently permits him to exhibit his individuality with complete independence.

The pianoforte thus became early the organ of musical conversational speech. It was the favorite instrument of composers at a time when its tone was still quite undeveloped, and the dissatisfied choice wavered between the harpsichord, with its incapability of nuance, and the more impressionable, but weak-toned, clavichord. We feel no surprise that Couperin and Scarlatti wrote for the clavier. Their compositions are adapted not only to the mechanism, but also to the timbre, of the instruments at their command. But even Bach and Händel did not despise them; the grandeur of their ideas produced the effect even in this miniature form, which quite failed to gratify the demand for a full and singing tone. The advantage of convenience in the clavier outweighed the objections to its tone. Centuries of endeavor in the art of instrument-building have now, indeed, developed the tone of the pianoforte to a perfection which it cannot overstep. But the inherent defect of its production by percussion, bars its advance to that modulatory fulness which the human soul requires when it would utter its emotions in tones.

True, the tone, once struck, continues to sound, but only in a comparatively weak degree. It is impossible to produce a subsequent swell. The tone is therefore dry in comparison with that of the bowed and wind instruments. While these incline more to a voluptuous fulness, the pianoforte tone retains an abstract quality.

But precisely this abstract quality has its peculiar advantages, when the unconditional serviceability of the tone in every mood to be expressed comes in question, and the sound shall appear coequal with the manner of treating the mechanism. The more decidedly the individuality of a medium favors the expression of special sentiments, the more will it tend to exclude other phases of expression. Thus the trumpet is one-sided in its power, the flute in its suavity.

The pianoforte tone is as good as free from a positive individuality. If it is not absolutely so, this is due to the fact, that its production by a blow of the hammer is always rendered observable by certain peculiarities in sound to be discussed later. With vocal music it has little more in common than the mathematical relation of pitch. It hardly inclines to the expression of any particular mood, and is therefore excluded from none. The pianoforte tone is thus, in a measure, objectively neutral. Though lacking the suavity of the flute, it is nevertheless so delicate, that an idea intended for the former does not suffer by transcription for the pianoforte. Though not possessing the power of the trumpet, its volume, provided full harmonies are taken, satisfies all requirements. It entirely lacks the flexibility of the human voice; yet skillful treatment lends it sufficient fulness and tenderness, happily to interpret even a vocal strain.

In any event we must not forget, that the pianoforte tone,

apparently so uniform in timbre, becomes capable of most manifold effects when seconded by an appropriate style of writing and touch. Just this intermediate station which it holds between the various shades of timbre and expression, renders it adapted for expressing any mood. One might almost say, that the orchestra can express every phase of emotion by its inclusion of all individualisms of tone, whereas the pianoforte attains the same end by their exclusion.

It follows from the above, that the tone of our instrument allows perfect freedom of choice in the style of compositions intended for it. Every species of composition, every phase of sentiment, is worthily represented in pianoforte literature. As we have seen, the mechanical preconditions furnish an excellent basis for this universality. It is therefore natural, that orchestral works and the like can be effectively transcribed for the pianoforte. Though the original splendor of tone-color is lost, such arrangements still have for the friend of art much the same *raison d'être* as a photograph of a painting. For the popularization of music they are indispensable. True, they have absolute value only in the hands of a performer who, in contrast with the mutual dependence of the members of an ensemble, employs in an artistic manner his opportunity for freer interpretation.

It was intimated above, that the colorlessness of the pianoforte tone is, in point of fact, only relative. Colorless it is indeed, in comparison with the voluptuous tone of bowed and wind instruments. But on the other hand it is natural, that the tone should receive a certain type from its production by percussion. The pianoforte-making art endeavors, it is true, to thrust this characteristic as far as possible into the background, through the felting of the hammer-heads, in order to give the tone that capacity for universal expression referred to above. But its neutrality is, after all, not so complete, that it does not favor certain nuances of tone and sentiment.

An essential attribute of the pianoforte tone is gracefulness. This is due to the fact, that its fulness satisfies the musical necessity, without, however, making its materiality felt in the same sense as do the instruments having a sustained, singing tone. The deftly dancing tone accomodates itself to every style of touch. Even the striving after vocal and orchestral effects by no means precludes its use. Its effect is most lovely in pearling passages, whose sensuous charm forms one of the chief attractions of the pianoforte.

Further, the shortness of the pianoforte tone is more favorable to sharp characterization than to sentimental expression. For the pianist there is no more difficult, but at the same time more delightful, task than to draw from the coy instrument a sweet-toned song. Far more readily rewarded is his striving to attain an accentuation not only precise, but full of significance. The necessity for exact rhythm is an inherent property of the pianoforte style. The mere mutual dependence of the two hands, and the continual consideration of at least two independent parts, promote this requirement. The circumstance, that the tone when once struck admits of no further development stimulative to the ear or the emotions, forbids many rhythmical licences for which a singer would hardly be censured.

Having discovered in the pianoforte tone, despite the neutrality chiefly prominent, a preference for certain shades of euphony and expression, we must now consider, how far the mechanism of the pianoforte and the plan of its keyboard favor certain styles of composition, though not confined to any one in particular. The earliest attempts to write for the clavier were based on strict part-writing. Then appears the principle of two parts, as more appropriate to the instrument. Finally the passage is evolved, developing later a manifold diversity of form such as no other instrument can show.

Brilliancy is characteristic of the pianoforte style proper. The sensuous charm of the same, and the importance of personal dexterity, made the pianoforte for a time an arena for jugglers with effect. Now-a-days, of course, the sole value of virtuosity lies in carrying out the artistic intention.

At all times a close bond of affinity has subsisted between the clavier-maker's art and the style of clavier compositions and playing. The thin tone of the old French harpsichords engendered the agréments, which gave the tone more emphasis by repeating it in the form of a flourish. The passage developed itself simultaneously; for the conditions of its existence are not found in the tone of the instrument, but in the plan of the keyboard. The period of the Viennese Flügel produced great diversity in figuration, which diverted by its pearling prettiness, but left behind an impression of triviality rather than of serious meaning. Neither mechanism nor tone was adequate to the production of a full harmonic effect. As striking power the hand was too heavy; only knuckle and finger-tip were used in playing.—The introduction of the English action opened a new æra in pianoforte playing. The greater volume of tone, which does not, however, exclude the softest piano, is accompanied by a heavier touch. The wrist and elbow-joint are drawn into the technique. Pianoforte compositions and treatment expand into grandeur. Orchestral fulness of harmony produces an imposing volume of tone. The new timbre is peculiarly adapted for the characteristic rendering of vocal melody. The brilliancy of modern pianoforte playing is founded on harmonic fulness as well as on brightly diversified figuration; for both these technical specialties areequally seconded by the plan of the keyboard and tone of the instrument.

Having attempted in the foregoing to mark the boundaries within which the pianoforte affords a stimulus, or at least gratification, to the musical craving, there still remains for consideration one circumstance which renders it the most important of all instruments: namely, that it is in fact the most prominent educational agency in art. Its tones are prepared in pitch and, in a sense, ready for use. Besides, it always directs the pupil's attention to a Whole. By imparting to the senses equal stimulation for harmonic, melodic, and contrapuntal beauties, it develops musical thought in the highest degree. Even the brevity of its tone is of advantage to the pedagogics of music. An emotional revelry in the euphony of the individual tone is not promoted by the pianoforte. All the more does its tone emphasize the necessity of clear and succinct presentation. Even if the latter be not the highest aim of interpretation, it still forms the indispensable precondition of a genuinely artistic performance.

In many cases pianistic training must seek, precisely as its chief aim, not to develop abstract musical reflection at the expense of naïve sentiment. Now, this very brevity of the pianoforte tone is the occasion, that the development of an expressive touch occupies the reflective faculty in a direction, wherein a singer or violinist could confidently be guided by feeling. The want of continuity and capability of swelling in the tone presents a serious impediment to a true characterization of the emotional life. When modulatory effect is required in successive, not individual, tones, or the essential point is an effective exhibition of the accentuation, the pianoforte tone can afford direct satisfaction. It is far less adapted for the presentation of prolonged tones.

Let us take one example. The Bach aria for violin on the G-string begins with a long-sustained e. The tone commences *piano*, with a swell following. Thus its full significance as principal tone is marked. Both the tranquil entrance and the subsequent *crescendo* correspond to the sustained, devotional character of the piece. If the pianist had the same strain to play, he would have to attack the tone more powerfully than the violinist, otherwise it would lose in weight. Should he, however, attack with the same power that the latter employs at the climax of the swell, the devotional tranquility of the whole would be endangered, despite the most elastic touch. The very softest tone, if it but sing on and on, has a power far more intense than an elastic touch on the piano.

It is therefore the task of the pianist, to provide, by means of quantity and quality of accent, a substitute for that, which the continuity of tone readily grants to the violonist or singer. This point demands unremitting reflection. It cannot be denied, that certain geniuses instinctively overcome the above-mentioned difficulty. Neither would we assert, that singers, or players on other instruments, can do without reflecting on beauty and expression in tone-production.

The fact, that the pianoforte tone has at first a somewhat discouraging effect on a musician of naïve feeling, must in any event be accepted. The first step towards solving a problem is a clear recognition of its difficulty. Pianoforte playing admittedly favors a certain propensity to reflection, both as regards the total conception of a composition and the separate training in touch. But mature musical experience, and a sensitiveness of finger-touch developed by long self-observation, must lend to the performance the appearance of spontaneity.

Before passing from the general æsthetic survey to the historical sketch of pianoforte playing contained in the following chapter, we must notice an attendant art — the art of improvisation. After poetry, this art reaches its fullest development in our province, for the other instruments too greatly hamper its flight, partly by reason of mechanical inadequacy partly, like the organ, through stylistic one-sidedness.

The material which improvisation has at disposal is the natural vigor of the imagination, the elasticity of its creative power, and, more particularly, promptness and presence of mind for the spontaneous development of the idea; skill shows itself in clothing the ideas struggling for utterance under such circumstances in the garb of a rational form.

This material is therefore one of the highest manifestations of natural vigor, and its mere potentiality exercises a charm possessed by no other material influence. Its power and treatment are, indeed, two factors which may be present in very various admixtures and in a mutual relation more or less proportionate. Most seldom will their co-operation produce the result, that the idea, simply in itself, shall act in absolute clearness and unsullied purity. Although such cases are handed down by tradition from great masters like Bach, Mozart, and

Beethoven, the attendant circumstances are of too great moment in summing up the effect produced.

Improvisation is the gymnastics of the imagination, the arena in which it can display all its characteristic ingenuity of invention, dexterity in the mastery of all rules, and the deliberating Genius of Form, under every shape. And brilliancy of technique may adorn the whole with its bright play of color. Improvisation is the feature-play of the inner psyche, speech in tones without notes, which may improve all advantages of oratory, the effect of the moment, living as it does essentially in and for this latter; making amends through its own charm for that, which the performance may lack in finished artistic value.

CHAPTER II.
The History of Clavier Virtuosity.

An historical retrospect over the development of clavier playing must revert to the great masters of the latter, who in performance and composition marked out the path and direction which the multitude of their contemporaries was obliged to take, the pattern set by the teachers being authoritative for their emulators. To the history of the practical side of clavier playing, as exhibited in the personal example of the masters, must be added an historical survey of the written methods for the treatment of the clavier. The histories of practice and of theory naturally belong together, when a presentation of the historical picture is aimed at.

A description of the virtuosity of earlier times presents peculiar difficulties. Firstly, their contemporaries speak in hardly more than general terms concerning the clavier style of the masters, and even these reports are not always clearly intelligible; secondly, their opinions possess only a relative authority, inasmuch as this earlier period necessarily judged from quite a different standpoint from our own. When something new makes its way to the front, its effect must always influence, more or less, the objective calm of judgment. Such a judgment can claim confidence and acquiescence only upon the height of a completed evolution. Nevertheless it is beyond doubt, that the intellectual side is more likely to be judged aright, or perhaps even to be too little emphasized, when we consider, that even with our modern training the comprehension of a Bach and a Beethoven is but gradually ripening to maturity. The technical side, however, was assuredly overvalued; on the one hand, because the instruments of that period could have stimulated the same but partially; on the other, because the reporters lay stress on matters now regarded as self-evident elementary requirements.

The history of modern times naturally presents itself more favorably, personal experience being enabled, in part, to follow the swift process of evolution, and in part to add, from oral tradition, what was necessary in the way of correction and augmentation.

Besides the two last-named sources, there have been used, for the delineation of the following historical picture: Gerber's "Lexikon der Tonkünstler"; Forkel, "On Johann Sebastian Bach's Life, Art, and Art-works"; Otto Jahn's "Life of Mozart", Part IV; Brendel's "History of Music"; Marx, "Beethoven"; the pianoforte methods by Adam, Kalkbrenner, Hummel, and Czerny; and for the latest period the consensus of written communications.

Virtuosity properly so called begins with Domenico Scarlatti and Johann Sebastian Bach (the former born 1683(?), the latter 1685). Interesting as it would be to extend the historical notes to the virtuosity of still earlier times, the æsthetic aim nevertheless requires a certain limitation in the breadth of the historical picture. There is a point, where the historical and æsthetical search after knowledge have divergent interests, and it would advantage the latter but little to dilate upon the numerous body of ante-Bach pianists who treated their instrument in immature fashion.

Scarlatti is spoken of only in general terms. He is called the greatest clavier-player of his time, perhaps of future times as well. But Händel was undoubtedly also an eminent player, though he is not so emphatically recognized. Special details concerning the technique of both are lacking. In view of their works we can only surmise (as Jahn likewise does, P. IV, p. 5), that in regard to the fingering they closely rivalled Bach's progress.

Concerning the latter, tradition is more exact. Johann Sebastian Bach is called the greatest clavier-player of his time, perhaps of future times as well. The chief characteristic of his style is said to have been extreme distinctness of touch. This was attained through the following method. Bach held the five fingers so bent, that their tips were brought into a straight line, each finger being held in this position over its key, ready for striking. The method of touch accompanying this position was, (acc. to Forkel), that no finger fell, or was thrown, upon the key, but must be borne down with a certain sense of power and mastery over the movement. This power bearing upon the key, or the degree of pressure, must be sustained in equal strength, namely, by not lifting the finger directly up from the key, but causing it to slip away from the front end of the key by gradually drawing in the finger-tip towards the palm of the hand. In passing on from one key to another, this degree of power or pressure bearing on the first tone is thrown, by this slipping away, with extreme swiftness upon the following finger. This method, by means of which Forkel seeks to explain the great precision of Bach's touch, stands in direct opposition to our modern style, which founds the principle of touch upon the movement of the whole finger (not, as Bach did, upon the finger-tip alone), requires a distinct lift, and allows a drawing-in of the finger-tip only in special cases. The further statement, that Bach played with so easy and slight a movement of the fingers that it was hardly perceptible, can be explained only from the light action of the instruments then built. Only the end-joints of the fingers were in motion, the hand retained its rounded form even in the most difficult passages, and the fingers were lifted but very slightly from the keys, hardly more than in trilling. All other members of the body remained perfectly motionless. Bach's method likewise developed all the fingers to perfect equality. All were alike in strength and usefulness, so that double notes and runs, simple and double trills, even trills with accompanying melody in the same hand, were executed with equal ease.

Special importance was attached to Bach's new fingering. The greatest players of that period, not excepting Couperin, very seldom employed the thumb except in stretches. Bach, however, was forced to a perfectly free use of the thumb in playing, partly by the polyphonic spirit of his works, and partly by the system of equal temperament advocated chiefly by himself, which latter rendered it possible to write in all 24 keys. The great diversity in the figuration of his compositions had the result, that Bach knew no difficulties, and never missed a note either in free improvisation or in playing his compositions.

His favorite instrument was the clavichord. He found the harpsichord too lifeless (here the instruments provided with quills are doubtless to be understood), and the pianoforte was still too undeveloped and too clumsy, to afford him satisfaction. He considered the clavichord the best instrument for practice, and also for private musical entertainment. He thought it better adapted for rendering the finest shades of tone and conception, and despite its poverty of tone more responsive, than the other instruments named.

His free improvisations are said to have been in the style of the Chromatic Fantasia, but frequently to have surpassed it in brilliancy, expression, and freedom. He took very animated tempi in performing his compositions, to which he lent such a wealth of modulation, as to reach the expressiveness of speech. Strong emotion he expressed, not by an outward

manifestation of strength, but by the inworking artistic medium
of harmonic and melodic figuration.

After Joh. Seb. Bach his sons, W. Friedemann and K. Philipp Emanuel, are reckoned among the most eminent clavier
players of the period. The former is said to have been distinguished by his fantastic wealth of imagination and a neat,
refined style; the latter by brilliancy without remarkable depth.
It is known how the talent of the former, in consequence of
exterior conditions, never attained to the highest effectiveness;
a detailed characterization of K. Philipp Emanuel will be given
in the following chapter when discussing his text-book. The
technical standpoint of both was that of their father, although
the latter is termed the greater master.

Did we propose to divide the history of virtuosity into
epochs, the first might be closed here. Technically, it is distinguished by the thorough comprehension of the organic nature
of the hand now evinced for the first time. It lays down the
principle according to which the evolution could thenceforward
advance in natural and methodical progress. Intellectually,
the epoch is characterized by a profoundly religious, but one-
sided spiritualism, which is modified, in Friedemann Bach, by
a visionary romanticism, and in Philipp Emanuel by a more
entertaining brilliancy. The form, dependent upon a closely-knit
texture, confines the imagination to the devotional meaning.
But in this one-sidedness it attains, in amends, to the highest
expression, and presents the picture of religious ecstacy, of a
soul inspired by devotional presage, in the most lifelike manner.
Within its one-sidedness is developed the greatest diversity.
The soul has thrown herself with all her might and all her
faculties upon a single object, and succeeds in clothing it,
within one and the same style, in the greatest possible variety
of form. Alongside of the above-mentioned close-knit plasticity
of the same there is unfolded, strangely enough, with Seb. Bach
a contrasting form of free lyrical dream-life, e. g. in the Chromatic Fantasia, which in its unfettered freedom discovers a
fervent yearning of religious romanticism such as never recurs

in any department of literature. The sensuous charm of the clavier is still so slight, rather of a negative than positive nature, that thereby, too, the imagination is held back from extravagation in the material elements of beauty. The exoteric clavier-music of Seb. Bach is foremostly represented by his great Suites, which imbue the old dance-forms with the highest degree of grace and poetic meaning.

The greatest representatives of the second epoch are Mozart and Clementi (the former b. 1756, the latter 1752). Haydn (b. 1732) was, it is true, also eminent as a clavier player, but his peculiar greatness lies more in the broadening of the ideal basis effected by him in the entire conception of musical art. He is the great Reformer, with whom the modern æra begins. He tears himself away from the rigidly crystallized canon of ancient opinion, from the strict dogmatism of religious spiritualism, and endows the musical conception with the poetry of worldly charm in a freer, far more proportionately balanced form. Still psychologically considered, the evolution of the musical conception takes no leap, but transmutes spontaneous harmony, conjoined with the absolute form resulting from the earlier constraint of dogma, into that mood of the human breast, which, undisturbed by the harsh experiences of maturer life, inclines with the free impulse of a natural necessity to the bliss of constant harmony. This mood finds its natural expression in the poetry of children, and Haydn thus enriches music with an abundance of the freshest and most natural ideas, in contrast with the foregoing period. In a fairly inexhaustible stream flow from out his soul, in all the forms still prevalent to-day, tone-poems of childlike naïveté, full of youthful gaiety and joyousness, which transfer their style — analogously, to the preceding epoch, but in a reverse sense — even to subjects lying within the pale of religious earnestness.

Mozart enters the path opened by Haydn, and develops the harmony of his form to yet fuller completeness. The expression of musical feeling also gains wider bounds, the childlike naïveté of Haydn being wedded to the charm of a temperament more earnest and intense. The absolutely beautiful, and in the characteristic expression of gracefulness, permeates all Mozart's creations, from the deepest earnestness up to a gaiety akin to Haydn's mood, but inspired by an intenser fervor.

Unhappily, it is possible in a still less degree than with Bach to give a distinct and intelligible idea of Mozart's clavier style. Tradition mentions only a few characteristic traits. He laid his hand so gently and naturally on the keyboard, that it seemed fashioned for the latter. To follow it afforded the eye no less pleasure than the ear. Through the study of Bach's works, and especially by adopting his fingering, he developed his technique to perfection. Of Ph. E. Bach he observed: "He is the father, we are the boys". Praise is bestowed upon his quiet hand, the natural lightness and flowingness of his passages, and the correctness, clearness, and precision in all details. In keeping time he was always "accurat", so that for a *tempo rubato* in adagio the left hand did not relax, but held to the measure quite unconcerned as to the right, the whole nevertheless exhibiting finished expression and warm feeling. Delicacy and taste, with his lifting of the entire technique to the spiritual aspiration of the idea, elevate him as a virtuoso to a height unanimously conceded by the public, by connoisseurs, and by artists capable of judging. Clementi declared that he had never heard anyone play so soulfully and charmfully as Mozart; Dittersdorf finds art and taste combined in his playing; Haydn asseverated with tears, that Mozart's playing he could never forget, for it touched the heart. His staccato is said to have possessed a peculiarly brilliant charm.

Mozart's great rival was Muzio Clementi. These two confront each other as founders of so-called schools. There can hardly be room for doubt, that in technique Clementi was the more eminent. His perfect mastery of running passages, his quiet hand, the superior vigor of touch and fulness of tone, clearness, evenness, his exquisite rendering of the adagio, and his (though probably executed with the arm) dexterous octave-playing, all find praise. He is even said to have trilled in octaves with one hand.

What distinguishes Clementi from Mozart is the opposition of the English to the Viennese school, which, being based upon the action of the instruments, likewise exercises an influence on the character of the style. Mozart, the representative of of the Vienna school, embodies lightness, grace, brilliancy, and animation. These were favored by the light action of the instrument. Clementi, accustomed to the deeper keyfall (dip), the heavier touch of the keys, and the full, singing tone of English action, had a sustained, earnest, and really grand purpose in performance and composition.

Each school has its individual history. The Viennese school degenerated later, losing the spiritual elements of Mozart's playing, and keeping solely in view a superficial bravura style. Before this decay was consummated, the school attained in Hummel and Moscheles a somewhat more ideal height. The former occupies Mozart's own standpoint; idea and form are nearly the same; only the technique is developed to greater perfection, and already often appears for its own sake. His playing was distinguished for extreme cleanness and correctness, united with a lively rhythm of peculiar refinement in the *declamando*. Moscheles has more manifold nuances in tone and is grander in the bravura, but also tends on the whole more to delicacy and elegance than to a deeper meaning. In refined and carefully developed interpretation he surpasses Hummel, who despite all accomplishments cannot be acquitted of a certain monotony in rendering. Later, the school declined. In Mozart alone were technique and conception in true harmony. Hummel still holds most faithfully to this standpoint, and outrivals Moscheles, as regards conception, in a series of semi-classic compositions. Woelffl and Steibelt, and still more Kalkbrenner, Herz, and Czerny, cultivate technical brilliancy exclusively, and dilute the idea so far (with a few exceptions, e. g. Kalkbrenner's D-minor Concerto) that the technique must remain in the foreground.

The Clementi school is first continued in Cramer and Dussek. The striving after effect is here far less marked than in the Viennese school. A spirit almost antique lives in this virtuosity. Repose, deliberation, clearness, great conciseness, songful inspiration, and an equability of style, free from all extravagance, distinguish this development. Mozart's school uses the pedal but little, here it is more frequently employed. While Clementi is more eminent in power and grandeur, Cramer excels in suavity and the measuredness of style noted above. Dussek, who had a special fondness for the pedal, was celebrated for his rendering of the *cantabile* and lofty sentimentality, though his compositions are inferior in conception to those of the masters mentioned before. He is followed by Berger, whose development was radically influenced by Clementi; in playing and composition he cultivated a certain spiritualistic romanticism. In view of a higher tendency in conception, the Dresden Court-pianist Klengel should also find mention. But the most eminent virtuoso of this school is Field, whose touch (with fingers held vertically rather than bent) was one of the most delightful in the annals of clavier virtuosity, and who ranks as one of the greatest masters of all times in his picturesque diffusion of light and shade, in perfect finish united with the warmest feeling. Finally, Karl Mayer, the last representative of this school, must be mentioned; but only with reference to his first epoch, for his later development fell quite under the influence of the modern striving after effect, and this in its most superficial form. —

Between these two schools stands Beethoven, a phenomenon of characteristic and lofty independence (from about 1790 onward). Like his predecessors Bach and Mozart, he aimed at the harmonious coalescense of conception and technique. In his first period more akin to the latter, and later embracing Bach's elements as well, he first of all developed technical resources by larger forms, fuller in harmony and broader in treatment. True, the mechanical virtuosity of certain contemporaries, especially of younger ones like Moscheles and Kalkbrenner, had pressed on before, and far as Beethoven overpassed Mozart, he never exhibited his bravura for the purpose of showing off its sensuous brilliancy. But it can hardly have entered into any listener's head to apply the standard of such an elaborate and elegant precision to Beethoven's performances, which, by the magic of most potent pregnancy, made abundant amends for anything left to be desired in the former regard. His free improvisations, above all, were teeming with inexhaustible charms. Quite at variance with the superficial dexterity of his contemporaries, who shed around them a halo of splendor and renown by deft concatenations of swift passages and melodious commonplaces, like Hummel, Woelffl, or Steibelt, Beethoven conjured up images full of bold, original fancy, inexhaustible in wealth of imagination, and of such harmony and unity of conception as well, that in this province he proved himself no less eminent an artist than in those works which were evolved by deliberate reflection. It was, alas, granted only to his contemporaries to hearken to the revelations of this titanic soul, which aroused in all hearers the highest degree of suspense and of ecstatic gratification by the electric potency of eminent spirituality, and by the magic of a realm of tone inspired by and born of and for the moment, never to return; accessible to later generations only through description and tradition. Beethoven did not play with tones: he depicted, declaimed. One step beyond this limit plunges us into the reverse current of a later romanticism, grown incomprehensible through undue boldness; one step short would be a reversion to the creative energy of a Haydn and a Mozart, growing out of mere spontaneous delight in music-making. Although the description, thus expressed, of this peculiarity of his improvisation be but conjectural on our part, contemporary tradition being unable to measure the value of Beethoven's performances by the standard of future epochs, our assumption is nevertheless supported by the great wealth of his compositions. Far as Beethoven may have overpassed the bounds of his predecessors, and endeavored in theory to constrain musical art into rivalling in creative power the poetic word, in practice he never, or at least but seldom, over or undervalued the inmost essence of the spirit immanent to musical tones. What he gave, was the loftiest poetry, but in the genuine garb of music, not in the fantastic finery of a symbolical hybrid art, which vainly attempts to lend animation to its sickly physiognomy by borrowing the features, now of one art, now of another.

But that, which characterized his improvisations no less than his carefully considered compositions, was the spirit of unity. Only where this controls, does the work of art rise to its true conception; all other points of view, whence the momentary charm possesses a stronger influence than the survey of the organism in its entirety, draw art down from her ideal height into the sphere of sensual desires, even though these be speciously veiled. Spirit is unity in diversity, and its potency augments with the range of the latter, provided that unity be preserved. Beethoven's ideas often show, taken by themselves, but slight inventive genius and charm; but in combination as a whole they are always in place, essential, and precisely of that effect which the thought of the whole requires. After Beethoven this standpoint has never (by Mendelssohn only approximately) been attained in such perfection; and where the organism of the latter's works apparently exhibits even greater unity than Beethoven's, their range in regard to diversity is more restricted. The unity of Mendelssohn has less ideal potency, ·because more easily maintained amid the elements controlled by his imagination. Schumann, again, possesses the principle of diversity in a higher degree, but lacks ability to raise it to unity; the same may be said of Schubert in the majority of his instrumental works. In others, where unity is more marked, Beethoven's fulness of conception is lacking.

This characterization of the great virtuoso makes it ap-

2*

parent, that his pianoforte technique was developed only to such a degree of perfection as might serve to fulfil the requirements of his predominant idealism. Anything beyond this he probably thought neither needful nor profitable. To quote himself in a letter to Ries: "The high development of the mechanical in pianoforte playing will end in banishing all genuineness of emotion from music". Indeed, he is accused of positive negligence in points of technique.—True as his prophetic words have proved, a halt in the evolution of technical virtuosity would none the less have borne a doubtful look; moreover, the elements of higher progress do not develop simultaneously, but successively. In the development of pianoforte playing a temporary, one-sided predominance of technique appears the more natural, as the next-following period of sentimentalism and romance yielded elements of but scant fructifying energy.

Here concludes a second epoch of clavier virtuosity. Beethoven, it is true, occupies but an isolated place therein; for in Dussek, and even in Clementi, the technical side already becomes so predominant, that a rupture in harmony, such as Beethoven feared, seemed imminent. With another group the harmony between technique and conception remains more intimate; though the latter is not so pregnant as with Beethoven, still, the avoidance of all glittering pretension for its own sake on the part of a Cramer, a Field, and a Berger shows, that its due predominance is accorded to the conception; and this latter displays itself, in fact, in distinct and self-sustained lines. Setting aside the offshoots of the Viennese school, the course of virtuosity exhibits up to this time either a complete congruity, or at least a proportionate relation, between ideal productivity and material reproductivity. The pianoforte player was no less a mental than a gymnastic athlete.

The relations changed. Hummel and Moscheles extend technical skill so decidedly, that it attracts attention as a special art, apart from the conception. While, with Hummel, the rupture of this special art with the entirety of musical art, though already beginning, is still kept back by lending to the conception a form as dignified as possible under the circumstances, with Moscheles the rupture already grows more decidedly apparent. The harmony of the purely beautiful in music gives way to the merely charming, which heralds both the rise and the decline of an artistic epoch. Moscheles is able more fully to develop the sensuous charms of pianoforte playing; but in the same degree as he surpasses Hummel herein, is he inferior to the latter in point of conception. But the brilliancy of Kalkbrenner's virtuosity most effectually parts the special sphere of technique from the general foundation, and presents it, as a branch of art justified in a certain sense, by itself.

Technical dexterity seemed like a newly acquired faculty, artificially joined to the organism of the physical frame. It so far overstepped the limits of spontaneous naturalness in the direction of the miraculous, that the virtuoso appeared in the nimbus of a most eminent individuality. Moreover, by reason of the immediate effect, the feeling of admiration extended to the steady perseverance and the mastery shown in conquering innumerable difficulties of all kinds. An element of art lies in each victory won over the impediments raised by the intractability of natural forces. Now, if with the greater skill of the bodily apparatus a more powerful instrumental tone be combined, and if, conversely, the instruments present entirely new difficulties for the technique to overcome, and these two factors push, in their mutual emulation, to such a climax that something unheard-of and never before attained is brought about, it will surely come to pass, that in the domain of virtuosity not only music alone, but likewise the technique of the reproductive medium, will be taken into account. Their relation must needs be so adjusted, that virtuosity no longer remains a reproduction of ideal tone-poems, but becomes sensuous production; and it lies in the nature of the case, that the might of the sensuous presentation, as the specifically new element, must for a moment occupy the foreground.

Kalkbrenner still exhibits many really fine characteristics as a virtuoso, and his observations in his Method manifest the thoughtful artist, striving to maintain a connection with the normal groundwork of art. Little as an intentional abandonment of this connection is to be assumed or proven in the case of the virtuosi following him, the causes of its dissolution were part and parcel of the quality, and above all of the effect, belonging to the novel charms of the pianoforte.—But it would be unjust to designate this course as the general characteristic of modern virtuosity; although a great majority of pianists may really succumb to the temptation, precious germs are nevertheless found beneath the dazzling glitter whose lease of life ran throughout nearly two decades.—The historical progress was, in detail, as follows.

After technique had once parted, as a special art, from the common ideal, and brilliancy, velocity, and bravura ranked above expression, truthfulness, and harmonic unity, the former characteristics had by no means reached their fullest development in the last champions of the Viennese school. Modern virtuosity recognized this failing, and also a second, namely, that despite increased technique better taste must be displayed in the use of outward resources.—First, technical development was pushed to the utmost. But all progress depends upon intellectual perception, and all perception upon closer attention to distinctions. Thus the development of technique was furthered by taking up each of its details separately, and training it to the very height of perfection. While the Viennese virtuosi, like Hummel, Kalkbrenner, and others, had discovered more departments in the domain of technique than their predecessors, and done important work therein, Liszt and Thalberg seize upon each detail, as an individual form, with such eager and exclusive attention, that the earlier virtuosity seems almost like a microscopic portrait in comparison. Formerly the passage had appeared as a contrast to the *cantilena*, the instrumental principle to the vocal, movement to repose. Now almost all becomes movement; contrasts appear only in the various figuration of the movement. Technique develops in everything. The minutest detail is viewed from the gymnastic standpoint; the most unimportant shines in the brilliancy of technical training; mechanical finish draws the most insignificant atom within the sphere of material charm. What otherwise found room as an ornament hardly noticed betwixt the pillars of the artistic idea, is now seized upon and worked up in factory-like imitation and the running figuration of the Étude form, as a problem for that mastery of difficulties now grown to be child's play. The Étude form predominates. Its principle so permeates the wide-spreading ramifications of all forms, that its law quite dominates free productivity, and almost nothing is left of the earlier ideal method of composition. This revel of technical equestrianism hurries away in its mad career any modestly forthputting germ of ideality, and psychical expression becomes a rarity. Technique builds up its passages like walls; no sooner is one climbed, than another towers above it, and between such adamantine piles no tenderer bloom can flourish.

But this is not the end. Modern technique is not content with laying in a wholesale stock, as it were, of ornaments from the former retail dealers, through incessant imitation of the same, but further increases their number by new patterns. The old ones are used only in case of necessity, like remnants of an old stock transferred to the second-hand trade; invention continually discovers novel combinations. No longer the octave, but the tenth, is regarded as the normal stretch. The field of earlier technique seems from this standpoint, too, like a portrait in miniature. The demands upon physical energy and endurance outgrow all limits. Where the earlier masters thought they were putting forth tremendous efforts, the moderns just begin to take an interest in gymnastic enjoyment. The former methods of touch are supplemented by the stroke from the wrist and arm. Kalkbrenner had, it is true, pioneered the way in these, but perfection in the temper and flexibility of the muscles had not been attained till now. The gradual prevalence of the English instruments also influenced technique. The more poetic and diversified tone of the Viennese action, which despite its weakness was far more sensitively reponsive to the slightest vibration of the finger-tip, makes way for the brilliant, hard rebound and full concert-tone of the English action. In like measure as the hand ceases to be an organism instinct with the more delicate pulses of the psyche, and becomes merely a physical, artificial mechanism, must the art of instrument-building prepare the brilliancy of the pianoforte tone. The material effect of the tone already lies in the pianoforte action; the hand need display no special art, to develop this side. Yet the mechanism of the pianoforte demands absorbing attention and serious exertion in its treatment; woe to the pianist who has a weak chest. Health is a prerequisite for pianoforte playing. The player must first wean himself from the sensitiveness of nerve necessary with the Viennese action, and learn to translate all nuances into a coarser, but sensually more effective, medium.

Thus it comes about, that the spirit of composition also undergoes a change. The new school of playing cannot find free scope in the earlier works. The pianoforte has become an orchestra. A Thalberg or a Liszt draws from the keys a flood of harmonies which, though true in a measure to the main pianoforte characteristic, velocity, in contradistinction to the polyphonic orchestral style, approach the orchestra on the side of dynamic effect. Moreover, the pianoforte is actually treated, at times, in orchestral style, and employed for full harmonic combinations in a manner hitherto unknown. It develops, in particular, a polyphony of its own, by ornamenting vocal ideas with the abounding wealth of its figuration.—These two styles do not, however, quite exclude the old manner of treatment, and thus it happens that a fantasia by Thalberg, which economically distributes the entire stock of musical effects, sings, toys, gambols, outflashes brilliantly, thunders, etc. —Howsoever, this composer dictates the style, after which many disciples and members of a school of art operate. It must be admitted that, in the invention of figuration for the adornment of themes, and in his well-calculated cumulation of effects, i. e. in sensuous charms, he can claim the greatest originality, and that in reference to this department of taste none of his school have equalled him. Besides, his expression is free from sentimentality; the haughtiness of technique, the athletic repose, combined to effortless mastery of the greatest difficulties, and an aristocratic assurance that never falters, are traits of his playing. But his style of writing and playing banishes all higher spiritual flights. Their cantilena-like essence deprives his compositions of all the fire, the exaltation, of a presto. The most astounding technique plays about slow-moving emotional phases only, and in all cases the expression represents the same cool grandeur, which in the end grows monotonous. The former king of the salons, Herz, at least lent animation and grace to sensuous, superficial charm. His technique, too, was attractive, for, though more thin and mono-tonous, it displayed in rhythm more life and fascination. Herz was one-sided in trifling coquetry, Thalberg in grand repose.

Like Thalberg in a technical sense, but less tasteful in the distribution of effects, are Willmers, Kontski, Leop. v. Meyer, Döhler, Prudent, and others. Döhler sometimes works with a more artistic sense of style; but on the whole the Thalbergian spirit, which in its repellance of sentimentality shows an estimable trait, is blended, in the above-named fol-lowing, with milder, lighter, more superficial elements. A new figure, a novel effect, seldom appears.

It was inevitable that virtuosity should fall into ill repute; for the greater number of the pianists everywhere arising contented themselves with the less costly part of the task, i. e. with the display of mechanical skill. The performance of classic masterworks becomes infrequent, technique finding no gratification in them. A Beethoven sonata cannot approach Thalberg's and Kontski's fantasias in displaying all phases of gymnastics, all kinds of arm, hand, and finger-joint touch and caressing the keys. A comprehension of the masters is lost in the interest in gymnastics. The individual sensitiveness of the finger, its mission of conveying the emotions of the soul to the keys through subtle feeling, is swallowed up in its mechanical function. As a point of honor, the virtuosi play a number by Beethoven or some classic; they feel relieved on getting rid of it, and the audience is, in fact, chary of applause after such performances. Other masters of technique show, it is true, by superb isolated performances of classical works, to what superior excellence such interpretations can attain with modern resources; but they lack courage to risk their advantages, in view of a perverted public taste. Dilettantism distorts classic style, by treating it according to a technical, instead of an ideal, standard.

Such was in general the situation during a considerable period. Yet the healthy spiritual nature maintained itself, even amid decay, in some few elements; although at this time the better germs were more scanty and dispersed, they nevertheless present, gathered up in their entirety, a more pleasing picture. Precisely certain of the greater masters of technique, like A. Dreyschock and Döhler, exhibit in isolated performances, that the truth in music still lives, though at times neglected. But Dreyschock, whose tremendous technique outrivals Liszt in sensuous details, was still too fond of playing to follow his better genius with constancy. Not until the later period of his public activity does he elevate himself to the standpoint of making technique fully subservient to the idea. Promising germs are also found mated with the superficiality of a Henselt and Litolff.—The suffering condition of the gifted Chopin, Henselt's unconquerable dread of playing in public, and the similarly far too infrequent appearance of Th. Kullak, with whose style inimitable poetry was blended, offered too slight opposition to the dominant tendency. And finally, Liszt, the greatest of modern virtuosi, was at that time far too dependent upon the inspiration of the moment, to admit of the presentation of pure art in his style. Being more richly endowed with technical brilliancy than all the rest, his interpretation continually wavers between sensuous effect and spiritual flashes from a sphere kept in the background. The might of the latter could not entirely enthrall him, until he had departed from the arena. Nevertheless, Liszt remains that pianist, who has maintained the conception of his art in the most honorable scope and most enduring significance. Whereas the great majority of the others present for exhibition nothing but modernism, and this in the garb of their personal performances, Liszt's repertory embraces, even in his virtuoso period, the entire classic and romantic literature from Scarlatti, Bach, and Händel, Beethoven by preference, Hummel, Schubert, Weber, down to Chopin, Mendelssohn, etc. Together with most finished technique there shows, in all his performances, an emotional effect in exquisitely rhythmized declamation and accentuation, and also in his individual charm of nuance, so that the separation of technique from conception in less felt than was to be expected, in view of the exuberance of outward resources. A supernatural touch, an expression of gloomy sublimity, but changing on the instant to the brightest gleam of pure brilliancy, lend to his style the charm of a lovely poetic wilderness, wherein awful depths alternate with serene, sunny heights. In his presentation each object takes on the expression of his own grand lyric vein, and for this very reason virtuosity does not reach its most complete expression in Liszt. Everywhere is the arbitrary impress of a titanic spirit, which takes possession of all things, the sublimest and simplest alike, interpreting each detail with the prepossession of its own masterful virtuosity.

With regard to the literary productions of the better tendency, we find in Liszt's own works of that period, to begin with, only details of an original, mostly technical, nature; to these the pianoforte owes an extension of its capabilities. Liszt was not destined to attain to really eminent importance as a composer until he had turned his back upon triumphs of his career as a virtuoso. His most important works belong to a province far without the scope of this book,

—to oratorio and orchestral music. But the most prominent among his pianoforte compositions, as well, tower high above that standpoint which is content in the service of virtuosity. Salon music owes to Th. Kullak an ideal, poetic flight, which for a time has an epoch-making influence upon his contemporaries, and finds imitators. Henselt's Muse arouses hopes of novelty and beauty in the beginning only, from which she falls away; Stephen Heller exhibits many touches of amiable and delicate naïveté.

Of momentous import, however, and towering high above the whole London and Vienna school, are the achievements in composition of Schubert, Chopin, Mendelssohn, and Robert Schumann. During this entire epoch they maintain a spiritual counterpoise over against the extravagances of virtuosity; in this whole time they stand next to Beethoven in importance, and the romanticism, which already flashes forth in many traits from the monumental works of the great classic master, reaches full maturity in theirs.—Neither can Weber be passed over in silence. But his compositions are not sufficiently numerous, and in their spiritual essence call rather to mind that sphere, wherein the gifted opera composer displayed his grandest resources.

Schubert's sonatas breathe in many respects the spirit of Beethoven, yet their material does not exhibit the same weight and worth. Moreover, the period of Weber and Schubert precedes the full development of modern virtuosity, and does not fairly engage in rivalry with the latter. Of greater moment are Chopin and Mendelssohn.

The classic period, developed by the complete blending of form and expression, was long since in the sere and yellow leaf. Only to Mendelssohn was it granted, to utter things till then unspoken in classic form. The emotional faculty was already too far lost in retrospection, and had felt by far too intoxicating a delight in its own materiality, to hope to regain that self-control, whose outcome is artistic form.

Chopin's significance is due to the fact, that he augmented

the material of musical expression. Strictly speaking, he contributes merely new charms, isolated novel effects; but they are not simply material effects, though in this direction, too, Chopin's work was epoch-making, but belong to the ideal factors of music—harmony, melody, and rhythm—and the most direct result of these elements is the peculiarity of their action on the imagination. They sink the latter so deep into the innermost, secret heart of romanticism, that an entirely new phase of expression is developed. Melancholy is its distinctive mark, but in a countenance of such depth, ideality, and aristocratic refinement, as had never before been presented to view.— Expression predominating, however, as a *salient trait*, it is clear that Chopin's style must first of all break with the ancient form, he not being inspired by the ideal which found its full expression therein. His own is of a far more subjective, egoistic character. Therefore in his works the smaller forms, the Étude, Nocturne, Waltz, Mazurka, Scherzo, Ballade, Dead March, etc., predominate. Larger forms he adequately treats only in his two Concertos; the Sonatas, and even the Ballades, are without style, and charm rather by their details than as a whole.

Mendelssohn, contrasted with Chopin, is an after-bloom of classicism. In him the rejuvenated spirit of the past displays itself again in the beauty of form. Mendelssohn again kept the Whole in view, and the emotion of the instant does not rise from the depths as with Chopin. Now, these two factors are predestined to mutual exclusion; the harmony of the whole admits no predominance of individual effect, and the prominence of the latter disturbs the unity of the whole. True, it cannot be affirmed that Mendelssohn's individual effects lack an indescribable charm; one simply need recall the second theme of the D-minor Trio; but still there lies, in the entire nature of his most pregnant ideas, a tendency toward development, evolution; the most charmful theme of a Song without Words is instinct with the striving after rounded and finished formal development; and even where the listener would fain tarry, to follow out some special idea in tranquil enjoyment, Mendelssohn ever leads the delighted fancy to new paths of meditation and admiration of his skilful development and exposition. This is the pure beauty of form, in whose serene smoothness Mendelssohn ranks with the greatest classics. But in Mendelssohn himself we see, that Form does not exhaust the beautiful in its finish alone; that its faultless smoothness is the very cause and reason that not one idea can break forth in real grandeur. Or, conversely, a lack of grandeur in conception may in itself occasion the smoothness of form. And herein, again, Mendelssohn ranks below his great predecessors as regards sterling quality of material. The substance of his idea is a fond tenderness, an etherial romanticism, a feminine sensibility; the form seems to mirror itself coquettishly in its own smoothness, and though classicism be really rejuvenated therein, this is achieved only in so far as the venerableness of the earlier conception can be reconciled with the modern spirit. The antique soul, the sturdy originality of style, are wanting; an excitable flightiness, an emotional irritability, urge the imagination on into a realm of elvish and fanciful shapes teeming with romantic fondness and graceful coquetry, often lending its tender tinge to serious thoughts as well, which ought properly to be wrapped in reverent mysticism and monotony of tone.

In accord with this characterization, Mendelssohn's pianoforte compositions require a very high technical development in the singing touch, and in most exquisite, pearling velocity. Their gifted originator was himself a virtuoso of the first rank. With all brilliancy of technique at his command, he employed it only in the service of the noblest ideals. In his rendering of the classics he was the most objective interpreter of the period, and the art of improvisation attained in him a height worthy of his prototypes.

Robert Schumann can claim, on the strength of his works, to be named next to Mendelssohn. True, an envious destiny denied him the use of the right hand, and hindered his ele-

vation into the ranks of active pianists, yet his pianoforte works
were epoch-making in their influence on players through their
peculiarly ideal and romantic conception. Technically, they
call into requisition all modern amplifications, but demand
practice rather as regards strength, volume of tone, and stretch
of the hand, than in refinement in the elaboration of individual
effects of tone, in which Mendelssohn, and more especially
Chopin, exhibited such exquisite taste. In conception they are
noteworthy for augmenting the material, i. e. for creating new
effects in expression. Although, on the one hand, they possess
neither the depth nor the unity of style found in Chopin, and
never reach, on the other, Mendelssohn's beauty of form, they
nevertheless form an important counterpoise to the materialistic
and superficial tendency of salon music by their tender ardor,
and by the tints of emotional nuances of strikingly characteristic effect in individual cases. This expression often rises
in the gloomier, mystical spheres of feeling to impressive
reality, even to sublime grandeur, delineates objective situations,
and in every way enlightens the opinion of the period in
regard to the problem, to be solved in the near future, of the
further development of musical expression.

Taubert, too, has high aims on the whole, but does not
pursue them so consistently as the foregoing, and exhibits
similar talent only in details; the more valuable, however, are
his interpretations, as a pianoforte virtuoso, of classical masterworks. In this last domain Clara Schumann also proves herself
exceptionally gifted. Her thoroughly developed technique,
which only in the boldest tone-effects does not equal modern
masculinity in finish, is ennobled by an inner fire and a subtle
comprehension of all kinds of more refined music, so that her
rendering of the same attains to the significance of a standard.
Only in sustained movements does she not invariably reach a
similar depth of insight.

The sum total of the factors above enumerated had, as
their result, the decadence and obsolescense of virtuosity pure
and simple in the public taste. But the freshly emerging

champions of pianoforte playing maintain technique on a level worthy of their predecessors. A falling-off would have been alarming, if only because the best of the newer pianoforte music can seldom dispense with the attainments of the virtuoso period. Hans von Bülow deserves, above all, praise as an objective representative of the entire pianoforte literature. Seconded by the most thorough training, equally possessed of artistic inspiration and acute artistic intelligence, he disdains momentary effect while striving after self-forgetful interpretation. The early deceased Tausig outvied him in trustworthiness of technique, and perhaps strove still more after that tranquil plasticity of rendering not always compatible with Bülow's acumen and brilliant endowments. Ehrlich, as a pianoforte player, likewise followed the same tendency, which would sink the reproductive artist in the interpreted art-work. With Rubinstein the matter is different. Surrendering himself wholly, in playing, to spontaneous fancy, he keeps his own personality continually in the foreground. The inherent contrast between an objective and a subjective rendering, which, by reason of the natural indeterminateness of musical language, must obtain at all periods in musical reproduction, has hardly ever appeared so sharply as at the simultaneous public appearance of Tausig and Rubinstein towards the end of the sixth decade.

While an objective rendering strives only to follow the composer's intentions, as far as they may be directly specified, or are to be gathered from the spirit of the work, it is the aim of a subjective conception to give expression to that emotion, which the work awakens in the artist according to his temperament or mood at the instant. In the latter case it is not the work alone that produces an effect; this is done in quite equal measure by the personality of the interpreting artist. The cardinal element of the objective tendency is reflection; whereas subjectivity charms by the magic of spontaneity.

Both tendencies in art naturally have their limits. With regard to objectivity, the first question is, how far an exact knowledge of the composer's intention is possible. Outward signs of expression do not suffice. Therefore only the total character of the work to be interpreted can be authoritative. But how many works are there, whose conception is quite free from ambiguity? Even Beethoven's sonatas, whose self-consistent organism represents, before all others, a positive musical speech, grant boundless freedom to the player's subjectivity. Works like the Chromatic Fantasia are left entirely to subjective intuition. And there is this additional difficulty, — to exclude, from the individual performance, all personal impulses of the moment, and to meet the composition at every turn with suitable receptivity. Tausig assuredly carried this self-abnegation to an almost ideal height; but what his rendering hereby won in pure spirituality, it lost in warmth. The subjective element in interpretation likewise has its limits. The reproductive artist must not always be productive, at least in the sense of that improvisational production which stamps the artistic performance with the emotions of the moment. For firstly, there are many works whose emotional life is so clearly delineated, that the artistic interpretation must keep strictly within the clearly defined boundary; secondly, the spirit of the whole may so illumine a portion, in itself ambiguous, that its interpretation according to momentary caprice would also jeopardize the unity of style.—These parallel tendencies in art are equally justifiable. Let one player exclude subjective elements where he can dispense with them, and another favor them, where this does no violence to the work of art. What the former gains by observant criticism, the latter will make good through sympathetic spontaneity.

At present it appears unadvisable to pursue the history of pianoforte virtuosity further. A technique equal to the highest demands has become an everyday matter; it is no longer its own object, but a *conditio sine quâ non* for any good musician desiring to perform in public on the pianoforte.

The finest technique in the service of the loftiest ideal is a necessity of art, the highest aim to be sought by pianoforte virtuosity.—But hereby that one-sided, ethically tinged conception, which recognizes the Beautiful only in the loftiest ideal, ought not to be promoted. A continual parade of the loftiest ideals awakens suspicion of the error, that art is merely idealized morality; this standpoint, however worthy of respect from an ethical point of view, has happily been left behind by a right artistic sense. Even the beauty which finds its chief expression in sensuous charms, belongs within the scope of the pianoforte, and we may without scruple repel the view of many theoreticians, who, taking Beethoven as a precedent, are inimical to the technical progress of modern times. Pianoforte playing has various grades of beauty; but it would be a forcible invasion of the rights of the science of beauty, to neglect the remaining grades for the sake of the highest.

Thus the field of the present work on pianoforte æsthetics is, to explain the various forms of the beautiful, each according to its conception and claims, and to unfold the idea in its entirety by a review of the whole ground. It lies in the nature of the case, that stress is laid by preference on the highest ideal. But just because this latter can be developed only from the sum of its factors, they must not be neglected.

The principles laid down above undoubtedly find their practical realization through the discernment of modern musical training. Public musical life affords in this regard a fairly reliable standard; it shows us, that pianists of high and genuine merit are striving to realize the idea of the beautiful in its full extent.

It is the task of the following pages, to gather together with empirical exactness the results of such practical experience, to describe them, and to build them up into an orderly system.

CHAPTER III.

A Critical and Historical Review of Pianoforte Methods and Writings on Pianoforte Playing.

The history of practical pianoforte playing, as summarized in the foregoing, requires for its completion a review of the written methods handed down from the masters and teachers. Theory and practice complement each other; each serves to establish the other, and the recognition of both combined is needed in the complete historical picture. This fact will serve to justify the insertion of this chapter in the general part of the Æsthetics; and this justification calls for special mention, because a subsequent enlargement upon many details would make this chapter appear as a natural adjunct to the special course of instruction in the second part. Again, these details are not ample enough, so that their historical interest after all outweighs the methodical. But to place this entire section at the beginning of the work, under the title, let us say, of "List of Sources", seemed unsuitable, for the reason that the methodical system of the second part must assume a more self-dependent and independent position than is requisite for a purely historical presentation of its sources. Moreover, its placing at the head of the work would be as little justified by its critical bias, as a place in the second part by reason of insufficiently ample details.

The methodical works both of the earlier and later past are naturally various in value. We must distinguish between æsthetical life in theory, and the same in practice. Certain great masters of interpretation were either disinclined or unequal to presenting their ideas in writing. This is explainable from a certain dryness inherent in introspection, which, in contrast to the exuberant inspiration of artistic productivity, must be a strict and serious abstraction, to whose contemplation the fresh spirit of immediate enjoyment cannot always bring itself. Thus information is lacking from some of the most eminent authorities, and the opinions of contemporaries must be taken instead, trusting that they developed their theories, from the practical manifestations of the art, with conscientious faithfulness and the necessary insight. But these opinions, too, are founded on very various points of view, and for a due consideration of the æsthetic conception, the historical presentation must be similarly limited as in the foregoing chapter.

3*

Among the great number of methods and text-books only those require mention, which in form and substance appear important and independent, or at least owe their origin to real artists, whose mere opinion is worthy of consideration. We pass over those very numerous works, which, prominent through no marked originality, are subordinate to the chief works, and consist of repetitions or details of unnecessary excursiveness or insufficient brevity.

It lies in the nature of the case, that the chief works have unconsciously exercised, and must exercise, in a degree, the influence of sources upon the details of the next part, even had they been consulted simply to confirm the author's personal experience; besides, all knowledge has an historical basis. But the part in question is founded still more on the author's contemplation of masterly performances, and likewise upon observations made in teaching and close anatomical attention to his own playing; when speaking of sources, this foundation must be specially emphasized. And what is lacking, by the way, throughout the range of all the works mentioned below, is the tracing back of rules to the unity of æsthetic law; abundant as is the material accumulated by empiricism, it wears a more or less sporadic form, or, where more nearly complete, the stamp of pure experimental science. It is the requirement of our period, that the next step forward should raise this aggregation to unity of conception, and show where apparent practical arbitrariness springs from laws of art; and in this endeavor will be found the new element which distinguishes the following essays from the sources immediately to be cited.

Earlier sources mentioned by Forkel begin with a work by Doni (Giovanni Batista, b. 1593), and close with one by Rellstab (Joh. Carl Friedrich): "Anleitung für Klavierspieler, den Gebrauch der Bach'schen Fingersetzung, die Manieren und den Vortrag betreffend"; Berlin 1790. Among these, three are chiefly important, and a description of their contents renders that of the others superfluous. These three are by K. Ph. E. Bach, Marburg, and Türk. And among them, again, that by Türk has most claims on familiar acquaintance. While Bach's celebrated "Versuch über die wahre Art das Klavier zu spielen" is more noteworthy, in regard to originality, as the first erudite work of this kind, Türk's text-book forms a more complete summary of the results of the latter, and of Marpurg's experiences, arranges and adds to the same, and requires, although not so epoch-making as regards originality, the most careful consideration of all the older school-works. The report on the first two works will therefore be more brief and critical, and only the contents of Türk's Clavier Method mentioned more in detail.

Karl Philipp Emanuel Bach's "Versuch über die wahre Art das Klavier zu spielen" was published 1753 in a first, 1759 in a second edition, reissued in 1782 and 1787, and finally in an edition revised by Schilling in a perfectly unjustifiable manner. Haydn said of this book, that it was and would be for all time the School of all Schools; Clementi admits, that he owes all his knowledge and ability, his new touch, his fingering, and his so-called new style to this book alone. Gerber's Lexicon calls it the sole classical work of its kind; even moderns like Fink and the last-named editor of the work estimate its value very highly.— Its main interest lies, however, in its historical significance, and it is incomprehensible, how the latest editor could undertake to rob of its historical embellishments a work, whose absolute value no longer satisfies the demands of our time, and to lay it before the public in modern attire. Its chief merit lies in the fact, that it subjects, for the first time, the practical phenomena in the clavier style of the period to theoretical analysis in an intelligent manner. But what it lacks is systematic classification, scientific demarkation of its material, and the arrangement of the same under uniform æsthetic laws. An almost aphoristic form predominates, and most attention is given to that, which ought *not* to be done.

This excursiveness might have been avoided by a system of more positive tendency.

The work consists of two principal parts, the first treating of practical clavier playing, the second of the art of accompanying, free improvisation, and harmony. From these same titles may be seen, that the contents are not homogeneous, that things of general and special significance are thrown arbitrarily together. As the accompanist of Frederick the Great, the author lays a stress upon accompanying which is disproportioned to its present interest in a method. Both harmony and improvisation belong to the science of composition; the lines of scientific demarkation are thus confused.—The first part is the more important, and contains the following sections: (1) On Fingering; (2) On the Embellishments; (3) On the Rendering.

What is said in this part is, to be sure, true and correct, and confirms our remarks in Chapter I concerning Seb. Bach's style, namely, that the nature of the hand, in the harmonious co-operation of all its powers, is here recognized for the first time, and this in such a striking manner, as to remain authoritative through all clavier-playing ages. But it is not complete, as it restricts the mechanism of playing to the fingers, and necessarily leaves unnoticed a part of their capabilities having reference to tone-production on our instruments. Again, too great stress is laid on other matters, which now-a-days belong to the elements, such as the employment of the thumb. —There predominates here, as in Türk's method, the principle of theorizing on things which belong to the pure mechanical instinct. Czerny hit the nail on the head, by striving to develop everything relating to technique through innumerable exercises and continual repetition. This way is evidently far more rational, and renders quite superfluous the trouble taken to provide rules for fingering in all possible cases—an undertaking which never meets with full success. The fingerings are derivable from a single fundamental principle, and neither in Bach's method, nor in Türk's far more detailed theories, is the treatment clear and explicit, for the simple reason that it is too discursive.

The second chapter treats of Embellishments, i. e. of the manifold varieties of graces, mostly indicated by smaller notes or special signs, so much in vogue in earlier music, partly as a matter of taste, and partly to reinforce the thin tone of the instruments in another way: the majority of which are now obsolete. This chapter, interesting chiefly, though by no means exclusively, from an historical standpoint, will be more thoroughly discussed together with the method by Türk.

At the close comes the Art of Rendering. This depends essentially upon æsthetic perception, and the acquaintance with distinguished musical literature, both being advantages, in which the period in question could participate but insufficiently. Therefore the work is, in this part as well, neither deep nor comprehensive enough, although the correctness of its generalizations is deserving of remark.

Thus Bach observes, for example, that a good rendering consists in the audible presentation of musical ideas according to their true conception. He remarks, that music comprehends a multitude of passions and emotions, all which the player must bear within himself, and be moved by them, and govern his rendering accordingly. Evidently, this touches the matter only in the most general way. No sufficient distinction is made between the manifold manifestations of the idea; and the agencies of the rendering are also enumerated only as they appear superficially, namely, loudness and softness of the tones, their accentuation, the rebound, crescendo, legato, staccato, tremolo, arpeggio, sostenuto, ritardando, and accelerando. These merely outward distinctions in touch should be explained in detail, and their connection with ideal factors exhibited. The upshot of the whole matter may be expressed in the general phrase, that everything must sound well-rounded and tasteful, that one must hear good music—a rule which, in the lack of preciser directions, is repeated by most of the post-Bach authors.

While such precepts, together with a want of clear arrangement in presenting all sorts of rules (e. g. § 16, 17, 18), must be regarded as imperfections of this work, its fulness of material, and the fundamental idea that the performer should be trained theoretically, and an improviser and thoroughbass player, elevate it above mere historical interest. We now proceed to

Friedrich Wilhelm Marpurg's "Anleitung zum Klavierspielen, der schönen Ausübung der heutigen Zeit gemäss entworfen". 1765.

Had Türk's Method not enriched itself with the conclusions of this small, but methodically ordered booklet, it would well repay careful examination. But the rules on Fingering and Embellishments, which form, together with the usual excursiveness amid the most various elements, its chief substance, have been gathered into the successor's above-mentioned work, and will therefore be discussed with the same; here let it suffice to notice Marpurg's right of authorship.—Only one highly important point, which until lately has not received due recognition, deserves to be emphasized as a peculiar merit of the booklet in question. It concerns the technical rudiments. Marpurg insists, that in playing the nerves should be kept entirely passive, and that the fingers should feel perfectly free, as if they had nothing at all to do with the playing. This suggestion, though not expressed with precision, reveals deep insight into the mechanical requirements of playing, and will be presented more in detail further on. — Among the older methods the principal work has already been frequently mentioned. It is

Daniel Gottlob Türk's "Klavierschule oder Anweisung zum Klavierspielen". 1789. New edition, 1802.

Given as concisely as possible, the contents are as follows. The Introduction contains an enumeration of all kinds of keyed instruments, Guido of Arezzo being named as the inventor of the clavier or clavichord.—The directions for the player's attitude differ somewhat from Marpurg's, the distance from the keyboard being set at 10 to 14 inches. The hands should be a few inches lower than the elbows; the middle finger is held bent inward, the thumb straight, the little finger either straight or bent, as required. (Compare this rule with Marpurg's directions, and with Seb. Bach's manner of holding the hand, described in Chapter II.) The fingers must not be held too close together, and they only should play, all else being quiet; only in leaps a slight movement of the hands and arms is allowed. Moreover, the hands must be turned inward as little as possible, and must remain at the same height above the keyboard in staccato no less than in legato. The fourth and fifth fingers require particular attention; the strictest legato should always be maintained. Besides, the player's attitude must be erect, and his feet must be firmly planted.

Passing over some general hints on the course of study, let us turn directly to the actual exposition of the method of teaching. The first chapter treats of the ordinary rudiments, the second of Time.—The art of instruction in timing is a question not exhausted down to the present day, and what Türk says about it is worthy of notice: "Keeping time is more important than the development of velocity". As a preparatory exercise the pupil should beat time, while the teacher plays. A certain fluency in sight-reading is presupposed. The pupil should at first play notes of equal value, with one hand, and then notes of different values, the teacher playing a bass accompaniment; lastly, with both hands, notes first of equal and then of different values. Correct timing is more difficult with the lesser notes; a decided accentuation of the thesis, though a necessary feature, is no fully sufficient guide, and precision must obtain in each detail. Difficult passages combining notes of different value are to be avoided at the beginning. Loud counting by the pupil is useful in these, and must not be dropped until later, but should always be resumed in difficult places. On the whole, Türk does not lay sufficient stress upon counting aloud.

Here follows a section on the movement and character of a composition. Taken absolutely, the rapidity cannot be positively fixed; in this connection a quotation from Quantz is interesting, who fixes for each half-measure in an *allegro assai* the rapidity of a pulsation, and takes in *allegro* the time of a quarter-note, in *adagio cantabile* that of an eighth-note, in *adagio assai* the value of a sixteenth-note to one pulsation. Compositions in *alla breve* time, however, should allow a whole measure to each pulsation.

These sections on the theoretical and terminological elements are followed by very minutely detailed instructions for fingering.—It is well worthy of attention on account of the clear insight shown into the nature of the hand; its precision is matched only by Czerny's method. As already remarked in the case of Bach's works, an explanation in detail is, theoretically considered, impossible, and we abstain, in our analysis of this not unimportant chapter, from following the author into his extreme minuteness of detail. The following general principles are of more consequence.

The most convenient fingering is the best, i. e. that with which the hand can remain quietest. This convenience, however, is founded on the nature of the case, not on habits unreflectingly acquired. The fingering must always be arranged with reference to the succession of notes next following.

From these quite general principles are deduced the following ten principal rules:

(1) The first finger and thumb take a black key in case of necessity, e. g. in leaps, stretches, or when the highest tone in the right hand (for the left the rule must always be reversed) can be conveniently taken by the fifth finger.

(2) The same finger must not take two keys in succession. Exceptions are made only at rests and in staccato playing.

(3) When the fingers of the right hand cannot cover the notes in ascending passages, the thumb is turned under: "It is passed, turned, or drawn underneath, made to

creep unnoticed, as it were, under the other fingers".
It must not be passed under the fifth finger.

(4) When the fingers cannot cover the notes in descending
passages, the longer fingers are passed over the thumb,
excepting the fifth, particularly not when the thumb
is on a black key. The third may also be passed
over the fourth, the fourth over the fifth, or the third
over the fifth, provided that the shorter finger is not
on a black key. In case of extreme necessity 3 is
passed over 2*, or even a short finger over a longer one.

(5) The thumb is used by preference just before or after
a black key.

(6) In stepwise progressions the fingers are taken in their
natural order.

(7) Exceptions to this rule frequently occur, in which a
finger has to be used out of turn, e. g. 5 next to 2.

(8) With intervals wider than a second as many fingers
are left unemployed as notes are skipped; e. g. with
a third, one finger; but exceptions occur.

(9) With rapidly repeated tones the fingers are used in
alternation, the fifth usually remaining idle.

(10) Two or more fingers must often change quietly on the
same key, without repeating the sound.

Conformably to these rules, the fingering is explained in
detail for a great number of special cases. At first for the
scale, where among other fingerings for C-major the following:
2 3 4 3 4 3 4, is given, according to the old rule. Then
follow passages in doubled notes, in precise order from the
second up to ninths and tenths; next come three, four, and
five-tone chords, and the last section treats of the crossing of
the hands, and the distribution of the parts between the two
hands in polyphone playing.

The next-following chapters contain the theory, so important in the earlier clavier music, of the Embellishments or

---

* The figures indicate the corresponding fingers.

Graces; this being explained in such detail by none of the later methods, we review it briefly here.

Every note, taking for a time the place of the note following it immediately, for the embellishment of the melody, is called an appoggiatura. Its value is subtracted from the main note. This grace is employed to lend more connectedness, charm, and vivacity to the melody, and greater variety to the harmony through intermingling dissonances.

The long appoggiaturas. Here the appoggiatura takes half the value of the main note when the latter is divisible into two equal parts, and therefore its own value must be indicated accordingly, though many composers neglect this. Quanz, for instance, always writes an eighth-note. — With a dotted (tripartite) note the appoggiatura takes two-thirds; in slow, expressive strains the dot is prolonged by one-half, e. g.:

(All examples are followed immediately by the manner of execution.) The appoggiatura absorbs the whole value of the main note when the latter is tied to another of like pitch. Concerning its performance, it should be observed that the appoggiatura must be played stronger than the main note, the latter being lifted lightly. Türk remarks here, that Ph. E. Bach, Marpurg, and Agricola, require just the contrary, while Leopold Mozart agrees with his own opinion.

The short appoggiaturas. The distinction of these by means of a short stroke through the tail of the note is first mentioned by the author in the second edition as a mode of notation just coming into vogue. In the first edition he is unacquainted with it. Familiarity with the other directions given here may be taken for granted, and similarly those concerning the Nachschläge (after-graces), whose value is subtracted, contrariwise, from that of the foregoing note. — More important is the

Chapter on the essential embellishments. These are to lend the tones greater emphasis, to adorn the melody, to enhance the expression of the passions and emotions, besides endowing the composition with the proper proportion of light and shade. There are essential and accidental embellishments; the latter are sometimes noted by the composer, sometimes invented by the player, the former always given by the composer. In the choice of embellishments carefully avoid overloading, and employ them only in a manner befitting the character of the piece. For instance, in a *Largo mesto* no trills, mordents, or inverted mordents should occur, but rather dotted double appoggiaturas, long slides, and appoggiaturas. The tempo of the embellishments is accommodated to that of the piece. To avoid monotony, employ the embellishments in alternation. It is expedient to add the longer embellishments to long notes rather than to short ones. All essential embellishments written out in small notes enter on the beat of the main note, their value being subtracted from the latter. Now follow details concerning

(1) *The double appoggiatura* (Anschlag). It is formed by two grace-notes, one above, the other below, the main note. A distinction is made between the short and the long kind. In the short one the second note is a second above, the first shifting its place; it takes, according to Bach, Agricola, L. Mozart, and Hiller, less stress than the main note:

This appoggiatura also occurs reversed:

The long or dotted double appoggiatura has one short invariable, and one long variable, fore-grace. It occurs in slow tempo, and is executed slowly. The main note often retains only the smallest part of its value:

(2) *The slide.* This consists invariably of a stepwise succession of fore-graces:

There are the short undotted and the long dotted slide. The employment of the latter is quite similar to that of the double appoggiatura. The dotted tone is strong, the other weak:

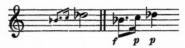

The main note often retains but a very small part of its value. If tied to another of equal pitch, the slide absorbs its entire value:

(3) *The inverted mordent* consists of the main note itself and its higher second, and is executed very rapidly:

Then follow the essential embellishments, which are indicated by a regular sign; and first, all kinds of

Trills. (1) *The trill without after-turn.* According to Türk, this always begins with the auxiliary note. Hummel is the first to give the rule, that it begins with the main note. It is usually employed where rapid movement admits of no after-turn. The sign is *tr* or ᷹, in more extended passages ᷹᷹᷹᷹᷹ etc.

(2) *The trill with after-turn.* The latter is either written out, or indicated by a hook ⌣. It is played in the same tempo as the trill, or even faster. When a trill over a dotted note is followed by a single note, this replaces the after-turn, which is omitted. E. g. 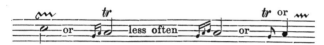 Chromatic signs are set above the trill-sign. Chains of trills, and short running trills like triplets, take no after-turn.

(3) *The trill beginning from below* arises, when to the trill two grace-notes are prefixed, the first a second below, the second on a level with, the main note. It is indicated in the following manner:

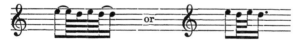

(4) *The trill beginning from above,* ⌣ or:

(5) *The double inverted mordent:* ⌣

is executed thus:

The signs ⌣ and ⌣ require no further explanation.

(6) *The mordent* is quite like the inverted mordent, only it begins with the main note and takes the second below as auxiliary. Sign and execution are as follows:

This is the short mordent. There is also a long one; it can occur only with tones sustained for a time. In this the auxiliary tone is sounded at least twice, with longer notes several times, but it must not fill the entire value of the main note, like the trill, but at most one-half of the same. Its sign is ₥, e. g.:

(7) *The acciaccatura*. In this two keys are struck at once, but the lower one released immediately. This grace having a somewhat harsh sound, it can be employed only in fiery, defiant passages. In fuller harmonies the lower tone is indicated by a line under the note to which the embellishment belongs.

(8) *The battement* differs from the mordent only by beginning on the auxiliary note: It has no special sign, and is written out in small notes.

(9) *The turn*. This is one of the most beautiful and serviceable embellishments. There are the following four kinds:

(a) *The simple turn*. It is indicated by the signs ∽ ? ∽ and also by small notes: Its execution in four notes: is incorrect. Several composers employ the sign of the trill for this same figure; this will be apparent, when on account of rapid movement the trill would be impracticable, e. g.:

When the sign ∽ is set to the right of the note, or over a dot, the turn should be played later, just before the following note. — To a dotted note, the fourth note of the turn is played exactly on the dot, e. g.: executed thus:

 The sign for the inverted turn is ∾.

Custom, however, has not attained to a precise distinction as regards the manner of writing the turn-signs.

(b) The "geschnellte Doppelschlag", also called the "Rolle", takes, before the turn proper, an auxiliary on a level with the main note:

(c) The turn with prefix from below is a slide with a turn, and there are, in analogy to the slide, short and long dotted turns:

(d) The rebounding ("prallende") turn is an inverted mordent with an after-turn. The two first tones are played very rapidly, the other two somewhat slower, but still so fast, that the main note retains one half of its value:

(10) The vibrato ("Bebung"). This effect was peculiar to the tangent-clavier (clavichord), and was impossible on the instruments later in vogue. It was indicated either by dots, or the word tremolo. The finger remained in contact with the key during the entire value of the note, but sought to reinforce the tone by oft-repeated, gentle pressure:

The following sign was also in use: Or, instead of the strokes: ∼∼∼∼∼.

(11) *The arpeggio* is the familiar figure:

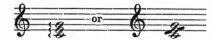

To prevent too long a pause between slow-moving chords, the chords can be broken several times in various ways:

(This grace has now gone out of use.)

When a long appoggiatura stands before any note of an arpeggio chord, the arpeggio is executed directly, i. e. within the value of the appoggiatura:

With short appoggiaturas the arpeggio is played thus:

(12) *The ribattuta* consists in the repeated alternation of the note written with its higher second. The given note is each time held longer than the auxiliary. This grace is used especially as an introduction to closing trills:

etc.

Arbitrary (accidental) embellishments are (1) alterations and additions introduced by the player for the embellishment of a composition; (2) embellishments or *fermate,* together with their transitions; (3) the so-called greater cadenzas. All these are sometimes written out by the composer himself. The number of their notes varies. If there are but few before a main note, they are subtracted from its value, e. g.:

if there are many, they usually stand after a main note, and are played within the time of the same. Those improvised by the player must be suited to the character of the piece and should on the whole be employed sparingly. Either notes are added, or those written down are altered, and this properly occurs at the repetition of passages. But variety may be lent to such passages by other means, such as loudness and softness, retardation, staccato, sostenuto, etc.

The author makes similar observations on the interludes at *fermate*, and the so-called greater cadenzas. Everywhere he notices differences, and enumerates cases and kinds, discussing them in detail, wherein the merit of exactitude cannot be denied him. More important, however, is the

Chapter on *Rendering in general, and the universal requisites of the same.* A distinction is first made between Performance and Rendering. The former is like the ordinary reading-off of a speech, the latter like its declamation. A good rendering requires: (1) Correct execution, a certain finish in technique, steadiness in time, and a knowledge of thoroughbass. (2) Distinctness of execution. (3) An expression of the predominant character. (4) The appropriate employment of the embellishments and certain other aids. (5) Natural susceptibility for all the emotions and passions to be expressed in music. Flowing execution, and attention to all marks of expression, are taken for granted.

Distinctness depends: (1) Upon the mechanical execution; (2) upon the emphasis laid on certain tones; (3) upon correct punctuation (phrasing). Emphasis is given: (1) To tones falling on the thesis or on the principal subdivisions of the measure; (2) to initial tones of sections and phrases; (3) to appoggia-

4*

turas, dissonances, and tones preparing the dissonance by means of a tie, syncopations, and tones peculiarly prominent from their high or low pitch, e. g.:

Emphasis can also be conveyed to certain tones through their imperceptible prolongation. This should, of course, affect only tones of peculiar importance. A slight prolongation is given, for instance, to tones called for by an accidental, or to particularly high tones; these may occasionally be prolonged by one-half their value.

This license must be avoided where it would occasion a faulty harmonic progression, e. g. where parallel octaves and fifths would result.

Correct punctuation is of high importance in exhibiting the interdependence of parts. Pauses must therefore be indicated similarly to those in rhetorical declamation. A phrase yet incomplete in sense must not be cut in twain by unseasonably lifting the finger. The end of a period should be gently lifted, and the following tone emphasized. Where the composer indicates the close by a rest, the last tone must be played shorter than it is written. At a perfect close the fingers are lifted sooner than at a half-close. When a fiery passage is followed by one of an opposite character, they must be divided more markedly than two of similar character. As a sign for smaller, less noticeable divisions Türk proposed the adoption of two short lines, and desired, in any event, plainer directions for punctuation from the composers. In music the period corresponds exactly to a spoken sentence, the half-close to a colon or semicolon, the phrase to a comma; there are cesuras like those in versification. — Clear insight into the punctuation is one of the most difficult matters. — Thereupon follows a section

On the expression of the predominant character. Characteristic expression is the player's highest aim. He must endeavor to immerse himself wholly in the dominant mood of the piece, and through speaking tones to communicate his emotions to others. So much herein depends upon feeling, that no rule can teach it.

Indispensable requirements are, however: (1) The peculiar measure of loudness and softness suited to the predominant character; (2) the staccato, sostenuto, legato, and slurring of the tones; (3) the proper movement.

Compositions of a vivacious, joyous, lively, determined, lofty, brilliant, haughty, confident, serious, threatening, spirited, bold, fiery, wild, furious character require a certain, though not fully equal, degree of force. This degree must be augmented or diminished according as the emotion is expressed in a more vehement or measured manner. A *forte* in an *allegro furioso* is stronger than in an *allegro*, which expresses only a measured degree of joy.—Compositions whose character is gentle, peaceful, innocent, naïve, pleading, tender, loving, affecting, remorseful, sad, plaintive, sorrowful, demand a softer interpretation, and the degree of softness is likewise variable.

It is impossible to give directions for each single passage. In general, animation shows in force; a tender, songful strain is more gentle. If a passage is repeated, the repetition is softer; though in many cases, on the contrary, louder. Significant tones are accented; dissonances are stronger than consonances — the sharper the dissonance, the more forcible in tone. Chords through which modulation is effected to a remote key, unexpected transitions, and interrupted cadences, are likewise forceful.

A distinction is drawn between a heavy and light style (rendering). The former results, when each tone is struck with a certain firmness, and held through its entire value. The contrary characterizes a light style. These varieties are thus opposed like legato and staccato, and are expressed through these agencies. Türk here gives familiar explanations on notes having dots above them, notes provided with a short stroke, and mezzo-staccato notes with a slur over dots. Some details are inexact; it is especially surprising, that he directs for the ordinary style, which is neither legato nor staccato, that the finger should quit the key a little before the end of the note. In modern theory, the legato is the ordinary style.

Whether the rendering shall be heavy or light is decided: (1) By the character or general intention of the composition; (2) by the movement prescribed; (3) by the Time; (4) by the note-values; (5) by the harmonic and melodic treatment. Furthermore, one must even consider the period in which the composition was written, the national taste, and the composer's style. Older pieces are heavier than later ones in freer style; those in the Italian national style require a medium heaviness of rendering; the French are lighter, the German heaviest of all.

Many remarks are of slight importance, in part a repetition of former ones, and the entire distinction made between heavy and light rendering really explains very little.

Other elements of a good rendering are: (1) A fine tone; (2) a free, unconstrained style of execution; (3) becoming gestures; (4) particular advantages.

An absolutely fine tone must be distinct, full, sensitive, bright, and above all agreeable; must not become harsh and grating in its highest intensity, or indistinct in its extremest softness; moreover, it must take on the characteristic quality of the composition, i. e. it must also be relatively fine.—He plays most beautifully, whose tone most nearly approaches vocality, compared with which all brilliant passages are mere trifling. To this end the player should often practice long-sustained notes, touching the key with only medium force, but pressing down until the tone gains its full intensity, and rises in pitch on continued pressure. (This latter result was attainable on the old claviers with tangents). — This holds good not only with the clavichord and fortepiano, but with the *Flügel* as well; although the last is not capable of great expression, a skilful player can lend some modification to the tone by means of variety in touch.

Besides tone-development, the following elements also influence the expression: (1) Playing without time; (2) acceleration or retardation; (3) the *tempo rubato.*

Free phantasies, cadenzas, *fermate,* and recitatives, must be executed according to impulse rather than in strict time. All the passages in which acceleration or retardation may occur, can hardly be definitely stated. In pieces of a very vehement character the most forcible passages may be somewhat accelerated. When passages in which gentle emotions predominate are interrupted by an animated idea, the tempo of the latter may be hastened, and similarly with such as unexpectedly express a violent impulse. Contrarily, passages of a tender, mournful character are retarded. Before the entrance of certain *fermate,* the tempo may be very gradually retarded, as if the energies were slowly sinking, and similarly with ideas which close a composition, and are marked *dim., diluendo,* or *smorzando.* A gentle, moving strain, between two passages of a forcible and animated ·description, is likewise retarded. Alternate acceleration and retardation is suited to pieces in which two contrasting characters are depicted. Transitions to the theme, and repetitions of naturally faint passages, should also be played *rallentando.* But deviations from the general tempo must never be too marked. — The so-called *tempo rubato* is also an agency of good rendering; it arises from a shifting of the tones by means of anticipation or retardation, and likewise from shifting the accents to weak beats. The general tempo, however, remains unaffected.

Türk concludes his work with an appendix containing a list of the terms whose knowledge is most essential to the player in connection with the rendering.

In the pianoforte method reviewed above *in extenso,* the earlier methodism attains to its fullest and most orderly systematization. With it the first epoch of written pianoforte methods closes. A merely hasty glance shows us that its characteristic feature is a theorizing, rather prolix treatment of the material, tending to lay stress on subordinate matters.

Much attention is everywhere given to the *agréments*, although these are not, in point of fact, immanent to the spirit of art. but to be memorized as part of the terminology. A decided want of perception for essentials is manifested in the attempt to teach things of a purely empirical, practical nature by theoretical methods. A theory of practical knowledge is quite possible, only it must not aim at skimming the surface of practical manifestations, but must follow them through the various stages of their evolution to their artistic perfection. None of the earlier school-works do this; they content themselves with a system of fingering, where they ought to follow up the theory of figuration and of mechanical forms, and the gymnastic development, from the rudiments to the perfect flexibility of the hand. True, their technique occupies, in comparison with our modern training, an infantile standpoint, and subtle distinctions can hardly be made so long as their contrasting manifestations are scarcely recognizable. Again, the theory of rendering finds expression in mere generalizations, and is far too much occupied with externals, where it ought to fructify the perceptive and intellectual faculties.

Neither do the next-following text-books complete the progress sketched above with reference to methodic conception. But what distinguishes them from the one just reviewed, is a greater accumulation of material, a broader consideration of the practical development in more numerous examples for practice, and here and there a deeper insight into ideal relations. In the transition period, as it were, from the earlier methodism to the ensuing epoch, falls the

Pianoforte Method of the Paris Conservatory, by L. Adam.

No date being given on the title-page, the year of publication can be fixed only conjecturally. The beginning of this century (1802 ?) seems probable when we consider, that the author cannot in his youth have written a text-book founded on experience. On the other hand, if we take into consideration the lack of that systematization which is, in any event, highly to be commended in Türk, and which forms no salient feature of this work, the hypothesis just advanced again loses in weight.

What further distinguishes this and the following methods from the previous ones, is the abbreviation of the chapter on Embellishments, and a limitation of the material belonging to the science of composition. A sharper demarkation of the departments is apparent.

Passing over Adam's theory of the ordinary rudiments, we proceed to a summary of the essential portion, isolated fragments of which result, in our combination, in the following general view.

First, the field of sensuous refinement is widened; this work, too, refers exclusively to instruments with hammers, whereas even Türk still occupies himself chiefly with the older kinds. This naturally has an essential influence on the production of tone.

While Bach (§ 17) says, that a stroke or pressure on the key amounts to the same thing, and Türk in the note quoted on touch has principally the clavichord on view, and even holds the *Flügel* to be not specially adapted for expression, Adam is the pioneer of theory in a new field, namely that of tone-production or touch. He says, that there is an extraordinary variety in the modes of touching the key and drawing out the tone. Only through the touch can a fine tone be obtained; only the power and pressure of the finger are to be employed.—The pupil must endeavor to play everything with expression, each note is important. His sole aim should be to imitate as far as possible the singing tone, developed by great masters on all instruments, and the manifold inflections of the voice, which is so tender and affecting.

Adam exhausts his vocabulary to express a conception of very general scope. He does not penetrate to subtle distinctions, or, in particular, to essentials of technique. Feeling is still the sole decisive factor; methodical acumen in the perception of mechanical details, as the responsive medium for the expression of feeling, is still wholly lacking. The several subjects of instruction are also confounded. Directly after the discussions on touch come the remarks: "Music is like Speech, characterized by similar laws. A piece must be interpreted faithfully, according to the feeling and style in which it was written", etc.

This manner of presentation is certainly no advance above Bach and Türk. Adam expresses himself throughout in general phrases without methodic arrangement. Furthermore, the remarks on rendering are dispersed in various places, and must be gathered together in order to gain a connected view. It is distributed among three chapters, one of which treats of time, and of the tempi and their expression; the second of the use of the pedals; and the third of style.

In this he remarks further: One of the cardinal virtues in rendering is keeping time. Only where the composer directs or the expression requires it should the movement be altered, and this effect must be used sparingly. The *ritardamenti* must not be employed throughout, but only in passages where the expression of a languishing, or the passion of an animated melody demands a different tempo.

An addition to the technical material is made by the invention of the pedals, which naturally could not be mentioned in the earlier text-books. It lies in the nature of the case, that the novelty of the charm should give rise to a greater variety and development of the pedals than we now have, their number being at present reduced to two, sometimes even to one. The period after Adam could frequently boast 6 or 7.— The method under consideration mentions four pedals, namely:

(1) The *forte pedal* (that indicated to-day by *ped.*) It is taken where the same harmony continues, and in slow tempo; it must likewise be treated *piano,* and is suited to singing harmonies with long sustained tones, such as *pastorali,* or in tender, melancholic arias, romances, and religious compositions.

(2) The *lute* or *harp-pedal.* This is for rapid chromatic runs, and for all passages to be executed neatly and cleanly.

The very dryness of the tone resulting from its use emphasizes the roundness of a passage, and renders it forcible.

(3) The *piano pedal*. Combined with the second it is superb, really heavenly. Again, taken with the *forte* pedal, it can perfectly imitate the harmonica, whose tone so strongly affects our fibres.

(4) The fourth pedal on the large pianoforte is employed only for the *piano, crescendo,* and *diminuendo.*

This description of the pedals is insufficient for one who does not remember their mechanism from personal observation, in case the historical interest requires a clearer insight into their operation. The second pedal probably operated by bringing a strip of cloth between the hammers and strings, and the third probably resembled our soft pedal. The description of the fourth pedal is obscure.

The author now proceeds, in another place: "The ripe student must create his own style, and not slavishly imitate other artists. Style is exhibited in two relations: (1) In the manner of rendering; (2) as the art, to give a piece its appropriate expression. The former is a matter of technique, the latter of feeling or expression. With reference to the second the following suggestions are offered:

"The *allegro* requires a brilliant, now a majestic, now a vivacious and fiery rendering; it excites astonishment and admiration. The *adagio,* on the contrary, must progress in sustained tones, at times sad, often melancholy. It interrupts the lively delight which the *allegro* gave, affects our fibres more powerfully, and awakens our emotions, together with a feeling of pain. The *presto* dispels all these impressions; lively and merry, it gives us something agreeable to hear, and returns in manifold guise. Lightness and grace it retains; when plaintive tones sometimes escape it, this is but to better expectation by delightful surprises of artistic transition." Then follow several sub-species of the given forms, and thereafter the remark: "Each composer must be interpreted according to his character, the one with deep feeling and forceful rendition, the other in a gay, romantic, often fantastic spirit, always with a fiery, spirited, refined interpretation, etc."

Thus the result is, if we choose to sum up our opinion, that, besides the technical additions, the work is animated throughout by a certain striving after poetic diction with a zeal for its subject, which is meant as a stimulus. Hereby it is distinguished from the earlier methods, but shows an advance only in the first-mentioned point. The second exhibits merely formal superiority in comparison with Bach's dry treatment, which often touched only the negative side, and with Türk's broader survey. Substantially it presents, on the whole, but few new points. Its phrases seek vividness of diction, yet often lack, where essential distinctions are called for, the slightest trace of a clear and striking contrast. On the other hand, they assume mere externals as a basis for teachings, which stand in need of general æsthetic substantiation, and which in this form do not even equal in fulness the material collected by Bach. The ethical side is of higher merit, which finds utterance in the appeal to loftier artistic aims and to composition. But noteworthy as this standpoint, which in later works recedes more and more into the background, may be, we must not forget that it carries confusion to the boundaries of scientific distinction, and that it rather lies within the scope of a pianoforte method to maintain the rights of its peculiar art by recording its elements of beauty, than finally to merge it in a universal subject whose treatment, as history proves, is by no means so profitable.

Among subsequent works

Cramer's Clavierschule

was for a long time that most widely disseminated, and still enjoys wide popularity on account of its concise and elementary treatment of the topic. The directions for the attitude of the body are as follows. The player should sit gracefully in the middle of the keyboard, neither too far nor too near. The elbows should be somewhat higher than the keyboard, the feet firmly planted on the floor, the arms held neither too close to nor too distant from the sides, the shoulders slightly sloping. The hands should be carried in a line with the elbows, and the knuckles of the second, third, and fourth fingers pressed down. The keys are touched with the extreme fingertips, but not with the nails, and the thumb must always be kept above the keys.—

What Cramer says otherwise, concerns the rudiments, and is not of eminent importance. His rules on using the pedals, of which he mentions five, are similar to Adam's. The popular tendency of the work naturally excludes a conception of deeper penetration, and even the technical part, by reason of too great brevity, no longer satisfies the needs of the period. Some generalities regarding accentuation are further discussed, but in this respect the work is far inferior to the earlier one by Türk.

The following three great Pianoforte Methods by Hummel, Kalkbrenner and Czerny, are more important, and even at the present time well worthy of attention as universal school-works. We first take up

J. N. Hummel's Ausführliche theoretisch-praktische Anweisung zum Pianofortespiel vom ersten Elementar-Unterrichte bis zur vollkommensten Ausbildung. 1828.

This work is distinguished from those hitherto named by its great number of exercises for practice, and establishes thereby, for the new conception of pianoforte study, a standpoint quite different from that assumed by earlier custom. Only Hummel still lacks the practical insight shown in Czerny's method, which trains the mechanical faculties by a shorter system, and in this respect laid the foundation of all modern progress. Hummel still slights the mechanical side; with him the development of the hand has not yet become a product of purely technical work, that turned it out as a perfected mechanism through the aid of a later systematization of method which, though intellectually deadening, nevertheless works quickly. He divides the whole course of study into far too many departments, still loses himself too often in contemplation, takes too little account of the advantages which the experience gained in one chapter should carry over to the next, bestows far too little thought on saving time, and despite all breadth does not include the whole range of modern pianoforte technique. — By not sufficiently considering the pupil's increase of strength derived from a thorough elementary training, he retards his development by too many minutiæ, and, after his laborious and tiresome toiling through all the little exercises of the first two large volumes, still leaves him in jeopardy of everywhere exhibiting extreme awkwardness in practical matters, and of having to perfect his training according to a quite different method.

We proceed to the examination of some details.

In the first part Hummel gives the advice, not to urge practice to mechanical hebetude, but to limit the same to a regular, though attentive time of at most three hours daily. Hand in hand with the mechanical should also go the musical in the study of pieces. The eye should be fixed on the notes, and the fingers must find the keys merely through feeling. For this reason, too, learning by heart is to be suppressed. Easy pieces and slow practice must form the beginning. This resembles Türk's remarks; as regards learning by heart, quite a different view prevails to-day, as we are aware.

Respecting the attitude Hummel directs, that the pupil must sit in the middle of the keyboard, and 6 to 10 inches distant from the same (as Marpurg directed). The feet are planted firmly, and children's feet must be supported. The elbows are turned in towards the body, but without touching the same. The muscles of the hands and arms must be quite free from constraint, and only be exerted so far as is needful to carry the fingers without laxness. The hands must be held a trifle rounded, and slightly turned outward, like the feet. The thumb and fifth finger form a horizontal line on the keyboard. A flat stretching out of the fingers, and boring into the keys with the hand hanging down, are utterly wrong, and cause a weak, lame style. The thumb touches the key only with the edge of its end-joint, and is always held bent in, inclined underneath the second finger. All violent motions of the arms and hands are to be avoided; their muscles must not be more exerted than a quiet and free posture of the hand requires. The fingers must move easily and loosely, and not be lifted too high from the key. The touch must be decided and even, all pressing and thumping be avoided, and neither hands nor fingers be brought out of their natural position. To this end, Logier's chiroplast may be usefully employed. (Here, for the first time, we meet with an artificial mechanical aid.)

Now follows the usual exposition of the terminology and other elements; the first part must be termed the most valuable on account of its collection of practical finger-exercises and little pieces, and its practical hints of all kinds. But how little Hummel's mechanical method recognized the distinctions of the modern system, is apparent, for instance, from his observations on the dots or strokes which indicate the staccato. Without discriminating, the author simply directs that the hands are not to be lifted, but the finger only filliped inward very lightly from the key.

In the second part a view is opened over the entire domain of Hummel's technique; by devoting ten chapters to this subject, with a large selection of finger-exercises, the author at the same time dispatches the question of fingering. This evidently proves better insight into practical requirements than is exhibited in Türk's and Bach's methods, which lay down the most various rules, without practically training the instinct of the fingers.—The ten chapters are as follows:

(1) Progression with fingers in like order in successions of figures of like form.
(2) Passing the thumb under, and passing fingers over thumb.
(3) Omission of one or more fingers.
(4) Changing one finger for another on the same key.
(5) Stretches and leaps.

(6) Use of the thumb and fifth finger on the black keys.

(7) Passing a long finger over a shorter one, and a short finger under a longer one.

(8) Alternation of two or more fingers in repeatedly striking the same key; repeated employment of one finger on different keys.

(9) Interlacing of the fingers, and crossing of the hands.

(10) Distribution of parts between the hands, and licenses in the order of the fingers in the legato style.

We have already noticed the discursiveness of this arrangement. In developing the hand a certain elasticity and looseness of all playing joints should be aimed at, and this is promoted not only by the different figuration of the exercises, but by influencing the manner of touch. It may be assumed, that one who has thoroughly studied the first part, and, in the second, chapters 1, 2, and 5, will also be able skilfully to master the exercises given in chapters 3, 4, 6, 7, 8, and 9. Aside from this, exercises of quite different character are found combined in one chapter, e. g. in the eighth. Nowhere is a difference in the styles of touch spoken of.

The third part of the work is devoted to the Rendering. Unhappily, Hummel here, like his predecessors, again brings up the theory of the embellishments. But in this even Bach and Türk were clearer in their conceptional distinctions, and did not subsume this part under the Rendering. The embellishments are a matter of pure memory, and contribute least of all to the spirit which the rendering is to reproduce. We therefore skip this section, particularly as it is by no means so fully developed as in Türk's work. It should not be overlooked, that this was in accord with the progressive spirit of the period. We observed under Türk's theory of the trill, that Hummel begins the trill on the main note.

Entering deeper into the real subject, Hummel distinguishes between a correct and a fine rendering. "The former is based on the mechanical element in playing, and can be indicated precisely by signs. The beautiful is referable to the rounded form, to the spirit appropriate to each composition, each passage, to tastefulness and agreeableness, particularly in the embellishments, and can only be suggested. Expression is the immediate outgrowth of feeling, and requires impressionability for and a reproduction of that which the composer intended. This expression can be stimulated, suggested, but not taught. Above all, one must hear fine interpretations, especially of vocal music, and perhaps have sung in one's own youth. Hasse, Naumann, Gluck, Mozart, both the Haydns, and the most celebrated composers of all times, sang in their youth. The mastery of difficulties does not alone make a master. Mock emotion, as expressed in gesticulation, too much pedal, and a superabundance of embellishment, is to be condemned."

There follows, not quite in unison with the above: "The chief foundation for a fine rendering is complete control of the fingers, which must command every imaginable gradation of tone by touch. The fingers must obey for the lightest and loosest touch, as well as for the firmest stroke with straining muscles. Let the player study the character of the piece, and consider whether he is performing an *allegro* or an *adagio*. The first demands brilliancy, power, decision, and a pearling velocity of the fingers. True, melodic passages may be played with a certain yielding *abandon*, though, for the sake of unity, not too far departing from the tempo. Withal, the tempo must be taken with decision, and not be permitted to waver throughout. The *adagio* requires expression, songfulness, repose. The tones must be sustained, drawn out, bound together, and made to sing by well-calculated pressure. The embellishments must be played more slowly, more meltingly and tenderly, than in the *allegro;* sometimes the finger must exert the gentlest retraction on the key—exercise the most exquisite sensibility. Ascending runs and tones are executed *crescendo,* descending ones *diminuendo;* though there are cases where the composer desires the reverse, or uniform power."

In examples now cited from his own concerts Hummel repeats, in part, matter presented in a general sense before,

marks the accentuation very appropriately, demands relaxation
in singing passages and acceleration in fiery ones; in *adagio*
a relaxation—especially in closing strains—is required, but an
accompaniment in strict time, and on the whole uniformity
of tempo is urged. With an uneven and crowded number of
notes in *adagio* their distribution should be considered before-
hand, and the greatest velocity saved for the close.

In another place the author gives some practical advice
for instruction, to awaken the feeling for declamation, but
without going into details, and finally discusses the use of
the pedals. Herein his taste differs from the general custom
of the time; for he declares, on the whole, against the pedals.
"Mozart and Clementi did not need this help to win fame as
the most expressive players of their period. The use of the
pedals cannot, to be sure, be entirely avoided, especially that
of the loud pedal in slow tempo, where the melody unfolds
itself on a broad, harmonic foundation."

This is the essential part of Hummel's observations. Much
therein is of permanent value; only depth of penetration and
systematic exposition are lacking. More careful consideration
of technique, and an attempt at a methodical survey of the
same, form the most substantial advance of this work beyond
its predecessors. In regard to expression Hummel shares with
his predecessors, and with the greater part of his successors,
the amateurish, indefinite notion of a sensibility which must
be present, but can only be led, not taught. Marx was the
first to arouse the sensibility to clear consciousness. It is
granted only to æsthetic perception, to follow him through
all details. Hummel, like Adam, starts from the external
names of the *allegro* and *adagio* to lay down rules for the
rendering, instead of analyzing the idea in its primitive elements, from which, as from one foundation, all forms of composition spring.

Neither does the rival school-work of Hummel's method,
of which we now propose to speak, pass beyond this standpoint. This is

Friedrich Kalkbrenner's Anweisung, das Pianoforte mit Hülfe des Handleiters spielen zu lernen. (Instructions for learning to play the Pianoforte with the aid of the Hand-guide.) This title awakens expectation of a one-sided conception of pianoforte instruction, and in fact one immediately perceives, if the prominence given by Kalkbrenner to his well-known hand-guide be considered, that the mechanical side will be more developed than with Hummel. Nevertheless, the examples accumulated by the latter show far greater industry and careful invention; herein Kalkbrenner set himself an easy task.

As regards the theory, we find, aside from some phrases which manifest, almost more than with his predecessors, an insufficient and merely general scientific education, observations based upon a finer and broader empiricism than Hummel's. Such phrases are, for instance, explanations like the following: "Music is the art of combining tones; Rhythm is the relation between two successive musical ideas; that music, whose rhythm is most marked, is most characteristic", etc.

The survey of the technical studies reveals, on the contrary, a more practical insight, although the examples for practice belonging to the same are not numerous enough. Kalkbrenner divides it into the following chapters:

(1) Exercises in five notes with quiet hand, as principal groundwork.
(2) Scales in all forms.
(3) Thirds, sixths, and chord-forms.
(4) Octaves with the wrist.
(5) Studies on the trill.
(6) Crossing of the hands, and ease in the mastery of all difficulties combined.

The development of the wrist is a very important addition made by Kalkbrenner to technique. The view given above is unquestionably simpler than with Hummel, though still insufficient; in Plaidy's works we shall become acquainted with one still completer. The author also gives a more thorough theory of fingering, which is excelled only by Czerny.

5*

Less deserving of notice, on account of their incompleteness, are the Terminology, the theory of Signs, and the explanation of the Embellishments. The term "Manieren" (agréments) now finally disappears.

What Kalkbrenner says on Rendering must, as with Adam and Hummel, be gathered together from various parts of the work, and yields substantially the following:

"The tempo of a piece is indicated above the same, and the player must govern himself accordingly. If he does not understand the Italian terms, he should gain a clear idea of their meaning from the dictionary." Here follow some explanations of abbreviations, as *f.*, *p.*, *cresc.*, etc.

"The employment of the pedals is indispensable, and the dryness of the tone of German instruments is lamentable, which in part have no pedals at all. For this reason he himself once nearly gave up a projected concert in Vienna, but hit upon the idea of inserting a bit of cork under the damper-rail in the treble, so that the two highest octaves hardly damped at all; only thus could he attain the desired effect in melody. The employment of the damper-pedal is to be recommended in two cases: either to connect the harmonies, or to augment the power." In his recognition of this latter point Kalkbrenner is beyond his predecessors.

"In performing, one must not be blindly hurried away by emotion, but carefully weigh the effect. All musical expression lies in the nuances, and monotony must be avoided above all things. The most general rules are as follows: Ascending passages must be played *crescendo*, descending ones *decrescendo*, so that the highest note is sounded most strongly, the lowest most softly. Music thereby takes on a certain undulatory movement. The longest tone must be the strongest; the notes of melodious strains should become a little slower; the first and last notes are to be more strongly emphasized than the others. The melody must be louder than the accompaniment, and the latter should not always follow the shades of expression of the melody. With frequent changes of harmony, or rapid successive modulations, the tempo must be retarded. The high keys must never be struck in a violent or hard manner. The sound of the fingers on the keys, which becomes too audible in the treble, must be softened as much as possible. All tones foreign to the key, or notes with accidentals, must be more marked. A note several times repeated must be shaded by swelling or diminishing the sound. Tied and syncopated notes are marked. Oft-repeated passages must likewise be variously executed, the right effect being usually attainable by varying the power. The player should sit quiet, and avoid all gesticulation.

"Regarding the rhythm, the punctuation must be carefully observed. Whenever the close of a musical phrase is put off, less power should be used; emphatic accentuation is only in place at the complete close. Pauses are the signs of punctuation. Such punctuation-marks are proper at: (1) Closes of movements, or perfect closes; these equal the period. (2) Imperfect cadences from tonic to dominant; these equal the semicolon. (3) Interrupted cadences or transitions, analogous to the exclamation-point. (4) Quarter-rests ending sections are like the comma. All these divisions must be punctuated with a view to their appropriate expression.

On the Touch the following may be quoted: "The tone of the pianoforte is by no means quite prepared; it is almost more capable of modification than that of any other instrument. By elongating the fingers or playing on the nails, but little tone can be drawn out; the key must be struck with the fleshy tip of the finger." Then follow the ordinary rules on quietness of the arm, hand, etc. Special attention is paid to the wrist-stroke. "The manner of striking the key must exhibit innumerable variations, corresponding to the various emotions to be expressed. One must now caress the key, now pounce upon it as the lion hurls himself upon his prey. Still, while drawing from the instrument all the tone possible, avoid striking it rudely and roughly. Bravura is not the highest aim; one should strive after higher ends—expression, emotion, and grand effects. In particular, variety of expression must prevail. The melody must always predominate; if one note has an expression-mark, the rest should not be likewise modified. One must at length attain to the expression of warmth without violence, strength without harshness, gentleness without weakness; this is, to be sure, the highest goal."

We see, that Kalkbrenner's material has become somewhat more abundant; but no further exposition is needed to show the same absence of thorough systematization, as in the the foregoing works.

We now come to

Czerny's great Pianoforte Method, Op. 500.

With regard to completeness, this work far surpasses the earlier ones; even if it does not thoroughly analyze the materials which it discusses, their mere mention is a striking manifestation of progress. Moreover, it embraces the modern features of virtuosity, and thus ranks pre-eminent, in range of material, among the works of the time. Czerny's style is not that of deep scientific penetration, but he is a practical man, and however slightly and superficially he may treat many questions requiring a lofty, artistic point of view, it cannot be denied that a certain practical talent shows throughout, and that this pianoforte method satisfies the demands of all learners up to a certain point.

The first part treats of the ordinary rudiments in a very perspicuous manner, and as it is more prominent in form than in content, we take the liberty of passing over this familiar subject.

The second part occupies itself with the mechanical training, and the principle is laid down, that the latter must be mastered by the player in such a degree, that the listener shall notice no exertion on his part. In form it exhibits, in the sequel, great similarity to Türk's method; namely, the system of fingering is raised to the position of the leading idea. Properly speaking, this is an antiquated standpoint, and the great master of playing, Czerny, might well have

considered, that not the fingering, which can be learned from
rules, but rather the gymnastic training of the muscles and
joints of the technical apparatus, is the requirement for
mastering the technical material. Here, no less than with
Türk and Hummel, it seems inadmissible to raise a secondary,
resultant idea to be the leading feature of a system founded
on a far more important conception. — Now follow, as with
Türk, first the general principles of fingering, and then their
application to the several forms of mechanical training; here,
also, the numerous examples facilitate comprehension.

Among the general rules the most important are: The
greatest practicality is the guiding principle. The most convenient fingering is the best, and in each individual case the
simpler is preferable to the more complicated, e. g. the use
of the fingers without passing under is better, where feasible,
than passing the thumb under. On adjoining keys the fingers
must be taken in their natural order. The four longer fingers
must not be passed over each other. No finger should be
used twice in succession. In running scales the thumb and
fifth finger are not to be employed on black keys.

The author now proceeds to the special chapters. He
observes, that for scales and similar passages just so many
fingers must always be taken as to reach the extreme note of
each passage with a convenient finger, in order to avoid superfluous passing under and over.—Every regularly formed figure
is to be played with a correspondingly regular fingering.—
When runs begin with an irregular finger, one should seek to
get back into the normal fingering during their course. When
the key changes during a run, the fingering must also change
to one appropriate to the scale. Where the same key occurs
twice in a run, the finger must be changed, etc.

The *glissandi* are executed with the nail, and the position
of the hand changed accordingly; with doubled notes only
one part is played with the nail.

The fingering of the chromatic scale is 1 2 1 2 1 2 1,
beginning on C, this being the standard; in very rapid runs

121212312341. The fingering 13131231 is not to be recommended, because the second finger gets too little practice, and the hand may grow accustomed to a slanting posture. Besides, both delicacy and velocity are too greatly embarrassed thereby.

We skip the greater part of what follows, as it must again appear in detail in the second part of this work. Czerny takes up in turn the broken thirds, fourths, sixths, and octaves (for which he recommends the fingers 1 4 on black keys), then chords, advancing doubled notes, double runs, change of finger on one key, the various trills, trills in thirds, in fourths, in sixths; the interlacing and crossing of the hands, the fingering for full chords (which is governed by the simple rule, that the interval of a fourth must not be taken by two adjoining fingers, excepting the first and second), the free entrance of the fingers on a key, the use of one finger on several keys, leaps, polyphonic movements, and the simultaneous striking of two fingers on one key.

The third part of this method has been, for several decades, the sole comparatively complete work for instruction on the rendering, and in it is found the chief evidence of progress.

It proceeds thus: The first two parts have taught only mechanical dexterity; these are only the means to the proper end of art, which consists in endowing the performance with life and soul, and thereby to influence the hearts and minds of the hearers. Yet we must not lose sight of the fact, that the rendering so greatly depends upon mechanical aids, that the two factors coalesce, the one appearing merely the natural result of the other.

Everything having reference to the rendering can be classed under two heads:

(1) The observance of all marks of expression given by the composer.

(2) That expression with which the player shall endow the composition from his own feeling.

The first point covers three kinds of signs: Those referring (a) to the power of tone developed; (b) to the degree of length or shortness of the latter; (c) to alterations in the prescribed tempo.

These three cases are now discussed in the first three of the 20 chapters constituting this part.— Those following take up the elements spontaneously added by the player to the rendering, the fourth chapter dealing with, The rendering of simple melody; the fifth, Expression in brilliant passages; the sixth, The use of the pedals.

The ensuing chapters bear the following headings: (7) On the use of Maelzl's Metronome; (8) On the correct tempo suited for each composition; (9) On brilliant execution; (10) On the rendering of passionate, characteristic compositions; (11) On performance in public; (12) On the execution of fugues and other compositions in the strict style; (13) On playing without notes; (14) On playing at sight; (15) On peculiarities in the interpretation of different composers; (16) On transposing; (17) On playing from score, and the other clefs; (18) On preluding; (19) On improvising; (20) On the good qualities, the preservation, and the tuning of the fortepiano.

However, it is apparent from the mere enumeration of the headings, that in this work, too, the spirit of practical empiricism predominates over that of scientific and æsthetic theory. Still, a certain right thereto may be conceded to a pianoforte method which necessarily keeps practical aims in sight; and a work in our own sense, which has been variously applied as a standard to the works heretofore reviewed, may require a different form from that marked out for such a pianoforte method.— This practical empiricism characterizes the part in question throughout; instead of entering more into its details, let it suffice to emphasize the wealth of the material collected therein, and to point it out as a source still of present value for the theoretic analysis of pianoforte methodics.

The fourth part is weaker in substance. In four chapters, each of which constitutes a volume by itself, it treats of Beethoven's style of rendering, of fugue-playing, and of the later virtuosi. After the poetic conception of Bach's and Beethoven's playing, to which Marx has accustomed us, Czerny's remarks upon each single sonata and trio by Beethoven may seem superfluous. The fourth chapter takes somewhat higher ground; it is devoted to fugue-playing, and the author gives eleven rules worthy of every player's serious attention. Their chief points may be summarized thus: The themes are strongly marked; where all parts enter, it is necessary to play with vigor, and less so with few parts. Long-sustained basses, even if in tied notes of similar pitch, may be repeated with each measure. Strict time must be maintained; a ritardando is allowable only at *fermate* and closing measures. The legato is always to be employed, except where rests or staccato-marks require the contrary. The arpeggio is to be avoided as much as possible, and likewise the pedal in older fugues; each note must receive its exact value. The regular fingering is quite disregarded. A special study must be made of changing fingers, or even hands, on one key without causing it to sound again. In particular, the distribution of the middle parts between the hands must be carefully considered, and definitively fixed when practicing.

The chapter which discusses the virtuosity of the newer school after Thalberg, does not rise above a certain amateurish twaddle. Modernism, according to Czerny, is based upon three characteristics: (1) The perfected development of finger-technique and bravura playing; (2) the art of weaving a brilliant accompaniment about a singing melody; (3) the extended employment of the pedal. To this he adds: Thalberg's works are calculated for extreme elegance and the tenderest gracefulness in rendering, and the most brilliant difficulties serve only as a means to that end. His appearance dates from about the year 1830.

Döhler was probably the first, in 1835, to write longer pieces for the left hand alone. His compositions are calculated for a very brilliant, piquantly clear, yet expressive rendering— for great velocity, bravura, and a fine trill, and must be executed with fire and animation, sometimes too with humor and roguish grace.

Henselt's compositions demand great sentiment and passion, a firm touch, great extensibility of the fingers. In his melodies feeling, rather than elegance, predominates.

In similar style he discourses of Chopin, and likewise of Taubert, Willmers, and Liszt, some passages from the compositions of these masters being quoted in illustration.—The chapter closes with the true remark, that all these attributes of the new school can be acquired but gradually, and that they are founded upon the foregoing period, like this latter upon the previous one.

Czerny, however, is by no means to be judged from his great pianoforte method alone. His numerous sets of studies, among which the most important are: The School of Velocity, preparatory to the "Fingerfertigkeit", Op. 636; the forty Daily Studies; the grand Études, Op. 746; the School of Embellishments, the School of the Legato and Staccato, the School for the Left Hand, the Studies in Thirds, for the Trill, Studies for the rendering of the Melody, 160 Eight-measure Studies, the School of the Virtuoso,—all these exhibit his standpoint as follows:—In the pianoforte player's career less depends upon the *knowledge*, how this or that form of technique must be treated (the point of view assumed by Bach, Türk, and Hummel, for example), than upon the *ability* to execute it. Now the latter lies, on the one hand, in such a flexibility of all active joints and members, that the same can overcome, instinctively and with equal certainty, every difficulty in any number of repetitions required; on the other hand, in a special, exclusive training in each individual figure and form, precisely such as Czerny supplies, to this end, in a whole work devoted to studies on the trill, another on thirds, etc.

All these works must be considered in connection with Czerny's pianoforte method, and only through a survey of their totality can conclusive judgment be passed on the author. The opinion arrived at is, that in the mechanico-practical development of our modern pianoforte style he has exerted the widest, most practical, and leading formative influence, and was also the first to attempt to systematize, in a complete school-work, all results till then attained.

With Czerny's Method closes an epoch. True, in the period next-following, other school-works appear, such as the methods by Moscheles and Fétis in Th. Kullak's edition, and the great Pianoforte School by Siegmund Lebert and Ludwig Stark (Stuttgart, 1858). But these works are limited, for the most part, to a grouping of studies worked out in composition-form; the former contains almost no theoretical details at all, the latter but few. Czerny's principle was, to occupy the mind as little as possible with deeper musical thoughts in his studies — the attention should be entirely pre-occupied with technique. This idea, being highly advantageous for practical purposes, has won undeniable popularity for several of these works. In the two school-works mentioned above, the musical contents again vie with the technical.

The works remaining for discussion have in part the character of monographs; such is the case even with Kontski's work, which reappears under the title of a school. These are mostly works treating of separate departments of the subject, — essays, supplements, and contributions to the understanding of pianoforte style lying at the foundation of the advanced, systematized training. We will first take up the preface to

Moscheles' Studies for the Pianoforte. Op. 70.

This finds mention here chiefly on account of the author's celebrity. In substance it ranks below Czerny's theories. The question of Touch, for instance, is treated with a superficiality which recalls the period before Adam. Only gradations of power are spoken of in the same. On the other hand, due emphasis is given to the legato, and to an exact reciprocal motion of the fingers. On the signs for the staccato and mezzo staccato follow observations already anticipated by Czerny. A chapter on the legato style repeats the opening remarks, another on time begins with the sentence: "Time is the soul of music", and for the rest agrees with Adam, Hummel, Kalkbrenner, etc., that a too frequent deviation from the original tempo is inadmissible.—Finally, some noteworthy suggestions on practicing pieces are given: The piece ought first to be played through slowly, the fingering then settled, thereafter the tempo, then individual passages studied repeatedly, and finally the connected execution undertaken.

More valuable is the preface to

Robert Schumann's "Studies for the Pianoforte, after Capriccios by Paganini." Op. 10.

Here we meet with a new element. In contrast to the one-sided preferment of technique, which became the characteristic mark of modern virtuosity under Czerny's influence, Schumann occupies a more ideal standpoint, toward which, as we shall see later, Marx also has a leaning. It was inevitable, that, even at the hazard of one-sidedness of conception, a counter-current to the exuberance of technique must somewhere make itself felt; and Schumann's individuality, his reformatory spirit, that also sought out original paths in composition, was born to take part in this opposition.

Together with the above-named preface, the appendix to his Jugendalbum must also be considered. Though we find in these two disquisitions no connected system, but rather sets of aphorisms, the fundamental idea is apparent, that not too much should be sacrificed to technique, but that the musical faculty, the imagination, should be occupied. Fewer exercises should be played from pianoforte methods, than invented by the player himself. Thus Schumann recommends, at a passage in thirds in the second Étude, to forbear from anxious practice of individual portions; "if the thirds are only struck exactly together from a loose finger-joint, their connected practice is better than such practice". In this "if" there lies, to be sure, an important presumption, and were it really easy to satisfy Schumann's requirements without mechanical studies, pianoforte playing would have inclined from the beginning more to the intellectual side. — And on the whole, Schumann surveys his principle rather superficially, nowhere displaying deep penetration. In the Jugendalbum he repeats, that a multitude of mechanical exercises continued to old age will not alone suffice; they resemble the A-B-C continually practiced for attaining greater fluency. Dumb pianofortes are also useless; one must *hear* what one plays. Instead of closetting oneself for days with exercises, one should rather plunge into the full current of musical life, especially with the chorus and orchestra. One should be able to sing the pieces which one plays; rather learn easy pieces perfectly, than more difficult ones fairly well; seek to win applause of artists rather than of the public; and live in an animated, universally formative, even poetical sphere, the emotional faculty continually occupied with genuine musical ideas.

All these are approved truths; but all presuppose, that the technique is either formed, or receives its due share of attention. For the talented they are adapted; for those less gifted — and with these the majority of pianoforte pupils must probably be classed — of doubtful value. Such phrases on ideality, though never so lofty in sound, are at bottom very cheap; an indescribably persevering industry devoted to technique is simply indispensable.

Schumann rightly distinguishes three grades of practice in all studies: (1) The mechanical mastery, especially an exact fixing of the fingering; (2) a higher technical standpoint, the execution attaining vividness and delicacy of touch, roundness and precision in details, fluency and lightness as a whole; (3) after overcoming all external difficulties, the imagination must assume easy and sure control, impart to its work animation, light and shade, and finish to whatever is lacking to a freer interpretation.

We now pass to the work, already mentioned above, by Antoine de Kontski, "Indispensable du Pianiste", Op. 100.

In appearance this school aims at a less mechanical point of view than previous pianoforte methods, being more concise and aiming in great part only at theoretical stimulation. The first section repudiates in playful descriptiveness all kinds of external aids, such as Kalkbrenner's hand-guide, Herz's Dactylion, the dumb keyboard, the Chiroplast, and even the school of finger-exercises, in which instructions are given for forming original finger-studies. This liberal standpoint is, however, only apparent, and in the course of the work we soon find one deficiency after the other, even contradictions, e. g. on p. 41, where the mechanical exercises in five tones are termed the most useful and indispensable. Admittedly, the work is not wanting in good exercises for practice and useful rules, but technique is on the whole too superficially estimated, and phrases often seek to replace what is missing by reason of insufficient care in the technical development.

A single effect, which Kontski describes in minute detail, is chiefly dwelt upon. We mean that shade of touch which he calls *carezzando*. The finger strokes the key, beginning in the middle of the same, sliding towards the front edge, and pressing it so far down that the hammer touches the string very gently. In his public performances the author did indeed thus attain an effect hitherto unknown in this direction, although a caressing of the key already appears in Kalkbrenner's method under the term *caresser*.

More important, however, is Kontski's theory for holding the hand, which stands in opposition to that in vogue since Bach's time, and, without knowing it, goes back to the style of the earliest period.—Whereas the other methods require the fingers to be bent, and the back of the hand horizontal with the forearm, some even demanding an elevation of the wrist, Kontski would have the latter held lower, and the fingers stretched nearly straight. He looks upon the finger-tip as the least sensitive part of the finger, and giving a dry tone, whereas according to ordinary experience a fine sense of touch is peculiar to this very part. And yet it cannot be denied that many advantages are connected with this view, which shall be spoken of later in detail, and that the author was well-enabled to illustrate his principle with the aid of a very delicate and flowing execution.

The section on Rendering lapses into the imperfections of Adam's method. Here we read, that touch and feeling are the main points. They render music irresistibly attractive; not rapid notes, but the noble sentiments and the heart of the player, are the factors requisite for comprehending and interpreting the sublime themes of music, etc.

Distinguished among the remaining monographic treatises is Theodor Kullak's School of Octave-playing.

The importance of the wrist-stroke, and the extended application of the same by virtuosi like A. Dreyschock and Thalberg, led the above-named author to the idea of subjecting this novel and effective addition to the modern school to an individual development; this work thus follows the training of the wrist from its first rudiments up to masterly facility. Theoretically and practically it is equally precise, and completely exhausts its topic.

No less worthy of mention for its development of fine scale-playing is the same author's work:

Rathschläge und Studien (Hints and Studies). Berlin: Trautwein.

although its predominant tendency is practical.

Likewise important are the

Materialien für den Elementar-Klavierunterricht (Materials for elementary Pianoforte Instruction)

by the same author. Their material of instruction is valuable, and excellently arranged. In view of Kullak's determinative influence on pianoforte methodics, the non-publication of the first part is to be deplored; this was intended to contain a detailed method for the holding of the hand, and for touch.

Somewhat earlier than the last-named work, i. e. in the year 1852, appeared the following treatise:

Louis Plaidy's Technische Studien (Technical Studies).

This Method, devoted to elementary instruction, is also of acknowledged importance. Here we first meet with a good exposition of the theory of touch. Although it contains only what Czerny had brought up, its methodic presentation of this subject is more distinct and perspicuous in form. Plaidy distinguishes four varieties of touch: (1) *The legato touch.* For this, only the first finger-joint is employed in striking; the others must neither be bent in, nor stretched. (2) *The staccato.* This is executed with the wrist, and in soft passages by a quick withdrawal of the finger instantly following the stroke. Some virtuosi play it with the arm, but this must not be imitated by the pupils. (3) *The legatissimo touch.* While in the legato one finger must relieve the other with the utmost precision, the fingers now stay down. This is practicable only in figurated chords. (4) *The mezzo-staccato touch,* indicated by a slur over staccato dots. Here the tone is developed by a heavy pressure of the finger, which must increase with the power of the tone to be produced, and is executed with a slight lift of the forearm.—

We shall, however, perceive in the following that this theory is insufficient. — Plaidy describes the attitude of the body and position of the hand more in detail than his predecessors. "The player should sit in the middle of the keyboard, and so far from the same, that his hands can easily reach its extremities." This direction is certainly preciser than that in inches, familiar to us in Marpurg, Türk, Hummel, etc. "The elbows should be held a little higher than the keyboard;" this is again the antiquated rule. "They must be held close to the sides, without touching them. The entire posture must be as unconstrained as possible. The back of the hand and the first finger-joint must form a level line; the knuckles must neither protrude, nor be drawn in; the two end-joints of the fingers are gently rounded, without touching the keys with the nails. The thumb must always be carried over the keys, held parallel to its key, and should strike the latter with its outer edge. All external mechanical aids are to be eschewed.—In the scale a new difficulty arises in turning over and under. For this the hands must be bent slightly inward,

6

and the arm held slightly away from the body. The arm
evenly follows the movement of the hand. The thumb must
already lie under the second finger when the latter strikes,
if it is to turn under and stand above its key at the right
moment."

Plaidy groups the whole field of technique in ten chapters:
(1) Exercises with quiet hand over five notes without supporting finger. (2) The same exercises with notes held down.
(3) Advancing exercises without support. (4) Change of finger
on one key. (5) Scales. (6) Figured chords. (7) Legato
thirds, fourths, fifths (diminished), sixths, octaves. (8) Chromatic thirds, fourths, fifths, etc. (9) Wrist exercises. (10) Trill
exercises.

Aside from the point, that No. 10 might be combined
with 1, and No. 8 with 7, this survey in exhaustive, and deserves preference before earlier ones. At the end of the work
are remarks on melodious playing, which ought also to have
been included in the theory of touch. Rules on the rendering
were not within the scope of the work, and are therefore
briefly disposed of. "Man soll gute Musik fleissig hören."

We may further mention, from the year 1855

Adolph Kullak, "Die Kunst des Anschlags (The Art of Touch),
ein Studienwerk für vorgerückte Klavierspieler und Leitfaden
für Unterrichtende."

Here the touch is treated of according to another principle than with Plaidy, or with Köhler in a work of his to
be discussed further on. The following seven varieties are
considered:

(1) The legato passage touch. (2) The melodious touch.
(3) The touch by drawing in the finger-tip. (4) The staccato
touch with the entire finger. (5) The wrist touch. (6) The
mezzo staccato. (7) The touch (stroke) with the arm.—In the
progress of "The Æsthetics of Pianoforte-playing" the author
will treat of the materials here enumerated in a more detailed
manner.

A very comprehensive and thorough work of its kind is
Louis Köhler's "Systematische Lehrmethode für Klavierspiel
und Musik." (Systematic Course for Pianoforte Playing and
Music.) Volume I: Die Mechanik als Grundlage der Technique. (Mechanical Training as the Foundation of Technique.)
1857.

Aside from a too abstract presentation of a subject in
itself already dry, one must in justice acknowledge the precision with which this work analyzes the mechanical art in
certain of its fundamental elements, and likewise in details
concerning its movements, forms, and most practical application. The limitations of the mechanical point of view have
the result, that the question of touch, which plays an important
part in this work, is also analyzed only from the side of its
external factors. The author consequently groups the varieties
of touch, according to the proportions of lever-length and lever-
movement, in four classes: (1) The stroke with the whole
finger from the knuckle-joint; (2) that with the tip-joint of the
finger; (3) the wrist-stroke; and (4) the stroke with the forearm from the elbow-joint.

But this classification is not satisfactory. Firstly, the conception of touch is quite as intellectual as mechanical, and a
one-sided apprehension does not exhaust it; secondly, even the
mechanical point of view is incompletely presented. According
to the latter, the touch ought to be dissected into its elements,
and determined in accordance with their distinctions. The
fourfold constitution of the striking lever is rightly given, but
tone-production is brought about either by a blow, or by
pressure. This gives a double series within the fourfold grouping.
Again, if we concentrate that principle of touch in which
pressure predominates, for the sake of practical perspicuity,
exclusively on the function of the finger-tip, we must recognize
at least five classes. That last mentioned would belong to the
singing touch. Moreover, there are other shades of touch
fluctuating between percussion and pressure, when the finger
slides or strokes, as in the *carezzando* and several kinds of

the portamento. Of these kinds Köhler's book makes no mention, neither does it speak of certain uncommonly interesting specialties of arm-technique; thus it does not exhaust its topic, despite various researches into very minute details.

Besides, a too pedantic standard is assumed for the position of the fingers and hand; theory is so stringent in her abstract claims, that practice can follow her only in isolated cases, and in spite of the greatest accuracy cannot reach the goal by the nearest way. The real gist of the mechanical side in pianoforte playing, of which we shall treat in detail further on, is touched upon too slightly.

A tendency diametrically opposed to this work is revealed by Marx, in the treatises entitled: (1) The Music of the Nineteenth Century. (2) Beethoven's Life and Works (Part II, Appendix). (3) A Selection from Sebastian Bach's Compositions (Preface). This author does not present his views in the shape of a coherent system exclusively devoted to pianoforte playing, but incidentally, to the extent permitted by the larger subject to such excursions.—We therefore possess only fragmentary observations, most important among which are those on the treatment of Bach's and Beethoven's works.

In the technical virtuosity of modern times Marx finds a deficiency, the individualization of the fingers not being satisfactorily developed. This is not to be understood as disallowing the independence and gymnastic training of the same; these are admitted; what the fingers lack is the *inspiration* of the tone. He might have expressed himself simply as follows: Modern players lack that psychic element which perceives and develops the poetic charm in the production of the single tone. —For the fingers by no means lack the capability for declamation; but the spirit lives more in figurate combinations than in the language of the individual tones.

In this regard Marx expresses himself thus: "In all pregnant melodies individual features, even individual tones, appear as the decisive elements, as luminous points in the total effect, which must as such be most distinctly and delicately felt and rendered. To this end, the contrary of that community and equality of the finger-mechanism becomes necessary. One must, so to speak, no longer play with the whole hand; each finger must be able to seize the emotional tone by itself, with the requisite degree of tenderness in accentuation, of individualization, or of melting into the next tone—must, as it were, have a soul and independent life of its own, to conduct through its nerve the soul of the player to the key. Far as the pianoforte is inferior to bowed and wind instruments in melodic power, as regards the blending of tones and their gradation in volume, much more may be achieved than one usually hears or believes, if the key be touched gently and caressingly, not dabbed at or struck; if the finger lay hold of it with intelligence, so to speak; if even extreme power be not expressed in rough blows, but issue from the native power of the musical conception. The key must be felt, not pushed or struck, it must be seized with feeling, as one presses a friend's hand only with sympathy—both in moments of mightiest and of tenderest agitation—otherwise the poetry of Bach and Beethoven can never attain full utterance."

As an external aid Marx recommends "that the hand be inclined, in particular, toward the side of that finger which is chiefly engaged nervously". Then, with reference to the polyphonic style of Bach's compositions, the rules are laid down, which Czerny had already formulated; each part should be brought out in independent and coherent distinctness, and the fingers possess such skill and readiness in following the interweaving melodies, that the spirit of the whole nowhere suffers interruption. The exchange of several fingers on one key, without repeating the sound, is very frequently requisite to preserve the connection, and needs special practice; and not less so a certain number of irregular fingerings, like passing the fourth finger over the fifth, and the successive employment of the same finger on different keys. (Czerny very truly remarked, in fugue-playing all rules are cancelled; this must naturally be taken as meaning that coherence, as the intellectual element, is the supreme guide, and that the technique has to adapt itself thereto in the way best suited to the end in view.)

Respecting the rendering Marx points out the fact, that the finished, neat, brilliant execution of modern virtuosity by no means suffices for a deeper apprehension of Bach. A fleet, showy style *en masse* is quite out of the question. The richer and deeper the conception, the more it finds utterance in single features, the less does it admit of superficial hurry to a sympathetic spirit. To penetrate into its essence, we must always ask: What reveals itself in these series of tones, and what can be made of them?

After this, the author subjects a part of his selection from Bach's compositions to analysis, turns our contemplation, by his consideration of rhythmic and melodic details, to the tempo and regulation of power, and leads the reflection to that feeling of unity which must form the basis of every finished work. Regarding the rendering of the fugue, he finds the rule, to emphasize the fugue theme, insufficient. "Each part carries out its melody consistently, through counter-subject and episode. This truly dramatic dialogue, animated throughout and in each part, is the very life and soul of the fugue. Each part must be studied individually, motive by motive, and its co-operation with the rest, in reference to the whole, calculated accordingly. Vague emotion is not enough; illuminating consciousness lights the pure flame of true inspiration." In opposition to many lovers of antiquity attention is finally called to the fact, that Bach can well bear an *accelerando* and *ritardando,* i. e. could lay claim to means of expression, which many grant only to the moderns. "Was our forefathers' temperament really otherwise constituted than our own? Was it not Bach's aim to depict joy, wrath, pain, and languishing melancholy? And is it not characteristic of the agitated soul, that its ebullitions now swell in vehement haste, now subside gently? Where equability of mood predominates, the player, too, must keep to the fixed movement, e. g. in Beethoven's great C-major sonata. Where the mood changes impulsively, the player must obey it."

Beethoven is similarly discussed by Marx. For this composer, as well, the brilliant side of the virtuoso's ability is insufficient. His spirit must be seized, and it is needful to live oneself into it. The view of many teachers, that the pupil should await his full technical development before venturing on Beethoven's works, cannot be accepted. These latter are in part well suited (e. g. the Sonatas Op. 10, 14, etc.) for a medium grade of technical skill, several indeed for one still lower, and they reach upward into the highest grades. The pupil should on no account be excluded from familiarity with and absorption in Beethoven; a one-sided practice of brilliant works often results in an incapacity to follow Beethoven's flight. In this connection Marx characterizes the defect of modern technique in a similar vein to that shown before with Bach: "The fingers lack individual training".

A thrusting forward of the melody, as in Thalberg's Fantasias, does not suffice for Beethoven's intention in declamation; the *cantilena* of the latter must be comprehended and chiselled out tone by tone, and stand in relief against the accompaniment. Then follow examples from the G-major sonata Op. 14, the first theme of the great F-minor sonata, the first episode in the first part of the E-flat sonata Op. 27, the first movement of the C♯-minor sonata, and the second movement from Op. 90. In all these each part of individual import must be individualized and carried out according to its inner meaning. Difficulties grow with the pregnancy and individuality of the elements making up the work; for the Finale of the sonata Op. 101, for instance, and the Fugato in Op. 120, the modern pianoforte hand, trained to correlation and uniformity, will not answer. The fingering, in frequent deviation from its general laws, must be so disposed, that the fingers take position where each can strike in most practically either in subordination or opposition to the others. Marx repeats here, that the hand, by its inclination and weight, should aid the fingers in emphasizing the decisive tones. Technique stands in need of poetry.

With reference to the general conception of Beethoven's works, one must be guided solely by the rule, that their spirit is the only determinant authority, and is to be followed rather than any oral tradition, even from Beethoven's own lips. But to apprehend this authority aright, technical and mental maturity are needful, and the latter discloses itself in a sympathy for the work and the desire to make it one's own. One must set aside all technical necessities, and study the work in another, a meditative, fashion. Three series of the sonatas are arranged here, beginning with those simplest in substance, and rising to the loftiest and most pregnant.

Op. 2, 13, 14, 22, 54, 53, 78; then Op. 26, 10, 7, 28, 31, 27; finally Op. 81, 90, 106, 101, 110, 109, 111.

On taking up any special work for study, let the pupil play it through uninterruptedly a few times, without regard to technique, in a tempo nearly approaching the correct one. This rule holds good no less for other compositions. As regards the tempo, our inner perception is the authoritative judge. The more the subject-matter of a piece is worked out in fine and minute detail, the less will it bear too rapid a movement. — Technical practicability is by no means the standard for the tempo (as, for instance, the first movements in Op. 13, 28, 90, and 101 prove). Beethoven often gave utterance to his dissatisfaction with over-rapid tempi. The mutual relation of movements frequently aids greatly in determining the rapidity of single ones.

Having gained deeper insight, the subject must be grasped with intenser vigor, the significance of the separate members analyzed emotionally and intellectually, and a fairly positive idea attained of the style of rendering adapted for each. Marx here gives an admirable analysis of the first movement in Op. 7, and proves the importance of each tone and the inherent necessity which guided the master's choice. This extends even to the embellishments, which with Beethoven admit of no modification, such as is possible with Hummel or Chopin, for instance. Further he rules, that an exact understanding of the architectural form must be gained by careful examination; some points are merely hinted at, others treated of in detail, e. g. the remarks on interpreting the Beethoven *cantilena*. An absolute essential in the rendering of Beethoven's compositions is rhythmic freedom. Several works, it is true, do not require it, such as Op. 22, 54, 53; but the majority, nevertheless. Freedom, not uniformity, of rhythm is a natural law. It roots in the undulatory nature of the temperament. Beethoven's own rendering was animated throughout by this freedom. Marx, who in all music views a striving of the tone toward articulate speech, specially insists on rhythmic freedom, it alone being able to express this striving.—After this, the author again analyzes several sonatas with reference to this rhythmic freedom, namely Op. 31 in D-minor, Op. 51 in F-minor, and Op. 90 in E-minor.

No further observations are required to show Marx' eminent importance in these episodes devoted to the pianoforte. Stimulation flows from his poetic diction, and from the productive power of his imagination as well, whose ready art endows the living tones of musical poems with language, meaning, and ideas. Even if they are not binding, and if the spirit of music inhabits a more universal sphere than Marx is fain to recognize, his example, and particularly the warmth of his language, promote receptivity for the nobler species of music, and lead the mind on, to gain a deeper insight into works of musical art. But he is entirely in the right in elevating the spirit to the court of last resort for pianoforte playing, and in wishing to see all technical effort directed to this highest goal.

We have now to consider a few shorter treatises, and shall begin with a work by

Thalberg on "Die Kunst des Gesanges auf dem Pianoforte" (The Art of Singing on the Pianoforte),

which was printed as an introduction to a series of paraphrases from his later period.—This affords a noteworthy contribution to the science of touch, inasmuch as it treats of the melodious touch, of all whose forms the above-named virtuoso was so complete a master. He lays down eleven rules as requisite for a fine singing tone, of which we quote the following points as the most important: "Broad, lofty, dramatic songs must be sung with a full chest; much is therefore expected of the instrument, from which the greatest possible volume of tone must be drawn, though never by roughly striking the keys, but rather by catching them closely and deftly, and pressing them down with power, decision, and warmth. For simple, tender, and graceful melodies one should knead the keys, so to speak, pressing and working them as with a boneless hand and fingers of velvet; in such strains the keys should be felt rather than struck.— To those occupying themselves seriously with the pianoforte we can give no better advice, than to learn, study, and thoroughly test the beautiful art of singing. To this end no opportunity should be missed of hearing great artists, whatever their instrument may be, and great singers in particular. As a possible encouragement for young artists we will add, that we ourselves studied singing during five years under the direction of one of the most celebrated teachers of the Italian School". S. Thalberg.

These few words sound, it is true, by no means so *spirituel* as Marx' observations on the rendering of Beethoven's melodies, but give rise to the probable conjecture, that the ingenious interpreter of the great tone-poet did not have a sufficiently accurate knowledge of the modern school. It cannot be asserted that *anyone* thoroughly trained in the latter is capable of executing Beethoven's *cantilena* correctly; but, on the other hand, it is certain that no one can perform them expressively, who has not practically applied Thalberg's rule to himself.

The second treatise is by the author of this work, and is entitled:

"Ein Wink für Klavierspieler" (A Hint for Pianoforte-players). (In the Berlin music-journal "Echo", Vol. VI, No. 26.)

It was written in answer to an attack in the Vienna "Blätter für Musik, Theater und Kunst" (No. 43 of the same year) upon a remark in the author's "Art of Touch", in which, in connection with the melodious style, the rule is given, that the finger should seek by a vibration of the key to obtain a *tremolo (vibrato)* in the tone — thus exacting from the pianoforte tone a beauty and pliancy, which it unhappily does not in fact possess.

This rule was attacked as unpractical and dangerous on account of its too ideal standpoint. The author's reply established it as æsthetically justified, and assured its scientific importance by a reference to that spiritualization, which is justified in inspiring within any material of art a tendency towards the next-highest sphere, thus endowing it with a more potent charm and spell.

Finally, we have to mention a treatise by Brendel, Studien über Pianofortespiel. Die Handhaltung und der Anschlag, die Ausbildung der Hand und des Handgelenks (Studies on Pianoforte-playing. Position of the Hand and the Touch, the Development of the Hand and Wrist.) (Neue Zeitschrift für Musik, Vol. 46, No. 22.)

Sundry new points render this treatise stimulating. "So many different directions for holding the hand, etc., have been set up as a standard by each individual master, that more or less uncertainty has arisen, and rules generally binding are not to be found. Hummel's playing could bring out no full tone in consequence of his way of holding the hand, which was jestingly called the 'Krabbelmanier' (grabbling style). For he did not let the fingers strike firmly on the keys, but drew them in after the latter were pressed down, so that the fingernail finally slid over the key. Field's style was exactly the opposite. He taught an absolutely perpendicular position of the fingers, so that they fell upon the keys like hammers*; he required that the keys should be pressed down to the very

---

* But this is impossible without the co-operation of the wrist!

bottom. By this method he gained great beauty of tone, wealth and variety of nuance, without attaining the brilliancy of the Vienna school. Moscheles has a fuller tone than Hummel; his touch is firm, pressing the key down to the bottom. But he, again, lacks Field's sensuous beauty of tone. Universal characteristics of all earlier masters are a steady, constant position of the hand, and a one-sided exclusiveness of style which strives to attain all shades of expression in one and the same manner. The modern style, with its far greater contrasts and gradations of tone, also requires another and freer manner of holding the hand. The marked emphasis of individual tones, with a stabbing pressure of the key; and in opposition to this an etherial *pianissimo,* with more elongated fingers".

In the further progress of the work the author recommends, for the first training, the holding of the hand with knuckles sunk in, and fingers bent, and dilates upon familiar matters.

It is not within the scope of this dissertation to review all the painstaking treatises, which contribute in their sphere to build up a vigorous system of training. The number of those works alone, which aim simply at a practical compilation of technical studies, has latterly augmented so greatly, that it were quite impossible to review them in detail. Among books on pianoforte playing lately published, the method edited by Emil Breslaur deserves special mention. The method pivots in a measure upon an essay by Breslaur on "Schulung der Hand, Bildung des Tones und der Technik" (Training of the Hand, Development of Tone and Technique), to whose principles experts will surely give their assent. This is accompanied by a great number of essays on pedagogics in music, written by eminent specialists, which offer abundant stimulus to aspiring teachers.

Dr. Hugo Riemann's "Vergleichende theoretisch-praktische Klavierschule" (Comparative theoretical and practical Pianoforte School) was originally intended only as a guide to the free use of the best material extant for instruction, but the author presents in the same many new and valuable points. The paragraphs relating to Phrasing merit particular attention. The work has appeared partly in book-form, and partly as a collection of technical and rhythmical studies, etc. Among later books on finger exercises Tausig's Studies, edited by H. Ehrlich, take the lead. They lay no claim to be judged as a systematic school-work, but pay chief attention to such exercises as do not occur in earlier collections of studies. Ehrlich gives an excellent commentary to this work in his pamphlet: "Wie übt man am Klavier?" (How should one practice at the Pianoforte?). Among other matters the following noteworthy principle is laid down: That in practicing, the upper arm should at times be held close to the side, which will render impossible various embarrassments due to a faulty position of the hand. Ehrlich has also published another interesting series of studies: "Der musikalische Anschlag" (On musical Touch), which equally constrain each finger to enter into the service of purely musical characterization.

In the Tausig-Ehrlich studies the highly instructive principle of transposition with retention of the fingering is laid down. Even in his earlier edition of Clementi's Gradus, Tausig provided figures analogously formed with similar fingering, regardless of the succession of keys. True, the finger-action meets therein with considerable difficulties in details; but hands of sufficient stretching capacity, which also play readily between the black keys, are easily borne over any difficulties by the consistent fingering.

The present appears an appropriate place for characterizing briefly some other efforts, which have led to an essential reformation of our views on Fingering. Firstly, a purely technical point of view is to be mentioned, on which earlier pedagogics laid stress only in exceptional cases; namely, the change of fingers at direct, or even indirect, repetitions of keys. Modern editors, led by Bülow, employ this aid to the widest extent for equalizing the touch; whereas it was formerly employed, at the utmost, when one and the same key was to be repeatedly struck in rapid tempo, i. e. in repetition passages. — For the reform of the fingering, however, another principle defined by Bülow is more essentially important—that not the technical convenience, but the phrasing, of a passage, is to be considered as the guiding principle—a rule followed likewise by Klindworth, Herm. Scholtz, Hugo Riemann, and others.

Still, rules for phrasing in details and in view of the whole have by no means been established with full scientific accuracy; on the contrary, no inconsiderable scope is left to subjective opinion. A very interesting work in this department is Dr. Hugo Riemann's "Dynamik und Agogik", whose merit must surely be acknowledged in having emphasized most strongly the "auftaktige" (anacrusial-fractional-measure) openings of most musical motives. Yet one will peruse the above-named work — like that by Dr. Carl Fuchs "Ueber die Zukunft des musikalischen Vortrags" (On the Future of Musical Rendering), which is written in much the same sense — with the feeling, that the last word on the question of phrasing has not been spoken; to both works, however, the reader will owe highly valuable suggestions.

The material here alluded to belongs rather to a general course in music than to pianoforte methodics; I therefore do not feel called upon to consider it more in detail at present.

PART II.

The presentation of the beautiful in pianoforte playing in particular.

Section I.

The Technique.

CHAPTER IV.

Arrangement of the following System. — Importance of Technique. — Theories on the Position of the Hand.

Pianoforte playing is a reproductive art. Improvisation on and composition for the pianoforte are subject to rules which extend into more universal spheres of the beautiful in music. Should these be noticed in the further course of the work, they cannot be treated of, to say the least, as if it were our intention to build up these branches of æsthetics from the foundation.

The subject-matter of pianoforte playing is formed by those material (physical) conditions and relations, which render possible the presentation of the beautiful in music, as found in creations intended for the mechanism of the pianoforte and the human hand; and the æsthetics of pianoforte playing has to trace out the general laws of the science of beauty in their application to this material subject-matter.— Thus pianoforte playing in its individuality (i. e. in its distinguishing characteristics) finds its sphere of action chiefly in the requirements for the actualization of the ideal subject, assuming correct conception of the latter. From the moment in which these material conditions are so far developed by æsthetics, that they can reproduce the musical ideal of beauty in the scope assigned to them, a further advance of theory would infallibly have to encroach upon the sphere of universal musical æsthetics. That it should keep within bounds, is the natural result of a sharp demarkation of the sciences; although it shall not be overlooked, that a certain participation in the universal and higher existence belongs to each special sphere of activity, and that the principle of scientific limitation would prove shortsighted, did it recognize as a right of the special sphere only its distinctive traits, and not a part of the common traits as well.

The special æsthetics now in question take a course deviating from that commonly pursued by universal æsthetics. The latter dwells by preference on the ideology of the beautiful, and in a measure arrives through theory at the phenomena of the separate arts. The development here following constructs its full conception of beauty from below; it begins with the first rudiments of art, and follows the operations of the will as influenced by the imagination step by step and ever higher, new ideas continually emerging from the subjects thus elaborated and assimilated, until at last the total conception is attained in its full scope. — Though the idea of universality and totality is more attractive, by reason of its philosophical charm, than the special subject which dwells on dry elementary relations, and consequently the course of universal æsthetics is made from the beginning more impressive, by an abstract nimbus, than the course of instruction to be followed here, the latter is, in amends, less subject to error, and moreover has the merit, of analyzing the beautiful in its material and actual details, a proceeding usually neglected by universal æsthetics, which is too busy with theories.

———

The idea of the work of art is transmitted by the material elements. The first act of the artistic energy is to grapple with these, their gradual subjection is its first and most necessary victory. The material must obey, and it is the task of every art, to wrest from it as much as possible according to the laws of the mystical bent of the psyche toward ideality. For pianoforte playing, the genius of universal music has elaborated the material, both in subject and technique, so far in advance, that the only material left to be immediately subjected to the will is the hand, as the agency appointed by natural conditions. The development of the hand is the course of that process, in which the inclinations and capabilities bestowed by nature upon that organ, but which are in part undeveloped, in part divided among manifold other requirements, are concentrated in velocity and strength to serve a single definite purpose. This purpose aims at thoroughly training, first the hand, but thereafter the playing mechanism entire, even with the muscles of the upper arm, to handle the mechanism given in the pianoforte keyboard in such a manner, that the production of tone can be achieved in all those relations, wherein they are demanded by the spirit living in compositions created for the pianoforte.

Tone-production on the pianoforte depends, on the one hand, upon the specific nature of the hammer-action; and the characteristics of the latter, provided that it is normally perfect, consist: (1) In the absolute responsiveness of the striking action directed against the strings; (2) in the shading and modification of the degree of power and rapidity proper to that striking action, and most intimately connected with its responsiveness; (3) in the equalization of each single member of the total mechanism, so accurately adjusted, that like exertion of strength gives like quality and quantity of tone,

7

the shades of the latter following the modifications of the former. — The medium through which the hand enters into communication with the hammer action, is the keyboard, a surface, which through its mathematically regular division into single sections likewise exhibits externally the principle of equality, and stimulates the sensitiveness of the fingers; the shape of the hammers, too, is founded on a corresponding equality in form-development.

The above-enumerated properties of a mechanical and passive organism mark out the task which the hand must undertake. In form no less than in power it has to develop precisely the same properties. The absolute responsiveness of the hammer-stroke corresponds to the looseness of the finger-motion; the shading of the striking movement to all degrees of power and rapidity in perfect obedience to the will, is no less essential to the technique of the hand than in the hammer-action; the equality in striking weight, the equalization of the individual fingers to absolute evenness of weight in their striking and pressing action, is the next task; and finally, the last consists in the outward expression of formal compliance with this requirement by the position of the hand.

Readily as a view of the first steps may be sketched in this manner, practical mastery can be attained only by a long, toilsome struggle of the will with the forces of the crude material to be subdued. Practical work conquers the path leading to the final goal by a wearisome process — little by little, step by step, but not in a straight line — by circuitous methods and with continual reference to other essential and incidental tasks simultaneously coming into view. This goal is not merely a technical one, but includes, in closest connection and co-operation with the technique, an ideal sphere of wide extent; and even aside from this, the apparent simplicity of the purely mechanical task resolves itself, through the manifold mutual relations of the live finger-apparatus, instinct with physical and psychical warmth, to the given lifeless key and hammer-organism, into a broad and fine-spun web of rules and forms, so that its theory requires precise systematization.—We proceed immediately to the latter.

Some theoreticians distinguish technique from mechanical training. To the latter they would leave the examination of the laws of finger-action, and of the movements of all members and joints needed in playing, and trace the same abstractly, without regard to their bearing on compositions, merely with reference to the given physico-mechanical purpose, to definite forms. Technique would then have to consider this mechanism as serving the ends of connected composition. A sharp demarkation of these two conceptions is not necessary, and is also hard to carry out. Where does mere mechanics cease, and technique commence? They are intimately connected; their separation would make it incumbent upon mechanics to abstain from all practical examples, for the very least connection of tones is an atomic germ of composition. And a course of practical study without examples is unpractical on account of its unstimulating abstraction. Consequently, the following method is not careful to hold these conceptions apart; the predominant character of the elements of the first species will be purely mechanical, with all the rest an encroachment upon technique will be unavoidable; it appears most practical to regard mechanics and technics as much the same thing, as practical precision is in any event more important than a precision of terminology applicable to neither sphere.

Mechanical training is the primary and indispensable condition of pianoforte playing. To the spirit of the same it stands in just the same relation, as the form to the substance, i. e. it is in itself, precisely like the substance, the Whole, and differs from it only from the point of view of another mode of contemplation, with which the observant understanding confronts the work of art.

The mechanical training must be perfect; the most subtle rhetorical genius can no more make an orator, when the

7*

tongue hesitates, stammers, or is even incapable of speech, than a pre-eminent comprehension of all compositions, or the most exuberant imagination, make a pianoforte player, when technique is deficient. When the slightest defect is perceptible therein, the perfection of the whole is marred; the most insignificant failing arrests the full development of the ideal; the most soaring flight of thought, the finest inspiration of feeling, do not avail, where a callous finger-tip, a stiff joint, an awkward motion, lay hindrances in the ideal course of the will. Where pure intelligence controls, and the fingers resist clumsily, the presentation takes on the nature of a repulsive hybrid, wavering characterless betwixt abstraction and art, a species of unintelligible symbolism, lacking in beauty because the balance of its elements is disturbed.—Dilettantism, indeed, often bolsters up its incapacity with the cheap parade of high-flown phrases. This is sheer superficiality. The ideal must be perfection in all parts, for the idea is quite as much material reality as the reflection of the same in the mind.

We shall now trace this material reality from its beginnings up to its passage into the supernatural.

The material to be subjected to the will, i. e. the hand, must first be examined as to its properties; and their careful consideration will show, in what way a rational beginning can be made with its new development.

The form and individuality of the fingers stand in opposition to the principle of equality, which occupied the foreground in the previous contemplation of the hammer-action. The third finger is longer than any of the others; the fourth comes next, and then the second. The fifth is decidedly shorter than those just named, while the thumb lies far back. A so various proportion in length necessitates a re-formation of the hand from its shape as naturally extended, aiming at its adaptation to the horizontally extended surface of the keyboard. All tones possess an equal right to existence; the keyboard symbolizes this idea by the mathematically regular distribution of the space appropriated for the same, and the hand must so adjust itself thereto, that it may be able to reach each single division of the keyboard with equal facility and under conditions which insure an equal power in effect. The theory of the position of the hand is a difficult point, not quite clearly defined even at present, as opinions conflict concerning it. If the principle of the equality to be attained in the vibratory and pressing power of the fingers depended simply upon their position, Bach's manner of holding the hand, with which we became acquainted in Chapter II, would be the standard. The equal curvature of all fingers, with their tips forming a straight line, are the conditions most nearly approaching those imposed by the keyboard. But there are various other points to be taken into consideration, and if we seek generally binding rules among the different theories in vogue, we shall be able to retain only very nearly the following.

Not the position of the hand, but the quality of touch and the tone-production, must above all be kept in view. The latter is the substance, the former only the form. The tone produced by touch must possess a well-defined quality, and from various individuality of the hands deviations in position will result. The requirement of one particular posture of hand and fingers as a standard must be termed either one-sidedness, or prepossession for theory without due consideration of practical needs.

This production of tone by touch, as the higher and sole ruling factor, must possess the following properties. Like the hammer-action, the finger-stroke must be perfectly loose, appearing to the eye much as if the finger were merely attached to the hand at the knuckle-joint by the supplest, softest, and most yielding fastening. It must look as if it moved on a hinge yielding to the slightest exertion of strength, and its lift should be effected just as loosely and quickly as its fall. The movement of the finger toward the key must exactly resemble a fall; so long as it looks like a reaching or stretching down, i. e. like any movement distinguished from falling by greater slowness, it is wrong, and one must seek to attain the end above named by assiduous practice. This fall of the finger is one chief characteristic. The second lies in the catching or pressing down of the key.—That is, after its fall the finger-tip must press upon its spot on the key so clingingly, firmly, yet gently with all firmness, that it appears to adhere to the key as if by suction, without slipping backwards or forwards. The finger must cling so closely, that its tip wears the appearance of a soft, semi-fluid, readily kneadable mass, which seems to lie quite stably wherever it lights. The touch thus exhibits two diametrically opposed manifestations: (1) A lightning-like vivacity of lift and fall; (2) utter repose and passivity during the act of pressing down. The powers slumbering undivorced in the unformed finger are thus developed into two most strongly contrasted factors — into an enhanced activity and an equally enhanced passivity, into mobility and repose, into most sensitive agitation and completest relaxation. — These are the mechanical characteristics of the touch, or its visible manifestation. The other side, which must combine with the above to form the full conception, has to do with the quality of tone. The tone produced by the means pointed out above, must be distinct, and bear an exact proportion to the force exerted by the finger. Both sides must take their departure from a normal mean. The movement of the finger must be neither strained nor too lax; it should appear natural as a native energy. In its movement the finger should develop only free, unfettered individuality, and the tone should develop accordingly a proportionate volume. For the recognition of this proportionality the ear must be so sharpened, as is the eye in the sphere of visible phenomena. The tone must have a volume corresponding to the length and strength of the fingers —with no suspicion of influence by the arm, or of weakening in the finger-tip. Above all things, it must be *pearling*. The fall of the finger should be audible, for an ear close by, through a gentle tap of the finger-tip on the key.

These regulations govern the fingers in their absolute manifestation of power. Side by side with them, however, exist the proportionate relations. One finger is to strike in just the same way, and produce just the same tone, as another. Consequently, besides strengthening and augmenting in detail the elasticity peculiar to each individual finger, an equilibrium must be established in the lifting and pressing process between these forces. Not simply an isolated manifestation of the liberated individuality comes in question, but a development of the feeling of community and interrelationship. The forces must be so nicely balanced, that the stronger individuality imposes moderation, the weaker exertion, on itself; the latter, of course, with the above-mentioned provision of perfect un-constrainedness and naturalness. This interrelationship lends to the fingers, despite all isolation and independence, a feeling of live tension. This must nowhere be lacking; it alone in-sures that characteristic of psychic animation, which must distinguish the fingers from the passive row of hammers. Fingers which fall only like lifeless wooden levers, will always have something wrong in their touch, despite all isolation and freedom. In their pressure on the key, and also in the act of mutual relief and succession of the fingers, the nervous tension must be visible which characterizes them, despite the subjection of those manifestations of strength which do not directly further their end, as individualities inspired by living emotion, and pulsing in warmest sympathy with the focus of the soul.

The individualization of the fingers finally has the result, that the physical activity of the player must concentrate itself practically and economically at the point from which the strength is exerted. This is the movement in the knuckle-joint and the pressure of the finger-tip.—Any other tension in the forearm, in the wrist, in the fingers not directly employed, is an aimless waste of strength leading to a roundabout and more difficult attainment of the goal. There must therefore be a complete relaxation of the entire playing apparatus from the upper arm down to the finger-tip, or, as Marpurg expresses it, the relaxation of all nerves must be the general fundamental feeling to be most emphatically awakened in every player.

As regards the connection of the tones, the movements must be so calculated in advance, that each is prepared, and does not fill out its allotted moment with jerky hastiness or the appearance of belatedness or hurry, but with the degree of equable repose and confidence appropriate to the length of the moment. Thus the movements, within their extreme economization, must possess a trait of equality while measuring the linear space allotted them. A "too early" shows the embarrassment of pupilage, a "too late" reveals a yet lower standpoint.

These are the rules most generally binding. If the question of the posture of hand and fingers is to be settled, the answer will be, that teacher and player must through personal observation arrive at those rules, which appear natural and self-evident according to the various individuality of the hands and the character of the tone-combinations under consideration. One fixed position of the hand is adapted neither for all hands, nor for all tone-combinations: and the strictest pedantry is not able to enforce a positive rule without exceptions in all cases.

But if the again recurring question as to the position of the hand is nevertheless to be answered theoretically from a positive point of view, and discussed pedagogically with special reference to the beginning of study, which always requires something definite, the following conclusions are reached.

In the sum total of all modifications to which the position of the hand is subjected, two principal forms are found which may be adopted as equally justifiable; and freedom not being the beginning, but the final and highest end of every method, it is expedient, according to the inclination and capacity of any pupil-hand in question, to decide positively for one of these forms, give strict training in the same, and only gradually allow a freer movement. In many cases it will rather be expedient to hold fast to one form for a time, then to train the hand to the other, and when fluency is attained in both fundamental forms thus sharply distinguished, gradually to leave the choice of either to the necessity of the moment. A thoroughly trained hand must be perfectly at home in either form; only in this case it will exhibit complete dexterity in the intermediate modifications brought about every instant by changing figuration and different degrees of dynamic shading.— A description of both forms now follows.

I. The back of the hand lies in a horizontal line with the first finger-joint hinging in the knuckle, with the wrist, and the forearm. The fingers rest upon the keys so curved, that the tip-joint touches the latter nearly perpendicularly. The growth of the nail, which differs in different hands, decides whether the finger-tip shall stand exactly or only nearly perpendicular. Should the nail touch the key in spite of closest trimming, the said perpendicular position must be so far modified, that the click of the nail on striking ceases. The finger-tips form only approximately the straight line insisted on by Bach. To speak exactly, they form a curved line, in which fingers 3 and 2 are furthest advanced, 4 standing somewhat, and 5 and the thumb still further back. The fifth finger lies somewhat flatter upon the keys than 2, 3, and 4. The thumb is also curved, only its curvature naturally takes from its position another direction; it turns inward horizontally rather than perpendicularly. The distance between the fingers is regulated by the dimensions of the keys. As point of departure the normal position is taken, in which the five fingers are placed on as many successive white keys. The hand is turned a trifle *outwards*. This is the rule for all figures in which the thumb is not passed under. Where passing under and over occurs, the hand is turned a trifle *inwards*. Each finger occupies precisely the middle of the front field of the key allotted to it.—According to a principle not only to be admitted, but to be recommended in all methodics, every task accompanied by any difficulty will be more readily and quickly conquered when presented, with reference to this difficulty, in a somewhat heightened form. This leads to the following application:

It happens continually, that the horizontal line, which should extend from the elbow to the end of the first joint of the third finger, is neglected by the pupil through lowering the wrist. Thus a slight elevation of the latter can be required without disadvantage, so that the forearm slants upwards a little towards the wrist. — Moreover, a constant inclination is exhibited to violate the prescribed horizontality in the contrary direction by the protrusion of the knuckles. In this case, too, the rule may be given, that the knuckles should be pressed inward to a certain extent. In this wise the horizontality first required is transformed to an undulating line, rising a little at the wrist, falling to the knuckles, and again rising in the first finger-joints.

Respecting the movement of the fingers in this form of the playing apparatus, the first joint represents the heft of a hammer, and the two others the descending hammer-head. The curved form of the fingers must be stringently retained, the feeling of looseness subsisting only in the knuckle-joint. Should the natural growth of the nail be such, that despite close trimming and even a somewhat slanting position of the tip-joints a striking of the nail on the key is unavoidable, this latter may be permitted at the beginning of the studies. This position of the hand holds fast in principle to an unchangeably curved form of the fingers.

II. The second position of the hand is as follows: The back of the hand slants slightly downwards from knuckles to wrist, i. e. in a direction just contrary to the foregoing. The fingers are more elongated. Nowhere is the slightest tension apparent. In the former position, the maintainance of the curve in the forward finger-joints was attended by tension; the horizontality of the line described from elbow to third finger, and still more the elevation of the wrist and pressing in of the knuckles, can likewise not be maintained without tension. Only after long habituation can this tension acquire the character of naturalness and unconstrainedness. In the second position, the guiding principle is an easy suspension. The crude material is from the beginning subjected as little as possible to rule, and its powers are developed out of : feeling of entire ease.

To both positions the striking movements stand in the following relations:—A lift of the first finger-joint is common to both as the first condition of the stroke; the down-stroke (fall) must consequently be united with a firm hold on the key, to produce a distinct tone.—But whereas the high (first) position, with bent fingers and knuckles pressed in, effects this lift with more effort, and cannot rise so high, the low position has much freer play and less effort in lifting. As the finger usually is a little extended, or the tip very slightly curved, it has a greater preparatory lift in striking, and more nearly approaches the hammer-action in its movement; while the bent finger moves less freely, but still more nearly resembles the latter in form. In the bent position the first finger-joint rises about so high, as to form a horizontal line with the bend of the wrist, providing that the latter projects, below which line lies the hollow formed by the sinking in of the knuckle. But where the back of the hand is exactly horizontal, the first finger-joint rises above the plane of the latter. The second position of the hand, with wrist hanging down, requires on the contrary that the finger-tip, at the instant of the preparatory lift, should rise high above the back of the hand, and fall down from this height. Here it is immaterial, whether the finger is stretched out straight at the moment of lifting, or bends a little; at the moment of falling, the curve comes of itself. A perfectly straight finger is very seldom used.

Now, with regard to catching the key, the bent finger is driven toward it as by a steel spring, on account of the reaction against the tension of the lift, caused by the pressing

in of the knuckle. The tip of the tensely curved finger strikes
with firm resistance against the key; the whole movement has
limited play, and the height of the fall-curve described by the
striking-point nearing the key is limited by the downward
bend of the finger-tip. We might say, that the finger deals
the key a blow.—In the other position, the fall of the finger
describes an arching line. If it is to strike properly in the
sense of this principle, it must act in the preparatory lift, at
least in *will*, as if it had to operate against a perpendicular
key-surface. It must lift as far as possible from behind, and
fall against the key. Thus no striking principle governs here,
but a falling principle.—But as the finger is not driven against
the key by any tension created in the knuckle-region, it
nevertheless loses the advantage (however great may be the
one which it gains on the other hand) possessed by the bent
finger in being driven downward. — True, the latter has the
greater exertion in the lift, but in the down-stroke needs only
half as much strength as the finger in the second position.
The long-stretched, high-lifted finger must combine a *pressing*
principle with the *falling* principle; in the action of its greatly
facilitated lift it must unite, from the very outset, the intention
of a forced downward pressure.—For the high preparatory lift
inclines but half so strongly to the down-stroke, as that combined with the tension of the bent finger.—The individualization of each separate finger, together with the equalization
of their manifestations of power, is of course the indispensable
task of both principles.—Neither do we need to mention, that
in connected playing that height of the lift, which was previously required of the long-stretched finger for practice, is
restricted in advanced work in such measure, as naturally
results from the requirements of rapid passages.—The strokes
from the wrist follow those of the fingers consistently in both
principles. —The more elevated hand allows of shorter lines
of oscillation than the lower, which impels the hand toward
the key through a quadrant-formed curve. In both the result
is likewise similar. The high form has the advantage in

striking power, and does not need that exertion of pressure which the hand having the higher lift must unite to the wider oscillation.

These are in the main the characteristics of the two positions of the hand.—Which is the better? This question cannot be answered with absolute definiteness. Each has its advantages and disadvantages; either may prove the better in the *proper place.* Hearing two players side by side, each trained one-sidedly in one of these forms, he with the bent fingers will have a distinct, rather sharply sparkling, sprightly tone: the other a softer, looser, not so sharply defined, but more pearling tone. In bolder effects the bent hand will produce a very strongly marked touch, though not quite free from the suspicion of exertion; the long-stretched hand will, however, also produce a great, though not so sharply defined volume of tone, and unite with power a soft tone, where a rapid legato is demanded. But in the staccato the bent finger will have the advantage of the pearling tone on its side, as it takes the key with a more decided, hammerlike touch; with the horizontal line of the stretched finger a trace of slovenliness will always be apparent in staccato playing.

It is, in short, necessary, that the gymnastic training of the hand should embrace both. Close-lying passages with more white keys call for bent fingers; black keys and spread figures impose upon even the most pedantic partisans of the first principle a transition to the second. The timbre of the rendering also helps in deciding. Hard, grand masses of tone forbid the touch with extended finger; soft-flowing, modern, romantic passages of expression are very favorable to the same. But above all, one must take into account the character of our modern instruments, and not concede too great importance to the theories of a Bach or a Hummel. The English action demands, both in regard to pressure and fall, a greater activity of the finger than the Viennese action, which could bear the so-called grabbling about with crooked fingers.

Finally, the peculiarities of the hand must be considered.

A strong masculine hand can produce an immense volume of tone even with bent fingers, where a weak hand must lift higher and press harder, i. e. employ the advantages of the second position of the hand. Similarly, it cannot be denied, that the sensitiveness of the touch is always more active in bent than in stretched fingers, and therefore the *pianissimo*, although not endowed in like measure with pearling charm, is still attainable in a perfect, even if peculiar, style.—What the first form affords, is outwardly more beautiful; its mere outlines and height augur grace and vivacity, the negation of gravitation, whose unloveliness is apparent in the lower position of the hand. The higher position also favors the training of the thumb.—It plays more neatly with the tip, it passes under more easily, because it finds freer room. In the lower position it strikes, to be sure, with a freer swinging curve; but as it falls on the key with its full edge, and not with the edge of its tip-joint alone, it shares the clumsy appearance which all the other fingers present, in a slight degree, in the low position.

Stiff, but naturally strong, hands which are submitted late to instruction, often attain a certain looseness only through the second position and more particularly by playing with stretched fingers; with bent fingers they torture themselves unsuccessfully for years.—Small hands are more apt to require the extended finger position than large, as they are obliged to do more stretching.—But the low position and extended fingers exercise most influence on that style of touch, which has long been one-sidedly trained in the first form, without being enabled to attain full looseness. In such cases a mere reform in the position often works wonders; one hardly trusts one's ears on hearing the same passage, that sounded so stiff before, so completely and suddenly altered.

These are the main features in the position of the hand. Besides the two chief forms mentioned, there are two secondary modifications.—While the first principle imposed constraint upon the form of the hand, but left the touch, which resulted almost spontaneously from this form, at liberty, and while the second principle left the form full liberty, but constrained the touch to exertion, the modifications mentioned mingle these two factors in the following manner. There result:

III. A position of the hand which leaves the finger-form at liberty, while imposing a rule upon the wrist; and

IV. A position, which regulates the finger-form, but leaves the wrist at liberty.

That first named results, when the wrist and forearm are slightly elevated, the hand slanting somewhat downward to the keys; and the fingers remaining extended. This form has a graceful appearance; the play of the fingers gives an impression of great lightness. But in the legato (and this is everywhere the authoritative standard) the touch attains to no particular fulness. This form, exclusively adopted by some modern players, is peculiarly adapted to flying passages with passing under and over, the thumb touching the key only with its extreme tip, and the entire movement often going over into a gentle, undulating line. To the singing touch, however, the almost standing form of the finger is well adapted, and yields twice the power wanting in the legato.—All bravura strokes with the arm also gain a peculiar power of tone, explainable from the thrusting touch with which the keys are taken. The marking of melody-notes with an erect finger is borrowed on suitable occasions, by each of the other regular positions, from this style of holding the hand.

Finally, the position described under No. IV lets the wrist hang down, but requires bent fingers. Beyond question, the densest legato is thus attained; even in the high position with bent fingers, whenever a particularly great volume of tone is demanded, an inclination will be observable to lower the wrist.

Here the general theory of the position of the hand may be concluded.—For all of these, the characteristics of the touch previously described remain an equally binding requirement, and we again repeat, that a perfectly trained hand must be equally at home in all forms. Each hand must study its nature, its capabilities, and the manner and form of outward aids by whose means it can bring out the timbre (tone-color) desired in the proper place; and choose its position accordingly.

For the methodical development of the hand it is necessary, however, to begin with a single positive form, and to keep to the same until it has become second nature. Then, and not before, should the resources found in the other forms be gradually added as extensions. A commingling of the different principles at the beginning would only create confusion. The quietness of the hand during all finger-movements is a prime requisite in all positions.—But it cannot possibly be attained, where no settled rule is followed for the position of the hand. Furthermore, true liberty is not possible until the rules are mastered, and a beginning must always be made with one rule. When quietness of the hand has been attained on the strength of one rule, the other forms can be taken up in due course.

True to this principle, the following system has decided for the position of the hand given under No. I, and will only gradually take up the extensions provided by the other theories, while consistently keeping in view the above-mentioned and carefully to be noted standpoint.

CHAPTER V.

Beginning of study. Individuality of the fingers. Space of the positions. Exercises with quiet hand. Application of the technical material to suitable compositions.

The hand, which in the ordinary course of life is abandoned to natural conditions and inclinations, is now made to assume a fixed and definite form. The fingers are bent, the knuckles are pressed in and form a curving hollow, the wrist stands a little higher, the first finger-joints slant slightly up from the knuckles, the forearm slants down slightly from the bend of the wrist to the elbow, the hands are turned outward, the fingers stand so far apart, as their appointed position on five adjoining white keys requires. The distance of the player from the keyboard is so calculated, that the arms can conveniently command their ground when crossed or mutually superposed; the elbows hang down easily, as if by their own weight; the feet are firmly planted on the floor, children's feet being supported; the whole bearing, aside from the observance of the prescribed graceful undulating line of the playing apparatus, must assume an appearance of unconstrainedness. Neither is the chest thrown out in military style, but is held easily, rather retreating than advancing; the general feeling is that of relaxation in all muscles, which must, however, be ready at each instant for prompt and energetic action.

The fingers must first practice promptitude in striking. Where the knuckles sink in with difficulty, this posture must be practiced till easy. It renders the finger-stroke prompt and elastic as a steel spring. — To this end, the hand is laid flat on the table, and while its palm remains in close contact with the table-top, the fingers (the thumb of course included) are drawn inward in their bent form. This exercise is excellent in bringing out the form, and can be practiced some time before introduction to the keyboard. — When the position has been thoroughly mastered in this way, so that the free hand can assume it on command, the fingers are placed on the keys, and in the beginning press all five down firmly, as if acting on a table-top. The exact mutual relief of the keys (fingers) is only gradually introduced, according to the relation of the striking fingers.

The stroke consists of the lift, the fall, and the pressure. Each of these motions must be practiced by itself. A perfect whole is attainable only through the perfection of its parts. — According to a principle mentioned in the foregoing chapter, the lift may be increased in difficulty in the direction of height. Frequently the mere holding up of the finger is an

8

excellent exercise, and should be practiced chiefly with the fourth or fifth fingers. The force of the down-stroke can be constantly increased so long as it does not shake the hand, which must remain perfectly quiet under all circumstances. The pressure exercised upon the key must be continuous, without wavering or letting go.—

The striking power must be equally developed in all fingers. Dynamic equality is the first ideal of the art here building up from its elements, and is comparable to the straight line in architecture, or the truly pitched tone in music. The former is a geometrical, the latter an arithmetical ideal; the equality of finger-power is a physical one. From the last, all further development in the art takes its departure.

The height of the lift must also be trained to equality. The first finger-joint must deflect distinctly from the line of the back of the hand, and each finger form the same angle. Previously the striking height was trained absolutely; it now enters on the second, relative, stage. Fingers 3 and 2 must restrain, 4 and 5 exert themselves, and practice until the original exertion passes into a condition of complete unconstrainedness. The pressing in of the knuckles to a hollow, though rendering the lift somewhat more difficult, strengthens the striking power of the fingers, and insures a forceful downstroke.—Later, the hollow at the knuckles takes on the normal horizontality proper to the original conception of this position, concerning which the foregoing chapter gives details.—Aside from the influences just mentioned, the inward bend of the knuckles illustrates the first victory of the will over the obstinacy and inflexibility of all sinews and muscles inherent in the crude material.

The forearm, too, will later be held quite horizontal. It should in no event lie higher than the hand; else it would mingle its influence with the energy manifested by the fingers, and disturb the isolation of the latter. Many are constitutionally disposed to a rush of blood to the fingers, which abates their power of endurance.—Holding the forearm lower is less disadvantageous; in the beginning it favors the isolation of the fingers, and is not unfavorable to natural needs till later, for other effects of touch.

The several exercises best begin with the easiest; the easiest beginning always insures the fullest accomplishment of the first step. The third finger is by nature the skilfullest and strongest. The style of touch which it possesses serves for a time as a standard for the other fingers. True, even its tone will not be exactly strong at first, but later, through practice, will attain that proportionate relation of strength and decision appropriate to its individuality, discussed in the preceding chapter.—All fingers must retain their fixed shape in striking; the more yielding and loose the movement in the knuckle-joint, the more tense must the curve of the tip-joints be kept, in order to present firm resistance to the key. Thus the striking-action will be concentrated at just that point of the knuckle-joint upon which it depends, and the individualization of the fingers arrived at by the shortest road. Should the tip-joints likewise move in striking, the strength would be diverted from the knuckle-joint and distributed at various points. The same would happen, if the hand or arm participated in the movement.

Among all the difficulties which the obstinate awkwardness of the hand opposes to the will, that residing in the knuckles is the greatest and most important. In no hand is the flexibility of the knuckles sufficiently developed by nature. The strengthening and loosening of their mechanism is a task requiring the patient toil of many years, would the player attain that soft flexibility in the lift and fall of the finger which was stated in the preceding chapter, before the theory of the position of the hand, as the general essential.

The remarks on the third finger hold good with the others. The second is the next-strongest and skilfullest. Its mobility is probably greater, but in strength it yields to the third. In this point, therefore, it must first strive to gain equilibrium

8*

with the third. Next to the second comes the fifth; but it has to struggle against more essential deficiencies.

Shorter and weaker than the former, it requires double perseverance for its strengthening; in addition, its somewhat straighter tip-joint allows from the outset less pressure on the key than is exerted by the central fingers. Consequently its lift before striking must be higher, to attain a correspondingly greater pressure. This peculiar feature, which must fairly become second nature, has in various methods given rise to the rule, that the hand should be held somewhat lower toward the thumb, slanting upward a little toward the fifth finger. The latter is, indeed, thereby urged constantly to take a wider sweep, through which it gradually arrives at equilibrium with the other fingers.

The fourth finger, however, is the worst. In its physiological peculiarities Nature has opposed an essential impediment to the human will. It occupies a far less free position in the hand than the other fingers, and is therefore weaker and stiffer. Its lift has the least height, its pressure the least strength. With no other finger is the hand so apt to move, or does the tip-joint so obstinately try to stretch out. If the fifth finger requires double, the fourth demands threefold perseverance.

The thumb has special peculiarities. In strength it ranks somewhat below the third finger, or even the second. This results partly from its shortness, partly from its low-lying position. In lifting it must exert itself more than the other fingers, because its lifting power is not so directly concentrated in one point as that represented by the knuckles. In pressing down, its exertion is also greater, because a straight finger, as explained in the case of position No. 2, does not strike with the tension of a bent one. Neither is it driven by the springiness of the inward-bent knuckle. Moreover, it does not follow in striking the natural bent of its motion, which inclines to turn inward, to close together with the fingers. Finally, it strikes with a narrow edge, and very often with a minimum of surface, and consequently misses the advantage of a nervous grasp of the key.—For these reasons the thumb needs special training, in order to rise to equality with the other fingers in strength and skill.—With reference to a *development* of strength, however, it finds consolatory compensation in another way. It moves in a soft, yielding, muscular mass of flesh, and its task is, to habituate the latter to equable manifestations of power. This task proves remunerative to persevering industry, as the striking-lift turns out to be very considerable. By reason of the great mobility easily gained, the lift must, in fact, be limited, to maintain the idea of equality with the other fingers.— Arm and hand should remain perfectly quiet when the thumb is lifted; the latter then reaches with its tip to about the height of the inbent knuckle of the second finger. The down-stroke is more difficult; great perseverance is necessary to obtain a pearling touch, the stroke always leaning rather toward a pressure than a fall.—To the above a very characteristic task is added, which requires double dexterity of the thumb; namely, the horizontal striking-action in passing under. Of this further on.

Practical work now begins with developing the strength of the separate fingers. Each falls perpendicularly on the centre of the front field of its white key. All the first exercises are played with fixed hand, i. e. all the fingers stand firmly on the keys pressed down by them, while a single finger practices the stroke. Thus, while the tension of the lift is brought into play, the hand is, so to speak, pressed down by a weight. To stand firmly it needs a firm foundation, and by the downward pressure of the inactive fingers the hand obtains a support.

The first exercises are performed very slowly and very distinctly as regards each separate movement; they increase only gradually to a moderate rapidity, beyond which they should not pass for some time. With specially unfavorable subjects, each single motion of the total movement should be strictly criticised by the teacher: namely the up-stroke, suspension, down-stroke, and pressure of each finger.

Each point must be mastered to a certain degree of perfection. Each, to be sure, slightly influences the rest by a bond of sympathy, but not one can be neglected. Though a complete isolation of every separate point cannot be expected in the first stages, such a good start must be obtained on the way to this goal, that whatever is lacking will surely be set right in the sequel.

After the fingers have gained some confidence in the normal position on five white keys, positions of different conformation must be examined and practiced. In the first position the fingers have to handle surfaces of equal length and breadth, of equal dip, and to be controlled from an equal height. As soon as black keys are added, the positions become more complicated. Narrower keys, higher placed, shorter and therefore further back, and set together in a twofold grouping of twos and threes, push forward between the broader white keys. The mechanical conditions become dissimilar, but the tone produced and the quality of touch must maintain precisely the same evenness.

There are in all the following five positions: (1) All fingers stand on white keys; (2) the outer fingers 1 and 5 stand on white keys, the central fingers either all or in part on black keys; (3) one of the outer fingers stands on a black key, the others on a white key; (4) both outer fingers stand on black keys, the central fingers either all or in part on white keys; (5) all fingers stand on black keys.

The last case most resembles the first in respect to its horizontal relation. The fingers have to deliver the stroke from the same height. But the narrow key-tops are more difficult to manage, and the distance between the fingers has also become unequal.

One of the most difficult positions is No. 4. The inner fingers have for their mark the narrow part of the white keys lying between the black keys. As with many hands the tips of the inner fingers are almost too broad for this space, the fineness of their sense of touch must be kept on the alert. The tips must strive after greater sensitiveness and flexibility, in order to avoid grazing the adjoining black keys. Both here and in No. 3 the position of the hand is normal. The inner fingers must learn to apply their power in a new measure; to secure evenness by a lower fall. The inequality of the local conditions must nowhere exercise an influence on the required equality of tone. Especially in rapid playing the inner fingers may easily exhibit a certain constraint and embarrassment, which must be conquered by careful strengthening.

The other positions are moderately difficult. When the outer fingers are set on white keys and the inner on black, the normal form of the finger-position is sacrificed for the first time. The tip-joints of the inner fingers lie upon the black keys slopingly — extended, but by no means quite straight. Here we have inequality in form and position, and the influence of both must be completely neutralized through the study of equality. The extended fingers must press harder, and they no longer share the advantage of the firm resistance of the bent finger-tip. In their lift they must also make greater exertion, as the striking surface lies higher, and the striking power must not be diminished in lift. The case is specially difficult where only the fourth finger has a black key, all the rest standing on white keys.—In all these cases the point requires consideration, that black keys always present a more difficult mark on account of their narrower surface, and need special study.

When the thumb has a black key, the entire hand is drawn into the region of the latter, and obliged to assume a posture turned more outward to the little-finger side. As in No. 4, the inner fingers have to conquer the difficulties in striking the narrow part of the white keys, the thumb having to stand at a slight angle with the black key. The thumb being inclined, from its position, to take white keys, this posture is decidedly inconvenient, and requires special treatment to completely master the problem of the free and equal manifestation of power.

Finally, when the fifth finger stands on a black key, and the thumb on a white one, the case may arise, if the former be considerably stretched, that its tip-joint is held quite horizontal, e. g. in the position f-g-a-b-d♯. Here its function enters into quite a new relation; if it would play with equal power, it must exert its full strength in lifting and pressing.

Thus the long chain of assiduous finger-studies is opened in five little chapters, from each of which abundant profit may be reaped. The fingers must become independent; they must respond so readily to the will-power aiming at evenness in tone-production, that they carry out its intention instinctively, without special exertion. The five playing-levers, of such various individuality and so differently built and placed, must renounce all differences of external conditions, and mutually offset and equalize their peculiarities and powers with such care, that they take on the mathematical equality of an artificial mechanism as their second nature.— Thus the natural condition of the material has entered upon the first stage of artificial training. The primary, undivided unity of the natural hand has been divided into a number of contrasts and distinctions; the original One is cleft into five individualities; through the long struggle of these opposing individual powers in their countless interrelations, unity is to be regained. This regained unity will, however, be an artificial one.

The fixed hand, i. e. practice with fingers held down, remaining for some time the foundation, the measure of this fixedness will, however, be decreased, and exercises previously executed with a single finger must gradually combine 2, 3, and 4 fingers; the absolute measure of power must constantly seek new expression through the attainment of relative equality.

A new feature now supervenes which, on the one hand, furthers this task, while being, on the other, in itself of the highest importance, as adding to pure technique the first elements of musical meaning in the form of Rhythm. Nothing so essentially furthers the accuracy, strength, precision, and the complete subordination of the fingers to the idea, as practicing in time; and simple as the tone-combinations hitherto attempted may be, they must already accustom themselves to this primary element of music. Herewith they lay the foundation of the most opulent later forms. The most rudimentary form of rhythm is the equal division of the tone-values. The time from one stroke to the next must everywhere have the same duration; indeed, it may even be required that the necessary motion within each separate stroke should be uniformly executed. A martial regularity must regulate in like manner the up-stroke, down-stroke, and pressure of each finger. The muscular action submits to a new law, and is strengthened thereby. Besides, the isochronism (equality of time-values), the positive similarity of the measure-units, the habituation of the senses to any measure whatever which breaks up the limitless extent of time, is the element from which all rhythm later springs.

Thus, in respect to equality, the mechanical action has now to carry out a fourfold ideal of regularity, namely: (1) Equality in tone-production; (2) equality in tone-lengths; (3) equality in finger-position; (4) equality in movements. The mere looseness and strength of the fingers is still comparable to a certain crude state of nature. These properties are nothing more than unlimited material, which requires form. Under the domination of rhythm this technical power first takes on refinement, docility, delicacy, and plastic beauty.

With a view to practical utility, whose rights,must always find recognition in a practical method, the sum of the isochronal movements will be divided into groups of four. Each movement is indicated by a figure; in even more rudimentary beginnings rhythmical exactitude may already control each separate motion; the up-stroke is indicated by 1, the downstroke by 2, the pressure by 3 and 4.

The fingers now unite, in all possible combinations, to execute in alternation simple successions of tones, and later simultaneous strokes. The thumb and second finger begin. Their unequal mechanical conditions will be especially apparent in the thumb, which has a constant tendency to impart its own motion to the hand. The player must therefore endeavor to bring the powers of both into mutual equilibrium. After this, the thumb combines with the fingers 3, 4, 5 under like conditions, then the second finger with the third, fourth, and fifth, etc. This is the most practical combination, and it will be a good plan to arrange the first practical exercises according to the following simple table of combinations:

I. Separate finger-exercises with the fingers 1, 2, 3, 4, 5.

II. Combinations of two: 1 2, 1 3, 1 4, 1 5; 2 3, 2 4, 2 5; 3 4, 3 5; 4 5.

III. Combinations of three: 1 2 3, 1 2 4, 1 2 5, 1 3 4, 1 3 5, 1 4 5, 2 3 4, 2 3 5, 2 4 5, 3 4 5.

IV. Combinations of four: 1 2 3 4, 1 2 3 5, 1 2 4 5, 1 3 4 5, 2 3 4 5.

V. All five: 1 2 3 4 5.

At the beginning each hand must practice for some time alone; the perfection of the whole is the greater, the more carefully the details are developed.—If we consider, that the invention of finger-exercises has perfectly free scope, in varying the combinations of figures found in the above five groups by repeating single or several constituent parts with doubled notes, with all possible transpositions, in the form of three or four-part groups, it is not surprising that there is quite a large number of works, which contain nothing but finger-exercises.—

With the fifth group the exercises without supporting finger begin. They form the second stage of finger-technique. It is utterly wrong, to let the latter begin with these, as was the habit of earlier works on technique.—The quietness of the hand must be established, before giving up the supporting fingers, for a free-hand exercise is harder than one supported, when the retention of the quietness of the hand comes in question.

The exercises without supporting finger follow the previous

method at all points, although for the reasons stated above the form of the hand must at first be watched more carefully, that any needless extension of unemployed fingers, or purposeless movement, may be suppressed. With all outward freedom the greatest firmness of form must prevail. These exercises admit of more manifold variation than the foregoing, and combine with the same to form a complete cycle of exercises with quiet hand.

For the entire mechanical art the law holds good, that each of its parts is equally important and essential; that while a progressive method from easy to difficult, from the simpler to the more complicated, may be established on account of systematization, the whole must still be held in living remembrance and practice. No form has meaning solely as a preparation for a higher one. The chapter on fixed exercises must therefore by no means be considered as closed when the free-hand studies are entered on, nor these latter upon making acquaintance with the following steps. True, in practical study new matter must sometimes be favored, but the old should always be repeated and perfected. For the one influences the other, and a proof of the true mastery of every new task will always consist in its simultaneous furtherance of those preceding it.—All forms are most intimately connected; the latest are founded on the first, and these are perfected by all coming after.

The exercises with quiet hand embrace a very extensive material, and its mastery is a highly important result. Therewith the first and most difficult step is taken on a path strange to the natural hand. The independence of the fingers thus gained is comparable to the creation of a material, henceforward to be moulded and fashioned; the main point was its creation, and the merit of this achievement falls to the elementary exercises. They are the foundation of all, and the teacher can not sufficiently insist upon consistency and patience in their conscientious mastery.

From theory to practice—from the rule to its application. This principle belongs to every method, whatever subject it may treat of. All mechanical art is dead, if not endowed with the musical spirit. Herewith we would not condemn theories which aim at turning the hand really into a machine, or even external appliances, which, according to peculiarities in the make of the hands, are often employed successfully, often uselessly. Only the moment must not be missed, when mechanical art should enter into the service of the spirit.

So soon as the fingers have taken the first step towards individualization, they must learn to exercise their capabilities in the service of higher requirements. The musical side must not only be stimulated together with the gymnastical, but the latter must seek its aim in the former. It cannot, of course, be the intention of the present work to exhaust this task in its full extent. The musical essence will be subjected to special analysis; to carry out the parallel between technical and musical progress at all points is inadmissible, for the reason that each individuality follows its peculiar course of development, and precepts universally binding can be arrived at only through a separate consideration of the technical and musical sides. Therefore a suggestion for combining the mechanical with the spiritual will be thrown out only for the first stage, the other chapters merely presupposing in general a retention of this combined course of instruction.

The rigid exclusiveness and rhythmical conciseness of mechanical studies, and the predominant monotony of dynamics and measure in these rudiments, are of but one-sided formative power even in a purely technical sense. Firstly, it is the rhythm of the practical little pieces of music that are now taken up, which in its greater variety exercises the tractableness of the fingers in quite a different manner from the one-sided equability of mechanical timing. The movements in forceful and persevering precision are the part of the finger-exercises; their liberation, naturalness, yieldingness and grace are perfected only through the practice of compositions. The two sides of pianoforte playing stand in the relation of rule and example, grammar and reading, the school and life.

The actual compositions employable at this stage naturally include a limited range, for the most part five-tone pieces. But that, which they add to the mechanical knowledge, is a greater variety of rhythm, a freer, less self-concentrated activity of the purely mechanical element, and the elevation of material means into the sphere of musical emotion.—In particular, the purely mechanical will receive new animation from the accent.

In the earlier technical practice no accent was required. Where an equalization of power is aimed at, the accent may act injuriously, as it easily throws the unaccented tones too far into the background. In any event, a certain power of touch and assurance of equality must have been attained, before the accent can be introduced.—When the finger-action is ripe for the same, it doubtless obtains therein a very essential promotor of strength and elasticity. Thus in practical work the accent becomes necessary for a perspicuous presentation and a deeper insight into rhythmical relations, and from this point may also be adopted into the mechanical studies. The beginnings and main divisions of all measures are marked by an exertion of strength beyond that for ordinary tone-production; the remaining tones are taken with a firm, but less marked distinctness. Technically and intellectually a new element is thus introduced.

Moreover, the gradual emancipation of the pieces from the parallel movement of the hands calls forth a finer instinct of locality in the fingers and a freer activity of the mind; the machine-like movement in the accustomed track gives way to an intellectual need.

Actual compositions bring a further gain in the addition of sustained tones. The slow movement of the finger-exercises at the beginning was a different matter. It flowed from mechanical requirements, and the mind was directed thereby only to external precision of performance. The tones were

significant only in the sense of their mechanical importance.
But they now obtain musical significance through their melody.— Two powerful main factors have forced the germs of
music to stately growth — melody and instrumental developments. The latter were introduced in the finger-exercises and
the more rapid notes of the pieces; melody is now added in
the long notes. Or at least, it more decidedly asserts its rights
in them than in melodic touches, that may have been found
here and there in passage-like figures. The fingers are therefore obliged not only to play, but to sing as well. A sustained
holding of the keys now already forms a preparation for that
pressing power, with which, as the essence of the melodious
touch, we shall later become familiar.

Thus in practical work the fingers obtain the rhythmical
and musical augmentations mentioned as supplementary to the
mechanical art, and the player's ear is stimulated by melodic
and harmonic beauties. That which was explained in detail
in connection with the elementary standpoint, is regularly fulfilled in the sequel, for which, as stated before, a constant
passing-over of the mechanical into the musical is presupposed.
The latter always tends to perfect the purely technical, which
would take on a certain coarseness if too exclusively cultivated.
The taste should not simply keep pace with the progress of
technique, but rather press on before.

The next extension of mechanical training consists in
spreading and narrowing the space covered by five fingers
with a quiet hand. The narrower position arises when the
five fingers play within a narrower space than is occupied by
five white keys, e. g. *c-c♯-d-e-f♯*. The narrowest position is
formed by a chromatic succession of keys, *c-c♯-d-d♯-e*. Wider
spread positions are formed when the fingers are spread beyond
the space of five white keys, e. g.: *c-d-f♯-g♯-a♯*. It is no bad
plan in practice to write out the finger-exercises from the beginning in figures only, and to regulate the position in which
they are to be executed according to requirement.

To enumerate all possible positions is quite as unnecessary as to practice them. It is not likely that any normally formed hand has ever studied all possible finger-exercises in all possible shapes.—Each principal class influences the rest; perfect smoothness of all movements and readiness in the obedience of all members and joints is the main end, and this is often attained rather through the quality than the quantity of the mechanical exercises. Besides, hands have different characteristics. One already gains the essential through half of the exercises till now enumerated; another will require their entire extent, in order to get the proper quality of touch.—Similarly, the need of perseverance in one and the same kind of exercises differs; what one hand acquires with ease, costs the other inexpressible difficulty.

The limits just mentioned may be extended in either direction, and new tasks come in view. By omitting fingers the narrow position can be yet further contracted, and the spread position still further extended by giving up the simultaneous holding of all five keys. For instance, by leaving out the second finger a narrowing can be effected from c to $d\sharp$, by leaving out several fingers from c to d, in its narrowest form from c to $c\sharp$, the thumb taking c, and the fifth finger $c\sharp$. The mechanical training must make trial of all chief distinctions, even though it may not be necessary to practice in detail all cases to be found in each class. The narrowest position, too, must first be practiced slowly, increasing to the velocity of a trill. This leads up to cases having in common the form of two chromatic neighboring tones played as a trill by two fingers not contiguous; for example, in the following combinations: 2 and 5, 2 and 4, 3 and 5. In these the hand may be fixed, half fixed, or free; several fingers may hold their keys, or one, or none, e. g. b and d can be held by the fingers 1 and 5, while 2 and 3 trill on c and $c\sharp$. These exercises lead to trills in general, which in point of fact belong to the chapter on exercises with quiet hand. They must likewise be practiced with all possible combinations of fingers, i. e. with the following groups: 1 2, 1 3, 1 4, 1 5, 2 3, 2 4, 2 5, 3 4, 3 5, 4 5, and with half as well as whole tones.—They will not, indeed, attain to perfect beauty during the first studies in technique, but attention has already been called to the fact, that while advancing to new tasks the earlier ones must continually be kept in view, difficulties not quite conquered forming a constant material for practice. The same is true of the tremolo exercises, which often occur in their simplest form among the finger-exercises, and also claim special attention in future as an independent branch.

The same is to be said on the stretches, which form, rather than the trill and tremolo, a separate branch, being the foundation of a widely extended class of forms. As such, too, they will later receive special notice in the proper place. Their first trial by the hand is more tentative than serious.— So long as the fixed hand still covers the space in which it plays, the stretch assumes only moderate proportions. In a more extended form it obliges the hand to give up its quiet position, and to move somewhat towards the side of the extreme tones to strike the keys.—In the middle the fingers may or may not hold their keys down; the former case gives best practice in stretching the outer fingers, here the chief consideration. But the stretching distance between the other fingers must also be increased by industrious practice at the pianoforte, and away form the latter at any level surface, or even with the aid of the other hand without support from any firmly resisting object.—However, at the stage now reached, such studies should be made merely incidental, stress being laid chiefly on the form of the hand, and the exercises being confined to the compass of a sixth, seventh, or at most an octave. For the bent position of the fingers, and the springiness of touch, are sacrificed by further efforts.

Where the normal position is combined with a wider or narrower one, or the last two occur in direct succession, a new class of mechanical studies arises, consisting in a sideways movement or progression of the fingers. Hitherto the striking action held fast to the perpendicular line; now it must combine with the same a horizontal motion.—In the following example each finger advances, as soon as the figure at *b* begins,

horizontally a little towards the right, and would have to retreat again just so far to the left, on a return to the narrow position. At first, the horizontal motion must exactly precede the perpendicular, and the fingers must carefully assume the quiet posture necessary for a position, before proceeding to the perpendicular stroke. But that, which a good method divorces at the beginning, must later blend to a single movement. In the fluent execution of such figures the fingers are forced, in reality, to a curvilinear striking movement.

The moment that the technique would overstep, in any direction whatever, the limits until now observed, it needs new resources. We first consider the case of finger-action within still narrower bounds than are set by two neighboring chromatic tones, and then proceed to forms ascending and descending the keyboard.

The first case occurs, when a single tone is repeated by one or several fingers. Both touch and tone-production are here forced essentially to modify their former mode of operation. The tones cannot be connected, and the finger-stroke requires a co-operation of the tip-joints, which hitherto remained passively bent, their strength showing in mere passive resistance without active movement. This exhibits two important deviations from the rule previously followed.

The second case, in which freer scope on the keyboard is opened, forms the transition to that field wherein the musical in pianoforte playing has its true foundation, and in entering upon which the conditions for the reproduction of real compositions are arrived at. Although both cases are natur-

9

ally evolved from the elements hitherto treated of, they
nevertheless announce, in their form, something so peculiarly
new, that an important advance in the mechanical art is
apparent therein, and they are therefore assigned to a new
chapter.

CHAPTER VI.

**The staccato from the knuckle-joint and with the finger-
tip. Repeated strokes on a key. Advancing exercises.
Finger-action in passing under and over. Scale-playing
and its importance.**

All forms previously discussed belong to the category of
connected or legato playing. This latter forms not only
ideally the most appropriate beginning for the studies, as
representing the elementary relation of successions of tones,
but also best develops the fingers, because they remain in
direct relation to each other.

The exact opposite of this is the staccato or detached
touch. Here one tone is not sustained until the next comes,
but between the two there lies an interval not filled by any
tone. The stroke of the fingers effects this, the lift of the
one entering before the fall of the other. In the feeling of
the fingers the immediate relation of the one power to the
other is no less missing than between the tones. The ear,
aided by the combinative understanding, has to re-establish
this connection, and in the union of two contradictory factors
lies the peculiar character of the staccato. Assuming the
natural connection of the tones to represent the simply
Beautiful, the impression of the staccato would be termed the
Charmful.

The feature of equality must likewise characterize the
staccato. Without it nothing beautiful can be developed on
the pianoforte. The equality of the staccato resides in the
equal power and duration of the separate successive tones,

and conversely in the equal length of the empty intervals. The fingers have therefore to acquire equal mechanical conditions in all points of their striking-action; the lift, the fall, and the rebound must be similarly developed in force and scope.

In tone-quality the staccato varies with regard to character, timbre, and expression, and its mechanical execution exhibits corresponding differences. The mental and mechanical must, of course, be intimately blended, just as the gesture should fit the thought.

It does not lie within the scope of this empirico-practical method, already to specify all these kinds *here*. They will be taken up in turn in the proper place; we begin now with that kind of staccato to which the preceding course of technical development leads up.

At the repetition of one nnd the same tone by several fingers a staccato is unavoidable, and two modes of execution are possible to the hand in its present stage of training. The first is distinguished from the accustomed connected style only in the feature, that the striking finger shortens its time of resting on the key. Otherwise everything remains as before in regard to form and movement. The finger lifts, darts down and back again, the following one does the same, etc. The tones recur in equal intervals and power. The repose of the hand must be retained. In the other mode of execution the finger-tip is drawn over the key and thrown up toward the palm of the hand, so that after the finished stroke the nail forms an acute angle with the key. In this manner one finger makes room for another; the hand aims with 2, 3, 4, or even all 5 striking-members at one and the same point, i. e. when one and the same key is struck repeatedly. During the stroke of the following finger the first again rises ready to strike. This staccato is, besides, of very general importance, and is also used with different successive tones.

In the first style, the hammer-like up and down-stroke of the first finger-joint at the knuckle was the leading mechanical feature; in the second, the mechanical action of the finger-tip, the gymnastic dexterity of the tip-joint, or of both forward joints, was the decisive point. The former is founded on the solid touch hitherto employed; the latter on greater brevity, delicacy, and flexibility.

Our horizon is now essentially extended, and we must inform ourselves regarding its full scope.

First of all, each class shall be named. The first is called the staccato with the finger-joint; or, to speak more exactly, the knuckle-joint. It may also be termed, as the finger on the whole retains its form, the staccato with the whole finger. The finger, like a casting of set form, is the striking-lever.—The second kind is called the staccato with the finger-tip.—But there is still, exactly speaking, a third staccato, which is not hard to guess, it being formed by a combination of the first two. The first finger-joint rises, and while it falls the tip-joint is thrown inwards. However, we will only term this kind a modification of the second, as it more nearly approaches the latter in sensitiveness of the finger-tip, and always appears of itself where greater power of tone is required.

Earlier theory, which noticed only differences in tone, and not the processes in the mechanical execution, classified the staccati according to the degree in which the tone was abbreviated. The staccato with dot signified that one-half, with the wedge-like stroke that three-fourths of its value should be substracted from the note. No positive rule for the mechanical action results from this; one cannot assert that the staccato with the stroke is to be executed, as some demanded, with the finger-tip, or the dotted staccato with the entire finger or with the wrist. The shortest is probably obtained with the wrist, the most delicate with the finger-tip. — These distinctions do not at present concern the technique; the matter now in hand is, to begin the study of the staccato.

The staccato with the entire finger requires no new

exercises; it can employ the studies with quiet hand. The touch must at first be powerful; the other rules of form remain unaltered. The staccato with the finger-tip requires for the first time a modification in the position of the hand, and this in the practice studies. Till now the finger-form was looked at as a whole, as a hammer, whose first joint acted as the hammer-heft; the participation of the two forward joints was not active, but merely passive. Now it is different; the first remains passive, and the two others, especially the tip-joint, become active. But the bent position hinders this activity; it admits of no full lift, and robs the striking-curve of half its sweep. The tip-joint has rather to stretch out quite, or at least nearly, straight, and to dart inwards for delivering the stroke. After striking, the edge of the nail lies near the key. To lend this exercise plastically defined form, let the whole front of the finger come in contact with the key, the tip pressing down the key during the inward spring so far, that the tone is sounded. This touch will produce the softest tone. Later, the finger more nearly approaches its bent form, and has still to master a series of exercises for regulating the power of tone. The tip-joint has to attack the key in various fashions, sometimes striking with a stronger touch, and again more gently drawing or slipping with softer touch. Later practical work employs only the latter form; the former with straightened finger is recommended for practice because it most directly calls out the elasticity of the finger-tip. It gives excellent practice to play entire scales in this manner with the finger-tip.

Both forms can now be combined with the knuckle-joint staccato. To this end the first joint lifts, and the tip-joint participates actively in the stroke, either straightened out, or a trifle bent. This staccato is chiefly employed in powerful effects, but not exclusively; it must also be able to produce the very softest tone.

The thumb executes this touch with more difficulty and not quite the plastic definiteness of the other fingers. Its tip-joint also moves inwards, but at the same time diagonally downwards, for otherwise no tone would be audible. Its impulse is thus divided between two lines, whereas with the other fingers the curve was maintained in one direction. The action of the thumb, like that of the other fingers, adapts itself to the power of tone, limiting itself for soft tones to the use of the tip, and calling its entire leverage into play for stronger ones.

In its direct application, this form of the staccato is employed for repeated strokes by several fingers on one key. The hand assumes a somewhat contracted shape, because it aims with all fingers at one and the same point. In playing, the fingers naturally incline to reserve the thumb for the last stroke of a fixed succession of tones, and to begin the earlier with the fingers, the further they are placed from the thumb. This comes from the native propensity of the fingers to close into contact with the thumb; for it is contrary to the inclination of the fingers, to close together toward the side of the fifth. The same principle has decisive influence in such repetitions, as do not employ the thumb. — It is expedient in practice to lift the first finger striking so high, that its tip rises high above the level of the hand; to raise the other fingers before striking to an approximate height, and to repeat this procedure at every repetition. This strengthens them most, and also influences the elasticity of the finger-tip, whose participation was alluded to. The appropriate examples are divided into two classes; either a repetition on one key without other figurative elements, or combined with other figuration.

In this connection we again remark, that the principle of changing the fingers, without which rapid repetitions would be quite, or almost, impracticable, is likewise frequently employed now-a-days in easy and slow repetitions of notes. Even though the fingerings resulting therefrom may not be termed exactly essential, it must be admitted, that on the whole they lend softness and flexibility to the touch, and are in particular adapted to facilitate the legato in repetition passages. In the case of indirect repetitions, too, precision and lightness of touch are often more rapidly attained by a change of fingers. Hence arise inverted-mordent fingerings like the following: 1 3 2; 2 3 1; 1 4 3; 2 4 3, etc. Many highly reputable modern editions of the classics adhere more or less consistently to the above-stated standpoint; e. g. the editions by Bülow, Herm. Scholz, and Klindworth.

We now proceed to the second class of augmentations developed from the elements discussed in the foregoing chapter. The first class treated of the development of finger-power within the narrowest room; that following arises from the essential requirement of an extension of the technical range. Through the stretching of the hand this requirement was but partially fulfilled. The tone-figures were still bound to the same spot. The transition to a fully free control of the keyboard is effected by the *advancing exercises,* wherein the hand passes through its range with medium velocity.—They are distinguished from the exercises with quiet hand by the sidelong movement of one finger, which by this means advances out of the normal position by a step forward into a new position, drawing the rest of the hand into the latter. In the new position the same order of fingering is usually observed as in that preceding, and this procedure is repeated through a series of quiet-hand exercises, each advancing or retreating by a step in the manner described. Almost any quiet-hand exercise may be taken as pattern for a series thus formed; the advancing step may be given to any finger. Such advancing exercises may also be combined with repetitions on one key.— Generally speaking, they lead the technique out of the monotony common to all limitations into a field affording more abundant variety, and stimulate the fingers, by a rhythmical interest, to a continued practice, to which they had rather to be forced in the exercises with quiet hand.

The advancing exercises were also cramped by a limitation. The rapidity of movement across the keys was retarded. The musical craving strives after yet more unhindered progression. The most important step toward acquiring the same is made in learning the technique of passing under and over, and the standard succession of tones, which flows therefrom as an important musical no less than technical advance, is the *scale.*—

Primarily, it is based on the fundamental idea of the standard position on five keys. At the moment of passing under, the thumb performs an act by which one normal position is exchanged for another, wherein it follows the familiar rules. By again passing under, the thumb again changes the last position into the next one, which lies an octave higher than the first; and this process is now continually repeated. The technique therefore starts from a known position, adds thereto a new feature of movement, and must strive to apply this latter as a mediating agency between two known elements, in a manner agreeing with familiar principles. These principles require: (1) An entirely independent, free, and flexible individual movement of the member actively employed in producing the tone; (2) the complete passivity and repose of the inactive members; (3) the blending of the several mechanical motions to graceful ease and uniformity; (4) the equality of all tones produced thereby.—The conceptions of economy and regularity were essential to the first ideal elements of pianoforte playing. Economy is the most essential law of art, for the substance no less than the form, for internals and externals—the law from which all else flows.

These æsthetic rules are authoritative in developing the scale. First of all must be learned the movement of the thumb toward the palm of the hand, passing close under one finger. For this the whole thumb, even to the joint working within the hand, must acquire looseness and flexibility in moving horizontally to and fro. The chief share of action, however, falls to the thumb-tip, which must acquire the greatest individual flexibility in bending inward and backward. The first thumb-joint, (that lying in the middle between tip-joint and palm of the hand) also needs extreme flexibility. The thumb-exercises must begin with a slow rate of speed, and increase to the maximum. The thumb must therefore learn to pass under the fingers 2, 3, 4 and 5 in turn.—The second law mentioned above referred to the quietness of the unemployed members. Consequently, neither the back of the hand must waver, nor the other fingers lose their form. The first normal position is the starting-point, and the beginning must be treated like an exercise with quiet hand. The new feature then enters, by substituting the thumb for the fourth finger, and later for the fifth. As a preliminary exercise, the following forms may be practiced in numerous combinations:

The second feature consists in passing over from the first normal position to the second. Here the advance of the hand and arm must be regulated more precisely. The thumb is here, despite all flexibility, not the sole essential factor in determining the mechanical action; both arm and hand must also take part in the movement with perfect quietness and evenness. According to the third law given above, this can be accomplished only by their smooth and simultaneous reciprocal action. The main point is, the combination of activity in advancing with passivity as regards direct exertion of the hand and arm; i. e. the hand must be twisted neither to the right nor left, and no turn of the elbow corresponding thereto allowed.—The hand is placed, slightly turned inward, upon that spot of the keyboard at which the scale is to begin.

Whereas in the exercises with quiet hand its position as turned outward was the standard, the contrary obtains here. Then, the thumb was laid as far as possible upon the key; now, only its front part touches the latter. This inward bend must not be unnaturally exaggerated. This position aims at facilitating the passing under; for as the thumb plays a leading part therein, care must be taken to bring it nearer to its point of passing.—The hand being firmly set in the first normal position, care must be taken, that the angle which it thus forms with the keys remains the same at every instant. As a guide, the teacher may lay a pencil on the hand from the middle of the wrist to the knuckle of the third finger, and call the pupil's attention to the angle which this line forms with the keys. At the slightest turn, this angle changes, and the pupil's eye should be instantly directed to this deflection. The judgment so passed by the eye is thoroughly reliable.

The thumb supports and guides the hand and arm in like manner, as these conversely regulate the rate of movement in passing under by continuing the quietly advancing total move ment, leaving the thumb free to develop its dexterity. They too support the thumb by the passive power of the general position. Thus a relation of equilibrium and reciprocity sub- sists between the two, which is so far modified by a more powerful touch, that the weight of the hand presses down somewhat more strongly, whereas in an easy flowing style the arm and hand, by lifting themselves, divert the strength of the fingers upward from pressing on the keys.—The arm is, as it were, the branch, on which the fingers flutter to and fro like movable leaves; its undulation up and down must resemble the gliding of a vessel. This feeling, as of a firm branch holding its loose leaves, must grow to a living consciousness.

For the twisting of the hand, the commonest fault, the thumb is usually held accountable. This is an error; it often occurs when the thumb is perfectly flexible, and is caused by the faulty gliding away of the arm. It usually occurs the instant *after* passing under; now, this instant must be occupied, aside from the lift of the second finger before striking, by the simultaneously advancing glide of the arm. Usually, however, the arm wrongly stands still at this instant, and lets the second finger move on alone. This must result in turning the hand, which turns back again when the third finger strikes, and thus the faulty twisting of the hand arises. It can be avoided only by evenly advancing the arm, the moment the thumb passes under. — Where the arm moves with the hand as described, it will form, when the hand is far away from the body, a straight line with the outer edge of the hand, which line gradually recurs to the obtuse angle on playing back. The arm-movement after passing under has therefore to be practiced carefully by itself, and the second finger not allowed to strike before it stands perpendicularly over its key, with the hand turned inward.—

This is one half of the mechanical process in scale-playing. The other concerns the return movement of the arm in playing back, and the passing of the third or fourth finger over the thumb. The latter also forms the connecting link in passing from one normal position to the following; and its features must be examined in detail before it can take on smooth and uniform movement. At the moment when the thumb strikes, the arm and hand must have moved so far forward in the direction in which the finger turns over, and with their angle to the keyboard as given above unchanged, that the finger passing over shall have advanced a key further than the thumb-tip, and has only to fall perpendicularly. At this moment the entire length of the thumb is underneath the hand, for which posture a flexibility to be acquired only by practice is needed. The retention of the thumb-hold and advance of the arm are two reciprocal forces, which result in a contraction of the hand, such as occurred similarly in passing under. To connect the tones, the finger passing over, and that holding the key, necessarily cross. Even though the arm directs the general movement, the feeling in the finger-tips must be actively engaged, and so develop the finger-action that it becomes quite independent of the arm. More especially, the sense of touch must acquire delicacy and an instinct of locality in this so widely extended space. The strength of the knuckle-joint stroke continues the most elementary precondition. —The at first separately and slowly practiced movements must gradually assume an exacter form. In *ascending*, the thumb must already stand over its key at the instant when the third or fourth finger strikes; *descending*, the fingers passing over develop like precision, and the movement of the arm must resolve itself into an evenly gliding sweep—just as the scale itself is musically the symbol of a straight line.

The course described is primarily adapted for those scales, which require, like *C*-major, the thumb to be passed first under the third finger, then under the fourth, and repeat this from octave to octave. But this fingering is not suitable for all scales. In *B*-major and *F*-major, the fifth finger is not employed in the left and right hand respectively. In other scales, beginning on black keys, the second finger begins in the right hand, the third or fourth in the left. One principal rule requires, that the thumb shall not be used on black keys in the midst of a running scale. Its low position makes it inclined to slip through beneath, and this is not compatible with striking the higher keys after passing under.

It is not so practical, to enumerate all possible modifications to which the fingering might be subjected in scale-playing, as to establish a definite form for regular practice. Only ever-repeated habit develops that instinctive fluency which must first of all be acquired in scale-playing before venturing on exceptional additions. These latter do not arise until the scale-form is utilized in runs and studies of every kind, which do not employ it in the normal limits of its opening and closing tones, but divide it according to other rhythmical requirements. In such cases other notes may be touched in passing under and over. Even then it is most practical, however, to pass over into the familiar fingering, although circumstances sometimes prevent. In this last case the fingering follows the prin-

ciple, analogous to that foregoing, of a convenient and pro-
portional distribution of the places for passing over and under,
the fifth finger being best saved for the highest tone (in the
left hand, the lowest). Passing under the fifth finger is an
exception rarely occurring.

In scale practice the familiar methodical rule obtains, that
each hand must first attain perfect smoothness and confidence
in the mechanical elements by itself, and then proceed to
octave practice in unison with the other. After this is thoroughly mastered, the great variety of forms in parallel thirds,
sixths, and tenths, sometimes beginning together, sometimes
beginning and closing at different times in either hand, can
be taken up. The lines of movement may run parallel or in
opposite directions, or with a most various commingling of
these two forms.

Another important point is the rhythm. At first, each tone
counts as an accent. The equality requires this rule, as in
the exercises with quiet hand. The touch of the fourth finger
must not be too weak, nor that of the thumb too strong.
With bent fingers and a somewhat elevated wrist, a peculiar
deftness of the thumb-tip decides the entire character of the
scale. Repose, grace, and evenness depend on its quality.—
Evenness being attained, the accents now fall upon the notes
commencing the fundamental groups. This is a second stage
in the development of the scale. No great fluency is attainable
with tones which are all accented alike. It is best to adopt
the grouping of the notes in fours, as that of the most natural
rhythm; groups of twos or threes somewhat endanger repose
and evenness, and must not come till later. After them, groups
of six, eight, twelve, and sixteen tones are to be accented.
Sharp accentuation or perfect equality (the latter treated either
as if each tone were accented, or as if quite without accent,
i. e. *ff, pp* or *mf,*) form the rule for practicing.—The accents,
falling on the different fingers, develop their independence,
and render them obedient to the will in a higher degree, than
exercises with quiet hand. In the latter the accents coincided

with the similarly formed figures. But the scale as a whole, or as a long series, is *one* figure, and the rhythmical law is subject to other conditions than the mechanical law of fingering. This combination of two ideas renders the scale a difficult feature in mechanical training.

Where the strength of the fingers is not fully equalized, the system of training must pay more attention to the strength of touch, with well equalized fingers more to the quietness of the hand, and in no event neglect either. Fluency and a fleet, pearling smoothness of all tones are the final result to which all studies should lead.

It is now time to examine the act of passing under and over from a more general point of view. Both are means of connecting tones, and are employed where the natural succession of the fingers can effect this only with inconvenience or not at all. But they are by no means employed exclusively in simple scale-playing; on the contrary, both passing under and over must be practiced with all imaginable combinations of fingers, as cases may be found in practice of any or all forms resulting therefrom. — Passing a finger under the thumb is probably most difficult, because the thumb lies low; but it may occur when the thumb stands on a black key, e. g. (a)

The structure of the hand renders the passing of a shorter finger under a longer one most easy of execution; e. g. (b)

Passing a long finger under a shorter one can generally
be avoided. The example at *a*, however, contains an exception.
Under certain circumstances it is also allowable to pass the
third finger under the fourth. The passing of long fingers
over shorter ones occurs in all imaginable combinations.
By thorough training in the cases described the ability
is acquired to conquer any unusual difficulties occurring in
passing under or over, and a theoretical explanation of abnormal examples is therefore unnecessary.

In the mastery of scale-playing an important step has
been made. Musically and technically it forms an addition,
which essentially widens the player's horizon. On the basis
of the scale greater freedom and independence in the feeling
of the hand are developed, and the fingers more familiarized
with the extent of the keyboard.—The pearling touch, the inmost
and truest essence of the beautiful on the pianoforte, reaches
full development in the scale. The spring-power of the falling
finger, the quietness of the hand, precision in lifting the fingers,
and the easy, natural pose of the whole mechanical apparatus,
are promoted and fortified by scale-playing.

Throughout the pianoforte player's life the scale remains
a main stay, acquired by toil and, once acquired, retained
only by untiring industry. Leaving this perfected standpoint
out of consideration for the present, and reverting to an approximate estimate for a technical development beginning from
below, at least a year, or a year and a half, can be devoted
mainly to scale practice.

Of course, the study of actual compositions must run parallel to that of abstract mechanical action; as already observed, the dead form must always be conceived in the light
of its living meaning. The scale too, as moulded by the composer's art, must therefore aid in freeing the aspiring mind
from narrow limitations; for on the scale are founded the
forms of melodies and passages, the foundation arches of the
whole. The forms of composition thereby rendered accessible
allow such free scope for the development of the two factors

named, as to transfer the mechanical interest to a broad field of artistic formations. Czerny, above all, practically and charmingly arranged the Étude from this standpoint, with copious illustrations. In musical literature, properly so-called, compositions are now accessible by Clementi, Haydn, Mozart, Kuhlau, J. Schmitt, Hünten, Köhler, A. E. Müller, Schumann, Th. Kullak, Ch. Mayer, Krug, Dussek, Rosellen, Heller, and even Bach and Beethoven. Compare Köhler's "Führer durch den Klavierunterricht" (Guide for Pianoforte Instruction).

At first, mechanical exactitude must outweigh the technical requirements of the piece, so that the mechanical skill acquired may find effortless application. Only that which is easy to do gives a smooth and graceful technique; what is toilsomely acquired, retains a certain incompleteness even after praiseworthy efforts. Later, to be sure, the path will be toilsome enough; but as the technique will be further developed, it then incurs no danger of stiffening. At present there must be only a gradual transition from the easy to the less easy, or even frequently back again from the latter to earlier steps; and only on the assured basis of self-developed strength are more difficult tasks to be attempted by the player. Everything must sound graceful and natural; the touch must always call the freely swung hammer into acting as by its own weight, never acting upon the hammer in a greater or less degree than its precision of stroke requires. This alone secures the pearling tone.

CHAPTER VII.

The wrist-stroke. The singing touch.

The mechanical elements hitherto acquired do not quite suffice for the compositions mentioned at the close of the last chapter, if it be desired to lend grace even to the smallest details. First of all, the staccato must obtain a third nuance. For accompanying chords, attacks after rests, and single strokes freely thrown off, and for marking brief harmonies, neither drawing in the finger-tip nor striking with the entire finger will suffice. The freer lifting of the whole playing apparatus from the keys, and an acquaintance with a new vibratory power of the same, are the first requirement. A critical eye notes in the earlier training a too anxious and constrained connection with the keyboard, the restriction of pupilage. If the liberation from the ponderousness of the untrained crude material, and from the dead resistance of its natural properties, shall find ideal embodiment, the playing apparatus must appear as if it were free, quite abandoned to its own lightness and graceful impetus, and yet as if controlling with unerring certainty of touch the entire range at its disposal. The connection with the keyboard was an elementary law—but the strictness of this rule must appear like spontaneous volition; subordination to the necessity of form, and the approximation to the keys, must manifest themselves as playful freedom. Now, the outward manifestation of all liberty is movement, and thus the lightly soaring movement of the hand must first symbolize this absolution from the constraint of law. But on the other side, the tone finds a new augmentation through the influence of another line of oscillation and increased leverage on the keys. The theory analyzing both aspects of the movement is termed the Science of the Wrist-stroke.

Every manifestation of power must be traced to its cause, and redeveloped from its initial point. A correct recognition of the latter determines the nearest and surest way for such redevelopment. The free upward impulse of the hand hinges at the wrist, where the hand is separated from the arm. The wrist must therefore obtain springiness, elasticity, and flexibility, if the hand-stroke shall act with the same independence as the finger-stroke before it. The dynamic action must be entirely concentrated in the wrist; the forearm remains quiet, and the fingers are also not allowed to participate in the stroke by any active movement. The present relation of forearm to hand is the same, as the earlier one between hand

and finger; that of finger to hand like that between the first finger-joint and immovable finger-tip. The whole hand acts now like a finger, the arm assumes the passive function of the back of the hand.

Wrist playing has two nuances, to which two essentially different forms of the wrist staccato correspond. A distinction is made between a positive and a negative staccato. To speak of the negative variety first, it covers that sharp accent required in part by single tones, in part by slow staccato passages (comp. for example the variation-theme in Beethoven's *G*-major sonata Op. 14). A lift before the stroke is quite wanting. Before striking, the hand is placed in contact with the keys, and produces the tone in darting back. The abrupt endings of all kinds of legato passages require the same mode of treatment, for instance (to name one of the most usual cases) that tone of a chord, to which a slur extends from one immediately preceding. It also often happens, that the end tones of legato passages require a lift before the stroke. But this needs no discussion, as it comes under the head of legato playing. This is the shortest staccato, capable alike of the most graceful refinement and of manifesting any degree of power. In the latter case it possesses the special advantage, that the tone gains in purity, being free from any disturbing noise produced by the stroke of the fingers.

Wrist playing proper, however, and nearly all practical exercises bearing upon it, are concerned with the so-called positive staccato; here three factors are to be considered: (1) The lift of the hand; (2) the down-stroke; and (3) the time of contact with the key. For the negative staccato, practical exercises are superfluous from a twofold reason; firstly, its main feature, the backward dart of the hand from the key, is likewise found in the positive staccato, and secondly, no appreciable harm is done if the movement does not come purely from the wrist. We shall now consider the studies for positive (or proper) wrist playing. In these the hand should bend upward as far as possible, and the forearm be held so low, that it may lie a little lower than the knuckles at the moment the hand strikes. For this stroke is to be preferred, above all others, the position of the hand described under No. II in Chapter IV; the hand is forced to a curvilinear preparatory lift, and falls from outside, as it were, against the key. The wrist is forced into a loose posture, and the touch obtains in the shortest way a pearling, hammer-like effect. Only the fingers must, as hitherto, retain the form defined under No. I. They must be held strictly curved, in order to offer firm resistance to the keys; elongated fingers may under certain circumstances attain a softer, tenderer effect, but before such refinements of shading are attempted, a normal precision must have been developed. The striking power resides wholly in the wrist; the strength of the fingers is in their passive but firm tension.

The exercises are best so arranged, that at first all five fingers fall with the wrist-stroke simultaneously on the keys; later 4, 3, 2, and at last one, when the stroke must be practiced with each finger alone. Repeated strokes on one key form the material of the first studies; then single fingers may practice entire scales; and finally, the wrist-stroke with alternate fingers can be studied. The down-stroke of the hand must be made with spring-like elasticity, and exhibit precisely the same smoothness and looseness required for the finger-stroke as analyzed in Chapter IV.

Although the wrist-stroke is chiefly employed in octave playing, the technique of the latter cannot yet be taken up. As a peculiarly difficult branch of the mechanical art it will later receive special attention in the proper place. At this stage the pupil whose hand has the needful stretch can include octave playing only tentatively in the course of exercises sketched above.

The hand-stroke brings out a power of tone before unattainable. This power, as the primary and essential element in this stroke, must now be developed. — We have therefore to strike down upon the key from the extreme height of the preparatory lift, and with the greatest possible strength. The fatigue unavoidably resulting is to be gradually overcome by renewed practice, until the down-stroke attains that confidence and precision of aim which must be the general characteristic of any mode of striking.

The exertion of power, urged at the beginning to the maximum of its mechanical tension, subsides by itself into natural ease and restraint when the result last named draws near. The striking height, in particular, regulates itself in correspondence with the degree of tone-power—becomes greater in *forte*, and less in *piano*, but must in every case retain the pearling quality of touch. A delicate ear must distinguish, near at hand, the tap of the fingers on the keys in addition to the tone produced.

The strength and plasticity of the movement being assured, greater velocity may be practiced; but in the most rapid tempo the normal characteristics must be observed.

Thus we now have three varieties of the detached touch, each having a definite character partly in itself, partly in contradistinction to the others. The staccato with the finger-tip has a piquant, sharp, fine tone; that with the entire finger has a stronger, pearling charm, fuller even in the *piano;* that with the wrist combines the impetuous elasticity of the stronger touch with the ethereal buoyancy of grace, whether it be effected by the mere darting back from the key, or by a stroke operating from above.

However, a precondition for the effect of the wrist-stroke is the normal development of the fingers. It cannot be sufficiently emphasized, how entirely the later development of all varieties of touch and tone depends upon a finely individuated and highly sensitive finger-action.—Only a mechanical training reaching to the finest nerves and muscles of the fingers gives assurance of further progress.—Wrist playing without the preliminary training of the fingers is always awkward and rough. — This is true in a still higher degree of the freer varieties of stroke from the elbow-joint, and for this reason their analysis may be deferred, however near their kinship to the wrist-stroke may be. But even the smooth and delicate execution of melodies, to which we now proceed, presupposes a normal finger training like that already explained; and we state here, once for all, what follows in regard to the touch: The looseness of the knuckle-joints, and the correlation of the sense of feeling with their flexibility, form the common foundation for all varieties of touch. Wherever the latter is subsequently referred to, it is always to be understood primarily in this general sense. The distinction of the different shades of touch rests thereon as its fundamental condition, and however subtle may be the discriminations of theory, or even should theories differ as to their systematization, all rules generally binding spring from this foundation.

The compositions which employ the technique hitherto acquired contain an element not yet spoken of, although it forms one of the most essential constituents of all music: this is, Melody. Its discussion was put off, because the practical course naturally busied itself with the preceding mechanical elements, and the melodic treatment could for the present be content with the varieties of touch so far acquired.—A preciser theory of the singing touch now follows.

Attention has already often been called to the melodious and instrumental elements, or the sustained and the more flowing, passage-like succession of tones, forming the groundwork of all music, so that it does not appear necessary again to emphasize the importance of melodic art.—Besides, the significance of long tones was already pointed out in the study of the first small pieces. — But these rudiments will not suffice for an appropriate treatment of melody.

Repose and movement, in manifold proportions and relations, constitute an important portion of the musical motive power; and, in particular, an intimate blending of the one factor with the other, an inclination of the one to the other, forms an indispensable condition of existence for the musical spirit. The *cantilena* ever bears within itself the elements of the passage; the latter breathes the spirit of the *cantilena*. But they likewise occur in sharp separation, and theory seizes upon this case by preference for teaching, in order first to exhibit the opposite sides in their simplest conception.

When *expression* is spoken of, the term is immediately conceived as applying to the melody. And this conception is, in fact, founded on no error; in the most obvious and natural sense the elements of melody and expression are identical. Only in later expansion does the idea of the latter take on another form.

Until now the lift, the fall, and the hold, sustained an equally balanced mutual relation in the touch. Though the fall was chiefly decisive, it none the less required a proportionate lift, and the pressure exerted was the natural issue of these two manifestations of power. But in the singing touch the pressure takes the front rank in the mechanical action. Formerly the down-stroke was the characteristic feature; now it is the downward pressure. The hammer-stroke on the string was then produced by a stroke; now it is caused by a firm, short, close pressure on the key. The falling finger has a dashing, striking effect; a pressing finger has, firstly, in its feeling a more intimate relation to the key, and secondly, the predominance of pressure takes something of its hard, rough peculiarity from the stroke of the hammer. One can say, that a *part* at least of the sharp and thin-toned principle of percussion is obviated thereby.

The finger-tip, as the point chiefly engaged, requires long practice to gain the necessary strength; for the exertion of the finger is here a very peculiar one. In less motion greater strength must be manifested; the tone must be louder, while the outward activity of the finger is restricted. Just as expression is a matter of hidden psychic feeling, the technique of melody, too, resides mainly in the nerve-power of the fingers. Hence the advice of idealistic teachers: "One should press the key as one grasps the hand of a friend, with warmth, with feeling," etc.

The passage, in its pearling elegance, has in the main an external, objective import. It is a line, an outline, a plastic sketch. Its highest beauty is that of a whole composed of mathematically equal parts. Each tone is but a part of this whole. In Melody all is different. Each tone has its own meaning, and strives toward individual apprehension by the soul. The very slowness of the *cantilena* loosens the firm connection between the several parts. The passage is beautiful through its form or picturesqueness, the *cantilena* through psychic charm. Melody is the expression of a vague yearning for the infinite — the side where musical art passes into lyric poetry.

The melodic treatment therefore signifies an advance into the inner essence of music. For a clearer and fuller development of the latter to the learner's sense, the knowledge of the singing touch implants a precious germ in his breast. His impressionability must be constantly stimulated, now for the pearling beauty of the passage, now for the expressive meaning of the melody.

Regarding the actual execution of the touch in question the rule is to be laid down, that the finger should take the key with a close, short touch, and develop its full strength with precision of pressure. The key is taken with the soft and fleshy part of the finger-tip. Thus, on the one hand, cautious tenderness prevails; on the other, strongly developed power. Adroitness must here be paired with strength, and the union of two measurably contradictory inclinations renders the touch difficult. Earlier theory derives the melodic touch purely from emotion; it makes the matter easy for itself, but hard for the pupil. — A soft, yet full-toned melody can be acquired only by sedulous mechanical study; without having thus learned it, the truest emotion will often be at a loss. In this sense Thalberg's work, devoted to the exclusive study of the singing touch, deserves a warm welcome; and it must be termed a defect of the earlier teaching, that too little material bearing on this point has been collected.

The finger should act upon the key as if it were kneading it, or impressing itself on wax; it must press it lovingly, warmly. The conjunction with the key, the pressure, and the purpose of the finger-nerve, to conduct the soul through itself to the key, are therefore the essential characteristics of this touch. The imagination is still free to endow the key with a higher capacity than its precisely formed mechanism can possess, and to attribute to the same a sustained, singing tone capable of giving voice to all that is passing within the soul.

For practical study, the scale is held to be the best exercise. At first it may be studied slowly, with the ordinary fingering, in the manner described. In detail, a threefold tone-power should be practiced; a very soft touch, for which the nervous finger-pressure must be exercised with peculiar skill; a medium touch; and a very strong touch, full in volume, but without sounding harshly or roughly. But in order to practice its pressing faculty, the finger must sustain an equal pressure on the key throughout the time of holding. Thus a silent after-pressure is to be exerted on the key, which for the moment exercises no influence on the tone, but is only intended to promote the elasticity and clinging touch of the finger-tip. As a second study, single fingers, unaided by the others, should sing the scale up and down, as smoothly as possible. This renders the touch still more clinging.

In modern compositions it occurs with peculiar frequency, that one finger has to play several successive melody-notes. The last-mentioned scale exercise is intended as a preparation for these cases. The finger must do its best to cover up the separation unavoidable at the last instant, by deciding upon it as late as possible, and gliding swiftly to the next key. Besides, it must often quite change its posture; and in fact, the general treatment of melody-notes requires freedom in great measure from the strict form hitherto observed. The finger will often be obliged to stand on end, and sometimes to glide over to the next melody-note with a slanting, sideways movement. When the legato is to be effected by different fingers, the rule obtains, that the following finger should touch its key before striking, and that, in general, the advancing fingers must study this style of legato till fluency is gained. The finger-tips must cling to the keys like antennæ.

An essential facilitation of the legato consists in changing several fingers on one key, without again sounding the latter. This exercise must also be prosecuted until fluent. Every imaginable succession of fingers must be studied; and more than two fingers must practice changing without interruption, swiftly and dexterously, on one key without again sounding it; finally, the same change must be practiced with doubled notes and triads.

A no less excellent aid for the legato is found in the freer employment both of the wrist and arm. While the wrist was heretofore used, in running passages, chiefly in the free staccato, or at most the mezzo staccato, it is an agent of equal importance in refined legato playing. Its main use shows first in the delicate connection of a series of tones executed by a single finger. Let the pupil practice the following:

the first chord being taken with the wrist bent upward. Before striking the second, the wrist sinks completely, so that the cushion of the thumb almost touches the wood below the keys; here too the principle obtains, that the study of each movement is to be forwarded by its exaggeration. Let the second chord then be struck, with the same upward bend of the wrist, as the first. The wrist is again dropped while the second chord is sustained, and again lifted before striking the third, etc. For each separate chord, the wrist begins with its highest position, and ends with its lowest. Of course, only pressure is exerted; for a stroke would chop off the legato touch of the successive similar fingers. The fingers retain very nearly their firm, passive form. As a second exercise, play the C-major scale with any single finger and with the same oscillations of the wrist, which should be marked by counting aloud. Experience teaches, that this forced elevation of the hand gives the fingers a more clinging legato. For further similar studies all possible tone-groups on white keys will serve, first in chords, then in doubled notes and single tones, but always under the condition, that the legato shall be kept up despite the continued use of the same fingers. A different treatment is required when black keys occur.—Play a chromatic scale with the third finger. Whereas till now a double movement fell to each tone or chord, the hand now lays itself low on the white keys, bends high upward for the black key, and sinks again to the white key. Convenience may decide in each separate place, where chords are to be connected in which black keys occur, whether the upward bend of the wrist for each separate chord, or an alternate raising and lowering, is most advantageous. It were hardly possible, and in any event useless, to exhaust all cases. Let the foregoing suffice; for a suggestion is more valuable just here than pedantic accuracy.

The same wrist movements may be applied with brilliant success to that singing tone, produced by pressure, in which a legato is effected by different fingers. To begin with, all the scales should be practiced with the normal fingering, and raising the wrist for each touch, lowering it again, of course, while the tone is holding. Next, practice with the movements reversed, sinking for the touch and rising during the hold. Further, study the scale of C-major, for example, with a drop of the wrist on c, a rise at d, a drop at e, and so on. Let it be the aim of study, that each finger shall be practiced both with the rise and the drop in all positions on the keys; and that perfect lightness of wrist-play will be attained, which not only insures the best binding touch of the finger in the legato, but is also retroactively of essential benefit to the style of hand-technique previously discussed. The treatment of the melody-note demands full freedom from all constraint of form, which is unattainable with a rigid wrist. Study all varieties here mentioned, choose from these according to the individuality of the passage, and add new features whenever it may appear needful. Throughout, pressure without stroke is a *conditio sine quâ non*. A co-operation of the lifting and sinking of the back of the hand with the forms of striking-technique is likewise useful under certain circumstances; but more so for the reason, that the mechanical practice should, on principle, include all forms.

Now, while exercises like those enumerated aim at an absolute exercise of the strength of hand and fingers in the singing tone, it must not be forgotten, that a no less important element for the plastic presentation of the melody is found in the relation between melody and accompaniment. The melody must, above all, stand in relief. This condition does not, however, exclude the possibility of a most delicate, even ethereal, development of tone. The ear and a refined taste must consider by what means the melody may remain distinct even in *such* a case. The pianoforte possesses the twofold capacity of lending to melody wellnigh the might of the human voice itself, and of investing the same with its own specifically instrumental charm of tone. Thus, though simple pressure remains the chief form of the *cantilena* tone, no kind of touch, not even the fleeting sigh of a pearling, ornamental passage, is excluded. A distinction may accordingly be made between two varieties of melodic style: The purely song-like treatment, founded upon the marked contrast of a melody to a (usually) broadly treated accompaniment; and that manner of singing, which transmutes the vocal fulness of the *cantilena* into instrumental delicacy. In the great majority of cases these two varieties will be blended. The vocal style will sometimes be refined to the pearling charm of the pianoforte touch proper, and the instrumental melody rise at its climax to the power of vocality.

In grand climaxes of expression, and in cases when the accompaniment itself demands a considerable degree of brilliancy, even the first style will not yield enough power, and the varieties of touch with the arm or the wrist, to be spoken of later, will be employed. The main rule, that the melody must stand out in relief above all the other parts, holds good in all cases.

Where the *cantilena* is adorned with rapid pianoforte passages, the latter must be executed with the more delicate shades of touch, most frequently with the pearling tone. Strong pressure aiming at a vocal development of melody impedes the lightness and grace, which form the soul of pianoforte playing, and would mingle a charmless element, unsuited to its spirit, with the nuances of tone.

The pedal is also of material importance in the art of singing, and its employment will be treated of connectly in the proper place.

Concerning the performance of the accompaniment we must also add, that the same is only in general to be played more softly than the melody. In grand climaxes of expression its power likewise rises with the general intensification, and wherever it may expand in broader figuration, it must guard against monotony, in full accord with the general rules on the rendering.

CHAPTER VIII.

Contraction and expansion in passing under. The chromatic scale. Harmonic passages. Doubled notes.

A freer mastery of the range of the keyboard is to be attained, than the scale can provide. Mental and mechanical requirements strive alike toward an extension of their power and capabilities. The diatonic scale set the normal measure for the stretch in passing over and under. Our next step forward is found in the contraction and expansion of this measure, and the methodic course advances in the same way here as in the exercises with quiet hand.

The contraction of the normal stretch mentioned is formed most regularly in the *chromatic scale*. A detailed analysis of the mechanical process is unnecessary, its nature having been sufficiently explained in Chapter VI, in connection with the diatonic scale. Besides, the conditions for its fulfilment are easier now. It will therefore suffice to consider the different varieties of fingering.

The first is that with the second finger on black keys:

It is based on a certain deftness of motion due to the fine sense of touch residing in the second finger, and is favorable to the quietness and nice shape of the hand. Consequently, this fingering is to be employed in soft and graceful passages, and need by no means be restricted to the chromatic scale, but can be extended to such passages as are only mingled with chromatic elements.

The second fingering is formed by the exclusive employment of the third finger on the black keys; the white keys all have the thumb, excepting *c* and *f* in the right hand, and *e* and *b* in the left. This fingering has a firmer, stronger character; as the strongest fingers play, it is that best suited to a *forte*. Still, soft playing is not excluded.

A third fingering, which requires four fingers, indicates greater velocity:

Here, as in the foregoing kinds as well, the end of a run is commonly executed with the aid of all five fingers. While the chromatic scale was previously treated in its separate elements, point by point, it is now conceived as a whole. The great velocity of this last fingering exhibits the scale in plastic form, like a line or a thread.—

A fingering with all five fingers admits of yet greater rapidity, but is more inconvenient in passing over than in passing under. It is based on a regular series repeated with each two octaves. It best begins on $g\sharp$, where the fifth finger must be once omitted.

One more fingering must be mentioned, which also admits of extreme velocity. Its repetition also includes two octaves. It is really convenient to play only in passing over. For the right hand it runs as follows:

Its guiding principle is merely to use the fourth finger as often as possible in passing over.

The musical value of the chromatic scale is of a mechanical nature. Belonging to no key, it may be used in all, and shows everywhere as a light, pliant ornament. The tripping run of the fingers lends it a peculiarly neat prettiness. Calculated essentially for velocity, it is brilliant and sensuously charming.

Further chromatic exercises allow a similar diversity of forms to the diatonic, as they can be played by both hands at various intervals, and the linear direction of the passages can assume the utmost variety and complexity.

The expansion of the stretch in passing over and under occurs in its most regular form in the broken chords, whose figuration extends in uninterrupted succession through two or more octaves. The thumb here takes the range of an entire octave in passing under, and the finger passing over does the same. This widely extended form of the passage, which surpasses those hitherto studied in diversity of the mechanical relations, compares with the scales, as the figures in octave stretches compare with those of a fifth or sixth. The mechanical execution is founded on the fundamental laws for the scale: (1) The independent movement of the active members; (2) the quietness of all inactive ones; (3) the uniform evenness of all necessary movements; (4) the equality of all tones.

The main point in passing under is the elasticity of the thumb-tip bending inward toward the palm, and the reciprocal flexibility of the finger under which it passes. At the instant of passing under, the latter will assume a straight form inclined to the side. All twisting of the hand must be strictly suppressed; the chief points to be observed are to hold the hand turned slightly inward, and to keep up the steady advance of the arm at the moment after passing under. All this just as for the scale, only made more difficult by the increased stretch. In playing up with the right hand or down with the left the second finger must not strike its key before the arm has reached its position and the stroke can be delivered perpendicularly. For passing over, the rule is reversed. The hand must be so practiced in contracting and squeezing itself together, that it can do this with the utmost ease.

With short fingers a strict legato is at first, despite all efforts, impracticable, unless the twisting of the hand be recommenced. The will wavers here between two conflicting rules, and must see to it, how to reconcile them in practice. The best plan here is, to retain the quiet of the hand, and rather to sin against the legato. But the most serious attempt must nevertheless be made to secure the legato. In rapid execution a supple drawing together of the tones covers up any slight gap.—The normal method must, however, always be kept conscientiously in view. Evenness of movement must be so thoroughly developed, that the arm glides up and down in its horizontal course like a gently gliding vessel.—The thumb must be constantly nearing its point of passing under; i. e. at the moment when the second finger plays (supposing it to be the C-major triad), the thumb should be under the third, and, when the latter strikes, poising near the higher c. —The inward bend of the hand is so important, that twisting is often prevented by this means alone. Of course, it ought not to deviate too markedly from the normal position.

A certain bold aspiration is the mechanical characteristic of the broken-chord passages. The fingers fly over the keyboard as if endowed with wings. Freedom of position becomes more and more marked in the fingers. For a peculiarly graceful and light treatment the high position of the hand, with nearly straight fingers hanging down from above, will now be preferred.

But the other positions are not excluded, for each has its characteristic expression. — While the high position, with its gentle undulating lines, that revolve around the thumb as around an axis, suggest an ethereal delicacy of the mechanical sense, the low position with straight fingers will yield a soft, pearling touch, and the horizontal position with bent fingers a pearlingly sharp, crisp execution.—The inward bend at the knuckles, and the upward bend of the wrist, will gradually grow level.

In the low position the extended finger is able to produce a more sensuous fulness of tone by its broader, "fleshier" contact with the key. The fingers play with a very animated, fluttering motion, whereas in the high position the arm seemed to direct the whole.—In our course the normal position of the hand still remains desirable; in most cases the strict method must still be adhered to.

The harmonic passages form groups of three, four, and five tones. They are consequently derived either from triads, chords of the seventh, or chords with added passing notes. It is easiest to begin with the four-tone groups, first with the diminished chords of the seventh, whose regular shape best promotes evenness of mechanical action. At first the thumb must be taken on white keys only, the black keys being avoided until practice has matured the skill.—Then come the dominant chords and their inversions, and the minor chords of the seventh; finally, the triads and their inversions.

The inversions of the dominant chords are very difficult on account of the unequal distances between the fingers. As a preparatory exercise the single figure can be played up and down, e. g.:

The fingers must first be moulded in their places before venturing on the freer course. The feeling of form must be so far developed, that, after passing under, the hand every time recovers its plastic firmness with extreme promptness, and the fingers simply fall perpendicularly, without seeking their places.

By suspended and passing tones the field in question is greatly extended, and the difficulty often much increased by altering the intervals between the fingers. It is particularly necessary to practice passing both under and over the fifth finger, evenness of tone being unusually hard to attain. The fifth finger is here inclined to a weaker touch, and must be strengthened. The employment of the thumb on a black key is likewise difficult, and is best avoided by less advanced players; but it is sometimes unavoidable. For one characteristic rule regulates the fingering in all these passages. This rule is based on strict regularity, on the consistent recurrence of the same series of fingers. Nothing so develops the confidence of the fingers in running passages as the fixed track of their course of movement; hence it frequently occurs, that within a series of arpeggios, in all of which the thumb has the same place, the latter is obliged to take black keys. The increased difficulty of the single case is neutralized by the trait of habitual action pervading the whole.—Aside from this, the mechanical training must include such difficulties; a principle carried out under highly difficult conditions makes those less difficult seem easy.

Therefore, passages like the following should be studied as industriously as easy ones.

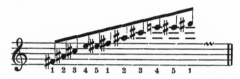

Concerning the arm-movement we must observe, that however economy, as an elementary law, may forbid the unnecessary co-operation of members in all forms of pianoforte technique, and demand, in particular, an entire suppression of the drawing backwards and forwards or the oft-mentioned twisting of the hands, exceptions must occasionally occur in the cases last alluded to. — For instance, if the thumb begins on a black key, and the other fingers have to play on white keys, as in this run:

it is very hard to strike the narrow part of the white keys between the black with precision. Therefore an exception to the above law may properly be admitted. To facilitate the striking of the white keys, the arm draws back from the black key position during play so far to the white key position, that fingers 2, 3, and 4 can play on the broad front surface of the same; when the thumb has to strike again, the hand goes back to the black key position.—This procedure certainly violates the quietness of the movement, and it must

be the aim of study to smooth the angular course of the line
of motion down to an undulating, rounded, and regular movement.—The trait of clumsiness proper to matter must be
refined here, too, by an artificial element.

A comparison of the chord-passages with scale-passages
gives the following result:—As an elementary idea of composition, the scale contrasts with the chord as the outline with
the color.—The scale is the abstract prototype of melody, the
chord that of accompaniment. The former therefore develops
a far more teeming profusion of forms than the harmony,—
just as the ᵛmacrocosm itself exhibits more abundant distinctions of form than of color.—But in regard to the mechanical
element the relation is changed. The arpeggios admit of
greater diversity in form than the scales. The two compare
as follows: The scale-passages bear a very even character;
respecting harmonic distinctions, only the two forms, major
and minor, are found in them; the linear tendency is equally
marked in both; the chromatic scale alone presents the line
in still more plastic form. Thus all scale-passages consist of
linear elements. The chords, however, possess in the very
character of their harmonic groundwork a greater wealth of
distinctions. Further, they admit, through all manner of transpositions and inversions, of a far more diversified figuration.

Both varieties have their peculiar characteristics. The
arpeggios are founded on a simpler regularity than the scale;
though they at first present more considerable difficulties in
the wider finger-stretch, the greater sweep in passing over and
under, and the boldness of their rapid flight, the mechanical
principle still rests on firm foundations. If we except zigzag
figures, e. g.:

the entire form is almost always repeated quite regularly with
each new octave, and the fundamental type itself is a firmly

11*

moulded, non-advancing figure. The circumstance last mentioned renders this variety easier than the scale. In the latter, the fundamental type of an octave is in itself an irregular form, because of passing the thumb under. The hand finds little support. The normal position on five keys is played actually through only at the end; the fingers assume a normal position, it is true, each time the thumb is passed under, but do not carry it out. One is hardly entered, when a fresh turn of the thumb brings the hand into another, to be played with the same incompleteness. For the chords, the fingers assume a fixed form, and as soon as this is once mastered, only the guidance of the arm is necessary—the passage runs almost by itself. The only irregularity is habituation to the idea that the thumb must take the fifth finger's notes. Otherwise the fingers have their definite places. The regularity of the spacing, as regards the equally measured octaves, is a sure guide for eye and touch. But for the scale the visible regularity of the key-groups stands in opposition to the rules of fingering. The fingering within an octave is complicated, and differs in *C*-major from *F*-major, and again in the latter from *B♭*-major, *F♯*-major, *D♭*-major, etc., and in the left hand from the right. This in a measure stamps each scale-passage with individuality; while the chords are more quickly seized by the eye and divined by the fingers. Even in playing with both hands the chords are the more favorable, thumb and fifth finger having like importance and in most cases (in octave unisons) entering together, and the grouping being easy to grasp. The grouping of the scale must be done by the ear; and the thumb-touch, technically so well adapted for the distinct division of groups, must quite suppress this function.

The zigzag arpeggios alluded to above are more difficult. Where only white keys occur, the principle of fingering is, that with each touch of the thumb a normal position of an octave in compass must be begun and played through. The difficulty lies in the varying distances between the fingers arising in each new position, so that with each thumb-touch the hand takes another form. — Where black keys occur, a position is sometimes not played to the end, i. e. when the taking of black keys with the thumb is to be avoided. But there is no necessity whatever to exclude this latter. Compare the fingerings in Tausig's edition of Clementi's Gradus, especially in the third Étude.

The above-mentioned difficulty in changing the form is notably diminished by the restricted range of the possible differences, to which the hand soon grows accustomed, e. g.:

Scale and chord are, each in itself, a source of many-sided formations; in their combination, the wealth of the latter expands to infinitude. For the mechanical action the rule obtains, that the fingers must feel at each instant that they are in the one or the other hand-form (position), and, in particular, that the higher standpoint of unconditional and easy obedience in every relation should now begin its serious development.

Mechanical work has till now followed the series of single tones, and has exhausted their fundamental types. The next step proceeds to the combination of several simultaneous series of tones. In teaching the legato, tone-series in several parts were already instanced; their essential characteristics shall now be discussed.

The simultaneous execution of several parts in a polyphonic sense properly forms the close of the technical course. This we shall not yet discuss. We have instead to examine that apparent polyphony of parallel parts, which has its own peculiar difficulty, and must act as a preparation for the former and greater kind. — It consists in the playing of doubled notes, and is classified as third, fourth, and sixth-playing. —

Octave - playing forms a class by itself, on account of its peculiar mechanical treatment.

We begin with third-playing. The rules obtaining for the single fingers are also applicable here to the simultaneous action of two. The bent finger-form, with knuckles pressed in, proves even more advantageous here than elsewhere. Needful as the relaxation of all muscles may be in general, a certain tension in the members held ready for striking is after all unavoidable; and now, when an enhanced manifestation of strength and the relations of mutual co-operation are in question, it can still less be dispensed with. The normal hand-form best induces this feeling of muscular tension; elongated fingers with a low hand are by no means incapable of learning third-playing, but, in general, experience sustains the opposite posture of the hand.

A full round tone is the first aim, simultaneity of touch (stroke) the second, the latter being an essentially new requirement. The conditions of the same are equal height of lift and an equally strong down - stroke with the two fingers engaged.

Third-playing is divided, like that foregoing, into exercises with quiet hand, and advancing and scale-like studies. The harmonic passages are naturally very limited.

In the exercises with quiet hand the following fingers are combined: 1 and 2, 2 and 4, 3 and 5; these combinations are first to be employed in practicing. In advanced study, however, the pairs 1 and 2, 2 and 3, 3 and 4, 4 and 5,— then 1 and 4, 2 and 5,—and at last 1 and 5, will be found indispensable.

Those combinations in which fingers 4 and 5 occur, require special examination, because the fingers mentioned are apt to have a weaker touch; indeed, a continual consideration of their disadvantageous disposition is the pianoforte player's duty throughout his career. The exercises are divided into series of two, then 3, and later from 4 to 5 thirds:

The weak fingers must intensify, the strong ones lessen, their lift and down-stroke, in order to equalize the conditions of touch. Rhythm and figuration may multiply the cases given in the above example to a great number of exercises, though the forms cannot be so numerous as with single tones. The elements here present are not as fluent as the latter, and are at bottom only three in number, whereas before there were five.—A large part of these studies has already been prepared in the quiet exercises with single tones; therefore further practice will be occupied with the newly added finger-combinations:

and the advancing figures.

The latter follow the normal laws of touch, but most combine therewith a sidelong movement of the fingers. In all third-playing the third finger is most used, and its special precision must be carefully watched over, as it easily inclines to lassitude. It places too ready dependence in its favorable disposition, overlooking the fact, that this latter is now doubly necessary for its double duty.

Too little attention is generally paid to this variety in the usual works on technique, although it really affords abundant material, especially when interspersed with chromatic elements, and with various development of the rhythmic forms. The simplest fundamental types are the following:

These exercises are followed by the scale. A passing over with two fingers together is here the newly-added element. The difficulty of the same lies in the binding. Even in the exercises with quiet hand, certain combinations of fingers ($\frac{1}{2}$ $\frac{1}{3}$ | $\frac{4}{5}$ $\frac{3}{5}$) permitted no complete legato. The aim of study must be, to make this unavoidable break as slightly audible as possible. The finger in question must cling to its key as long as it can, and divert attention from the momentary gap by the full strong tone of the succeeding touch. In slow playing it is very helpful to practice the scales of thirds with the singing touch, that is, with long-sustained pressure. In faster playing the finger must rely on height of the lift and a strong, precise down-stroke.

The most important feature, the legato, has in detail the following mechanical course. The form of the fingers is abandoned in passing over and under. The clinging to the key up to the last moment results, in passing over, in an almost straight form of the finger which is passed over. In the following example:

the fifth finger is bent quite down, so that it lies horizontally on the key; the third finger passes supply over it far enough to touch its key *a*. Now, and not before, it strikes. The gap occurs between *e* and *f*. In other cases, where the legato is perfectly practicable, the close connection with the following group of keys must be practiced in like manner.

The fingering of the scales is founded on the principle of the closest possible binding, and includes no other combinations than those mentioned under the exercises with quiet hand. A new element is found, however, in the combination of adjoining groups of exercises so as to form straight runs. The following combinations of fingers are the commonest: $\begin{smallmatrix} 1 & 2 & 3 \\ 3 & 4 & 5 \end{smallmatrix} \mid \begin{smallmatrix} 1 & 1 & 2 & 3 \\ 2 & 3 & 4 & 5 \end{smallmatrix} \mid$ $\begin{smallmatrix} 3 & 4 \\ 2 & 1 \end{smallmatrix} \mid \begin{smallmatrix} 4 & 5 \\ 2 & 1 \end{smallmatrix} \mid \begin{smallmatrix} 5 & 5 \\ 3 & 4 \end{smallmatrix} \mid$. The first quite alone suffices for *C*-major, the second finds application in the greater part of the other scales, wherein it occurs once within an octave in combination with the first, e. g.

D, *A*, and *E*-major are similar. In *B*, *D♭*, *A♭*, *E♭*, and *B♭*-major the groups $\begin{smallmatrix} 3 & 4 \\ 2 & 1 \end{smallmatrix} \mid \begin{smallmatrix} 4 & 5 \\ 2 & 3 \end{smallmatrix} \mid$ often occur; as in beginning *B♭*-major; notice must be taken here that the fourth finger is used twice. In many cases the grouping $\begin{smallmatrix} 3 & 4 & 5 \\ 2 & 1 & 3 \end{smallmatrix}$ also proves practical, and may be substituted for the fingering indicated, many scales thus admitting of more than one fingering; e. g.

In case of necessity all the scales may be played with the combinations $\begin{smallmatrix} 3 & 4 & 5 & 2 & 3 & 4 & 5 \\ 1 & 2 & 3 & 1 & 1 & 2 & 3 \end{smallmatrix}$, even those having 5 black keys.

Although the minor scales seldom occur, they should also be practiced for the sake of completeness; in ascending they follow the rules given above, though not with the same regularity; in descending they take the fingering of their relative major.

The diatonic scales are followed by the chromatic scale in minor thirds, the rules already laid down being simply applied to a narrower succession of keys. Czerny's fingering is that written over the scale:

it has the advantage of greater simplicity, whereas the one written below, which is taken from Chopin, gives an easier smoothness. The same scale in major thirds also applies no new principles. It seldom occurs.

The course in doubled notes next passes on to fourth-playing, which is ordinarily executed by the right hand, and supplemented by the left to chords of the sixth. The fingering is based on the following combinations: $\frac{4}{1}\ \frac{5}{2}\ |\ \frac{5}{2}\ \frac{4}{1}\ |\ \frac{4}{1}\ \frac{5}{1}\ |\ \frac{4}{2}\ \frac{5}{1}\ |$ $\frac{5}{2}\ \frac{5}{1}\ |\ \frac{3}{1}\ \frac{4}{2}\ \frac{5}{3}\ |\ \frac{5}{2}\ \frac{4}{2};$ cases also frequently occur, where the same fingers are taken twice in succession. Fourth-playing is employed, partly in diatonic or chromatic passages, partly in shorter figures combined from the elements named, which may likewise be used in more extended formations. From the nature of their harmony, fourths hardly ever occur in the left hand; it can only be in unison with the right, which will then play a supplementary sixth, or with the right hand crossing the left. — However, according to the principle of the equal development of all powers, the left hand must practice the studies coming under this head in their full extent.

In the following examples the ordinary fundamental forms are contained:

Two fingerings are usually practicable, according as the third finger is employed or not. — Both fingerings are given with the last example. — An employment of the third finger is often expedient in the scales. The latter are easily developed in accord with the combinations of fingers already given. The closest binding possible remains the guiding principle.

Diminished fifths are usually employed in chromatic succession; the other hand fills out, either with a single or a double parallel passage. The technical development is like that in third and fourth-playing.

By employing the third finger more or less frequently, several different fingerings are practicable. This exercise, like the previous one, is very useful for the flexible training of the third and fourth fingers, and also for the tips of all fingers engaged. The mechanical profit is more considerable than the musical, which in all these parallel series can employ hardly more than scale-like or chromatic elements. Parallel leading of the parts is in itself monotonous. But for the mechanical training the binding is valuable, it requiring an oblique position of the hand, a supple bending down of one pair of fingers, and an equally supple passing over of the other.

The same obtains in series of sixths and sevenths, which are also chiefly employed in chromatic figures, and need an accompaniment in the other hand to fill them out. The fingering for seconds requires a frequent employment of the third finger:

Sixth-playing is more important than the last varieties of doubled notes, as it admits of greater diversity of figuration. In this respect it stands on a level with third-playing.—Like the latter, it is divided into exercises with quiet hand, and advancing and scale-like studies, but in harmonic passages has a wider range than the same. Such passages are not quite suited to the figuration of third-playing, because in them the staccato is too predominant.

The exercises in sixths with quiet hand embrace firstly stepwise progressions (by seconds), then those in thirds, fourths, fifths, etc., and finally the manifold combinations of these forms, and their grouping according to the various requirements of rhythm. The chief types follow in this example:

All forms allow a perfect legato; but as the thumb often has to take two notes in succession in the advancing exercises, and the binding thus becomes only partial, the fingerings underneath the above exercises must also be practiced. The upper fingering insures a perfect legato.

The advancing exercises likewise admit of either a perfect or a partial legato. In the latter case the gap must be covered up as well as possible, in analogy to the familiar principles. The thumb can also be used more than twice in succession, which exercise is to be highly recommended; the dexterity of the thumb-tip is essentially increased thereby.

The scales in sixths have the aim of connecting, through passing over and under, the finger-groups practiced with the foregoing varieties.—Passing under concerns the thumb, which turns under the second finger, and the fifth finger, which turns under the fourth, or less often under the third; passing over is effected by the second finger over the thumb, the fourth over the fifth, the third over the fourth and over the fifth. The following preliminary studies may be taken up for practice:

After these studies, which are to be practiced with equal thoroughness by both hands, follows scale-playing, which forms the next object of study in all major and minor keys, with the closest possible binding. The mechanical action has, on the one hand, to observe the flexibility of the finger-tip noticed under the thirds, and on the other a pearling and powerful down-stroke. To this end it must alternate between the singing, low-reaching touch, and the passage-like, high-lifting touch. By the union of both studies, smoothness and brilliancy are acquired; the former touch is more conducive to purity of tone, the latter to brilliancy.

With reference to the second we must add, that for hands favorably shaped a perfect legato is attainable only in C-major, while in the other scales partial and complete gaps are unavoidable. For this reason, the touch inclines to a style wavering between staccato and legato, or even passes into a full staccato. The latter lends to the scale a very bold and brilliant effect, which does not appear in the legato, to which it is usually preferred; for the inferiority of the legato in brilliancy is not in unison with its superior difficulty.—But one should not forget, that the legato is the more useful, and an indispensable preliminary, exercise.

In scale-playing, too, more than one fingering is possible, particularly when the third finger is employed; where many chromatic signs occur, the use of the thumb on black keys is often unavoidable. This fact, together with the occasional necessity of using the same finger-group twice running, renders the scales in sixths more difficult than in thirds. The employment of the third finger is peculiarly advantageous for hands of wide stretch, and even the second finger may be used to advantage on black keys.

In chromatic form, passages of sixths are either major or minor. The series of minor sixths are the more usual. Their fingering is generally self-evident; where essential deviations are possible, they depend upon the shape of the hand. We therefore give no fixed fingering. Its elements are to be gathered from the foregoing observations.

The harmonic figures, from the nature of the chords, are not composed simply of sixths, but with an admixture of fifths or sevenths; the former in triads, the latter in harmonies of the seventh.— In the second case, fourths may also occur. The fingering is formed either by groupings in twos, or the same in threes: $\frac{4\ 5}{1\ 2}\ |\ \frac{3\ 5}{1\ 2}\ |\ \frac{3\ 4\ 5}{1\ 1\ 2}\ |$. Both kinds must be practiced; e. g.

Which is to be preferred, depends upon the nature of the passage; the fingering $\frac{3\ 4\ 5}{1\ 1\ 2}$ is the best, when it can be carried out completely at the end, or throughout the whole. For short passages the other fingering suffices. The highest note is best taken by the fifth finger, and this rule should govern when the fingering is decided on. Sometimes the succession $\frac{2\ 4\ 5}{1\ 1\ 2}$ is also suitable; e. g.

The chords of the seventh follow the same fingering, whenever they drop one interval within the compass of an octave:

The other case, in which all intervals of the chord appear in groups of fours within the compass of an octave, belongs, strictly speaking, to another chapter, the intervals all being narrower than a sixth. However, as it is not easy to find a better place, it will be considered here. The fingering is as follows: $\begin{smallmatrix} 2 & 3 & 4 & 5 \\ 1 & 1 & 2 & 3 \end{smallmatrix}$, for instance:

but $\begin{smallmatrix} 3 & 5 & 3 & 5 \\ 1 & 2 & 1 & 2 \end{smallmatrix}$ is likewise admissible.

The combinations of chord and scale-like elements and chromatic figures surpass calculation, and can be no more exhausted here than the diversity of passage-forms in general. Theory must content itself with the fundamental forms, and these can be taught by technique only in their most characteristic and essential distinctions. The pupil's imagination should utilize a knowledge of the same to exercise itself in figurate forms of the more complicated kind.

Sixth-playing is a technical acquisition of the modern school, and finds manifold employment in the literature of its first epoch, the high-day of Henselt, Th. Kullak, A. Dreyschock, Liszt, Thalberg, and Chopin.— The last-named composer and S. Goldschmid, and also Fr. Brendel, wrote Études for sixths exclusively.

The entire technique of doubled notes requires increased exertion of strength. In its legato treatment it is the highest exhibition of the specific power of the fingers, as an apparent representation of two players. The hand, which has to perform it alone or in co-operation with the other, tastes in its easy mastery the pleasure of an intensified self-confidence. In the first stage, the free and delicate grace of the simple runs will, indeed, appear somewhat hampered. Strength yet strives with matter; the principles of finger-flexibility and redoubled effort do not immediately admit of that easy grace which must be, in the last event, the goal of this as of all other mechanical forms. Not only the double exertion of the striking power is here to be taken into account, but also the constant heedfulness by each individual finger of its allies. Equality in the lift, in the down-stroke, in pressure, in retention, all seem like one common energy divided into two equal halves. This halving is a fetter, which does not permit the feeling of free individuality in the same measure as with the simple runs. It appears no longer as the Whole, but as the half of a greater power. Hence intrudes, at the beginning, the feeling of greater heaviness, of increased effort. Thus the double-note technique at first represents power rather than grace. But just by reason of this peculiarity it stands in fine contrast to the former simplicity, and constitutes a noteworthy addition to the material wealth of form.

The sixths form the transition to octave-playing. Firstly, they incline to the wrist-stroke in a similar manner; secondly, their interval approaches that of the octave; they are thus, both in sound and character of touch, in a sense related to the octaves. — Its numerous partial and imperfect bindings always render sixth-playing slightly disinclined to the legato. As greater striking power is also needed, real lightness and grace can be attained, by the mere finger-stroke, in no such finished freedom as by the wrist-stroke. Thus in conclusion the necessity becomes apparent, that after the legato the pupil should practice all the studies in sixths with the wrist staccato and with similar industry.

CHAPTER IX.

Octave-playing. Stretches. Leaps. The employment of the arm. The stroke from the elbow-joint. The shoulder-joint. The *mezzo staccato* and *carezzando*.

Another form of technique, very characteristic in its kind, is octave-playing, which we now have to take up in order.

12

Primarily, it is a further spreading out of the two tones from which the series of doubled notes are derived. — Its characteristic quality is the unisonance of its elements, and the wider compass of tone which it affects. These two peculiarities render its sound, on the one hand, clearer and more sharply penetrating, and on the other, its technique a still more bold and brilliant form of double-note playing. In the two-tone series of third and sixth-playing the attention of the ear is divided between two equally balanced parallel parts; octave-playing lacks, it is true, the harmonic fulness of the above varieties, but makes itself felt far more shrilly and clearly through all surrounding elements of tone. In proportion, more particularly, to the softer effects of sixths, it possesses something hardier, robuster, and stands in a much more appropriate relation to the steely force of its mechanical element. The sixths always have a certain soft sweetness, inclining decidedly to a tenderer treatment. The fact that the technique, in strong contrast to this peculiarity, tends to a brilliant staccato, deprives sixth-playing of a part of the firmly moulded and decisively characteristic effect, which almost every other variety of technical form can exhibit, and has, indeed, hindered it from attaining general favor. While all the other modern acquisitions have been zealously cherished, sixth-playing has been neglected, and came into vogue only for a time in the above-mentioned works of the virtuoso period.

Octave-playing, as the reinforcement of the single part, has just the same wealth of figuration as the latter in its simple form. This gives it wider scope than third or sixth-playing, which were restricted as to plastic development.— Besides, it is capable of all varieties of touch; all kinds of the legato and staccato are accessible to it. In it are thus repeated, with the necessary modifications, the entire sum of the mechanical elements hitherto acquired.

However, all these potentialities have by no means equal scope and equal rights in this department. Neither the legato nor the finger-staccato possess even approximately the same all-pervading importance for octave-playing as the pure wrist technique. The hand-stroke is the form in which octaves are most effective. It is also best to let the studies begin at this point.

Simplicity of action is characteristic of the wrist octaves; one and the same lever with one and the same movement is the sole agency for displaying this entire wealth of figuration. This simplicity is partly an advantage, partly an augmented difficulty. The former appears by comparison with the finger-action, wherein five separate individualities were to be trained and equalized, and the hand-form, the stretch, the fingering, etc. divided the technique into the greatest diversity of special arts. With octaves, nothing needs attention but the mere looseness of the wrist. Yet in this very simplicity lie magnified dangers. The cleanness of a complicated octave passage is far more uncertain than that of the most involved single run. The demands on the skill, elasticity, strength, endurance, and in particular on the precision, are enormously enhanced.

The first and most important step in practical study will now be the development of a function already touched upon— the wrist technique. The necessary movements need no further explanation. First of all, the repetition of one and the same octave must be pushed till the highest rapidity of vibration and greatest endurance are attained. Then study, with like requirements, C-major scales, before attempting black keys. As soon as the latter come into play, there enters, besides the elastic energy of the wrist, a new feature of no mean importance; namely, the thumb movement. The thumb must always progress in a straight line. It should strike the white keys close to the edge of the black, and the latter just on the end. Zigzag motions, with the inevitable joggling to and fro of the elbow, are strictly forbidden. The special thumb studies requisite here are best made in connection with Th. Kullak's Octave School (Part I.) Do not delay these until about to begin legato octave-playing; for while the thumb needs more attention then, its present flexibility is half the battle. In regard to the finger-

ing, the general practice favors the employment of the fourth
finger on black keys. A. Dreyschock, Th. Kullak, and others,
use only the fifth finger in wrist octaves. A special collection
of studies is unnecessary. Proceed from vibrations on one
key to C-major scales, then to the most various scale-like
passage, and finally to harmonic progressions. The industrious
player, who, by the way, must possess a healthy body for this
work, may find the goal of his ambition in the execution of
all simple tone-series in octaves. In his younger years A. Dreyschock played in this manner the difficult C-minor Étude
Op. 10 No. 12 by Chopin with immense bravura.

The freedom of the hand in its relation to the keyboard
is now increased to the utmost. Cleanness in playing is here
most difficult to attain; but this branch of technique has rightly
been regarded with extraordinary favor, for no other so fully
repays in brilliancy the toil expended.

The mechanical work in legato octaves is different in
principle. It is founded, to begin with, on the flexibility of
the thumb already mentioned, which has to give its part as
nearly as possible the sound of the legato. Indeed, its fleshy
framing favors it in so doing above all the other fingers.
Economy in movement is the main point in the technique.
The second principal feature is the play of the two last
fingers. The passing of the fifth under the fourth and the
passing the fourth over the fifth must be practiced in the
most diversified combinations. For this purpose, too, Part I
of Kullak's excellent Octave School furnishes the best guide;
in fact, this work treats all departments of octave technique
so exhaustively, that hardly anything of consequence remains
to be said. Each octave passage should also be studied with
the last fingers alone. Through passing over and under, a
legato is nearly everywhere practicable. In the worst places,
a skilful gliding must seek to smooth over the gap. Sliding
the finger from the black key to the adjoining white one is
often of great service. Above all things, take care that the
fingers alone play. Their development here obtains the final

polish. All other elements of movement must be avoided. To begin with the easiest, study first chromatic figures, then all scales, and finally progressions in various intervals and broken chords. The separate study of each of the two parallel series of tones must everywhere precede octave practice. It depends upon the individuality of the hand, whether the third finger can be employed or not. Opportunities offering for its use will be sufficiently evident. In rather slow tempo, the change of fingers on a key may be used as a further convenient means of binding; it is generally effected by the last fingers, but may also be successfully employed with the thumb. Kullak's Octave School contains, in the first Part, several exercises illustrative of this point.

Before proceeding to a detailed examination of certain specialties in octave-playing still to be taken up, it is necessary to review, in passing, the earlier observations on the wrist legato. In Chapter VII the high lift of the entire hand was recommended as an excellent expedient for binding successions of tones to be executed by the same finger, the clinging of the finger-tip being thus intensified. In the second place, it also proved advantageous even where the fingers could bind smoothly; for the freedom of the hand lends the tone more warmth, and perhaps a greater capacity for modulation as well. That octave-playing specially favors this mode of touch, springs from the very fact, that under the most favorable conditions a strict legato will be impossible in one of the two series of tones; it is therefore all the more desirable to facilitate the supple glide of the finger from one key to another.

The practical studies, for which all kinds of passages not containing altogether too many leaps can serve as exercises, are chiefly to be performed so, that the lifting of the hand coincides with the black keys and its sinking with the white; or, what amounts to the same thing in most, though not all, cases, to lift the hand for the fourth finger, and lower it for the fifth. This style of execution is the more practical, because even those figures whose exact binding presents no difficulty, gain in confidence and precision thereby, even though at first their cleanness be more endangered.

In genuine virtuoso pieces two more varieties of octave passages are found, which are calculated for deceiving the ear. The first, and the rarer, lies only in one hand, and arises from carrying out the full figure in one part, while the parallel part drops several tones, in most cases every second tone:

In rapid tempo the effect approximates to that of a full octave passage; great bravura is hardly attainable in this manner. The more brilliant is the effect of another kind of deceptive octaves, for which both hands are required. The actual passage is played by the regularly alternating thumbs, and each hand takes the octave of the tones executed by its thumb:

The effect of this variety is sharp but brilliant, though only in the most rapid tempo. Even execution is not very difficult; the more needful, for clean playing, is the training of the eye. For this, a most excellent study is contained in the second Part of Th. Kullak's Octave School.

For the full elucidation of octave playing, the differences in touch for melody and passage should still be noticed. It should be remarked, that singing tones, wherever progressing in octaves, must be treated precisely like single singing notes. A short, close touch and deep pressure of the key, together with the most clinging legato, form the unchangeable groundwork. — But with enhanced requirements of the melodic idea these limits, too, may be overstepped, and octave-playing may employ any variety of touch in the proper place. It is the peculiarity of pianoforte melody, that it imitates strains not only in a vocal sense, but may transfuse them with its instrumental charms and nuances. Thus the most delicate bell-tones of the wrist-stroke may carry out a melody quite as well as its full nervous impetus. Indeed, amid a broad flood of accompanying notes, even the weight of the arm may be called in, as is often indispensable in Liszt's and Thalberg's earlier works.

When passages are based on a wider interval than an octave, the *extreme stretch*, likewise an addition of modern virtuosity, arises. Until now, the compass of a fifth has been regarded as the normal stretch in exercises with quiet hand and in the scales; to this was added the space of an octave, employed in the case of chords. The sixths and sevenths lie as connecting links between these fundamental bounds, and for a long time met, with the latter, all the demands of technique. The extreme stretch widens the technical horizon by a full third fundamental principle, and forms the root of a most diversified growth of new figures.

First of all, the hand must outwardly increase its elasticity and stretching power by spreading exercises. Each finger must learn to stretch so far with the thumb as to form a straight line with the latter. To this end the inner face of the thumb and fifth finger must be set against the perpendicular front of the pianoforte below the keys, at their utmost stretch, and practice gradually increasing pressure upon the same until brought into contact with it throughout their entire length. An imaginary straight line, continued through the palm, will then coincide with both fingers. This process is to be carried out with all combinations of fingers with the thumb, and will meet with peculiar difficulty in the case of the second; but here, too, the requirements mentioned must be fulfilled.—The stretching power of each other pair of fingers must next be exercised, a right angle being taken as the result aimed at. Now the other hand may help the one practicing, first spreading the fifth finger from the fourth, then the fourth from the third, and finally the second from the third to the width of the angle mentioned. The palm of the hand must also be wrought as far as possible into convex form by means of stretching out and apart the straightened fingers; for elasticity in the skin of the palm furthers the general power of stretching. This latter can be judged of at a glance, with any hand, the moment it tries to take the form described. Later, stretching practice must be continued without pressure against firm surfaces or help from the other hand, and the required stretch also attained. Another exercise consists in bringing fingers 2, 3, 4, and 5 close together, and then forming the stretch of a right angle between each two in turn. The ability to keep the rest closed, while the one assumes the widest stretch without aid from the other hand, is, when effected with ease, a sure sign of the elasticity and independence of the fingers. In conclusion, caution is advisable in all stretching exercises, for under certain conditions the hand may be injured thereby.

All toneless mechanical practice is, of course, only preparatory; the studies on the keyboard are always the main point. On this now begins the first exercise in the arpeggio'd striking of the widest intervals; for small hands octaves, for larger ones ninths, for the largest tenths, elevenths, etc. Then follows the simultaneous, firm striking of the intervals named. The exercises mentioned in the first part of the mechanical studies (Chapter V), extended to wide intervals, must now be attacked in earnest. Formerly their most important aim was wanting, the chief purpose in their practice then being to make the fingers independent; now they are to strengthen the finger-muscles for striking in the most inconvenient positions, and to add in their elasticity a new element to the technique. Therefore, chords of the ninth and tenth, in part with some fingers held down, in part with free hand, now define the form, within which a comprehensive course of exercises is to be created in analogy to Chapter V. The exercises described above will be followed by attempts to execute, with a firm, pearling touch, such intervals as can be taken only *in succession*. These may be extended to intervals of the twelfth, thirteenth, etc.—The guiding principle is the independent stroke of the finger, whatever be the stretch of the fingers. The elasticity of the finger-tip now first attains its full strength and development. Co-operation by the arm is forbidden. Even in those intervals which require the aid of the arm, the sensitiveness of the finger must still be kept awake as the chief active agent.

Arpeggios of all kinds, beginning with double notes which touch only the extreme limits, up to five-tone chords which afford the hand full grasp, are the most important examples. The character of the great Arpeggio Études in Chopin, Op. 10, exhibits the measure of grace to which the first toilsome studies must rise.

The extreme stretch, besides the forms with quiet hand, includes advancing studies also, followed by others in passing over and under. The modern school furnishes abundant examples of all cases.

Examples:

This element by no means consists merely in the extension of the extreme fingers; it cannot even be asserted, that a stretch exceeding an octave is a condition of the same. Any stretch between two inner fingers already belongs within its scope; and thus even within an octave extreme stretches may be contained, as the second example before the last shows. In most cases, to be sure, the extension of the outer fingers —the natural spreading fingers—is also added.

While we can term, in general, any stretch of fingers 1 and 2, which exceeds a fourth, and any between two other fingers, which exceeds a third, an extreme stretch, the differences of different hands also limit the meaning of the term; for many hands much will prove easy, which demands of others the effort of a stretch.

The great diversity in figuration resulting from the principle of the extreme stretch gives proof of a manual gymnastic training which, both as regards strength and skill, may be considered as the climax of all technical performances. A strict legato treatment is here assumed as a matter of course. Where ninths or tenths are executed with the wrist staccato, they belong to the technique of octave-playing. As the extreme stretch sets in motion still wider ranges of tones than all earlier forms, the boldness and bravura of its technique attains still more brilliant effects. The hand runs, in an outspread form which makes its five fingers seem almost spider-like, with the strangest meanderings over its smooth and slippery course. The form of the hand now quite departs from the original rule. The finger-tips only *feel* a striving in the direction of a downward or inward bend, but are in reality nearly straight. The sensitiveness of touch aroused by the foregoing series of exercises remains active, it is true, even in this posture; but a real bending of the tip-joint is very seldom practicable. The pace of this technical form has the most winged sweep possible within the bounds of the legato. When wrought into the weft of the divers artistic forms of technique, this variety possesses an effect of sensuous charm quite its own, a character contrasting through bravura with all others, and blended, besides, with a fuller euphony.

Where the extreme stretch overpasses the last-mentioned limit, a detached style of playing becomes necessary. A connection between intervals is required, which can be effected only by the aid of the arm. This leads us to the leaps, and, in a wider sense, to the technique of the arm, to which, in the foregoing, allusion had to be made several times in advance. We have now to discuss the same more comprehensively.

The arm can participate in playing in a threefold manner. Its movement is either horizontal, or vertical, or a turning on its own axis, in which its direction to the keyboard remains unchanged. Till now the player has employed the arm almost exclusively as an external, supporting lever which, without individual activity or participation in the execution, was but the parent stem of the more finely organized branches serving as the playing apparatus. The nerve of the play dwelt in the knuckle-joint and in the finger-tip. To these factors was added, as second in order, the wrist; and now this case is repeated on a still larger scale, showing the player, that the above-named sensitive nerve-system does not alone constitute the entire playing organism, but that in the latter the idea of a many-jointed, longer lever finds expression.

When speaking of arm-playing, the forearm is meant. In its stroke it is subjected to conditions similar to those for the finger-joints and the hand. Its movement is governed from the elbow-joint in the same way as the hand from the wrist, or the fingers from the knuckles. Flexibility and smoothness, united in case of need with intense power, but always with the utmost precision of aim, must quite as markedly characterize the movements at the elbow as the other striking movements. The forearm must swing and turn easily in its joint in every direction; in this regard it has a still wider function than the hand and the fingers, because it is forced to take a broader horizontal sweep.

The former functions of the arm were mainly of a negative nature. Its task was restricted to maintaining the quiet working of the mechanical apparatus, thus giving more independence to the fingers or hand. It served, besides, to bear the hand back and forth over the keyboard, though mainly as a passive agent. This last function becomes more important in leaps, whether the latter are formed by notes played singly, doubled, as chords, or in octaves.—We shall now begin with the technique of the elbow-joint in the horizontal curving throw. The absolutely prompt and precise traversing of the space from one point of aim to another requires in the throw of the forearm lightness and strength, the two factors, which are indispensable in every branch of technique. In the operation of the elbow-joint, therefore, must be acquired the same looseness, independence, and smoothness as required at first in the other joints. In the mechanical practice the hand assumes a firm form, in order to offer proper resistance to the impulse of the striking weight. Were it not the foremost principle of all technique, that the living consciousness of the fingers must never be suppressed, one might say, that here the relation between arm and finger-action discussed above is reversed. Now the arm only is held loosely, and firm immobility is expressed in the fingers and the hand.

The leaping exercises are first occupied with single notes. The leap is effected either between the outer fingers, or one middle and one outer finger, or two inner fingers, or by the repetition of the same finger.

But in many cases the fingers too are held quite loosely, and the stroke is effected no less by the action of the knuckle-joint than by that of the elbow-joint. This occurs particularly in isolated leaps, incidentally interrupting the legato. Only in a continual leaping movement is the chief share in the execution concentrated in the elbow-joint. By its elastic sidelong bend the wrist also aids in the case previously mentioned. More undivided attention can be paid to the arm-technique in chord and octave-leaps. The chords, in particular, require a firmly-moulded, unvarying form of the fingers and hand; but the wrist-action in them, and still more in the octave leaps, cannot well be dispensed with, and may combine with that of the elbow-joint. Only for a sharper touch will the latter be exclusively employed. Throughout the theory of this great compound lever the rule obtains, that a combination with the more delicate joints does no harm, even if it may be dispensed with in many cases.

Until now we have discussed the function of the forearm in reference to *space*. Its *dynamic* function, to which we now proceed, is more important.—The mere direction of the fingers by the arm does not constitute its own independent technique; the observing eye will always view the leaps mainly as an art of the fingers. The beauty of the line of leaping is a charm which operates only in the latter sense, and is altogether, from the material standpoint, the highest expression of movement of which the fingers are capable. From an ideal standpoint, the leaps confessedly rank below most of the other passage-forms in their essence, for they exhibit thinness and poverty of tone, and lack all variety.

In considering the arm in its dynamic intensity, we arrive at the theory of the arm-stroke proper. The same is governed by conditions quite similar to those of the wrist-stroke; it only expands the measure of the inward and outward manifestation of the latter.—But as its *natural* function much more nearly approaches the stroke, it has by no means like value, from an artistic point of view, with the wrist and knuckle-joint, which had first to be freed from the shackles of Nature. The most skilful arm-stroke, compared with that from the wrist or knuckle, savors somewhat of roughness. It is also a mistake to class the variety in question, in the theory of the stroke, together with the stroke from the knuckle or wrist. It must be explicitly stated, that the arm-stroke requires far less artistic skill than the finger-strokes; neither does the physical construction of the arm stand in just proportion to that of the keys. It is a too massive lever for the keys, with which the fingers alone stand in direct and actual connection. In its ponderous stroke the arm therefore represents a shade of tone-color, but not the primary color. The latter resides entirely in the fingers, and only great and isolated contrasts claim the aid of the former.

On examining the mechanism of the arm-stroke more closely, the elbow-joint is found to be the point whence the familiar functions of the up-stroke and down-stroke issue.— Before precisely elucidating the form of these movements we must, however, consider that dynamic influence of the arm-power, which in its invisible manifestation causes an augmentation of tone-volume.

As long as the fingers execute a pearling legato, the co-operation of the arm is not allowable. Should it take place, the evenness and independence of the finger-strokes would be lost. It is, however, a different matter with separate long-sustained series of singing tones or accents not gliding on in unbroken flow. Here the weight of the arm aids the pressure of the fingers and augments the singing tone. This occurs most often with singing notes in the modern style, where they are to penetrate through a full figurate accompaniment, and are held long. The gesture unconsciously follows the impulse of the thought. As already remarked in speaking of melody, expression is outwardly symbolized in the feeling of pressure. Moreover, the wrist unconsciously rises higher while holding the important note, and together with the arm presses down on the finger-tip.—Externally and internally a co-operation of the whole nervous playing apparatus is involved, which exercises a delicate influence on the production of tone. A series of tones thus played will be distinguished by softness, fulness, and melting melody.—But not only singing notes in the modern sense call for this treatment, but all notes of deep, soulful expression, and a simply figurated chorale by Bach will often afford ample opportunity for the same.—In fugue-playing it is, of course, still more frequently employed.

Such is the influence of the arm on the finger-stroke, the chief agent. Its working, though sensible, was still invisible. The first active function of true arm-playing is exhibited in its upward lift after short notes and at rests. This symbolizes, as in the wrist, though in a yet higher degree, full liberation from the constraint of the rules of form, and needs no further explanation. But the lift of the arm presupposes a still stronger, more vehement stroke than that of the wrist. The note, which in rebounding throws the arm upward, must possess greater intensity than that which only throws up the wrist. The greater the masses shaken by a brief shock, the greater is the intensity expressed by the latter. The wrist represents medium power, the arm the highest. Therefore, chords of special shortness and sharpness will most frequently employ the latter.—On the other hand, the case is sometimes reversed. Where an extremely soft touch is combined with the lift of the arm, the airy, ethereal nature of such tones is thereby expressed, and here, too, the arm more perfectly symbolizes the expression than the wrist. Hand and wrist movement often combine, then resembling in function the arm alone. The greater flexibility then observable on the whole, will lend a tinge of gracefulness to the grandeur of lofty harmonies.

Finally, the arm exhibits its most characteristic striking action when it executes both striking movements. It raises itself from the elbow-joint, and falls from on high upon the keys with its full weight. In order that the latter may operate quite independently, and not be weakened just before the blow by a cramping tension of the forearm, the movement in the elbow-joint must be loose and pliant. This demands industrious practice. For sufficient stress cannot be laid upon the fact, that beginners check the arm-stroke just before touching the key, and take a fresh and lower start, with which the stroke is carried out. They do not gain full benefit from the height of the arm-lift.

The arm-stroke is employed either for single notes, chords, or octaves. Singing notes, which have to penetrate through broad masses of tone, take the same (e. g. the author's Étude "Lore-Ley", Op. 2), and chords, whether they have the melody, or are in general to be strongly accented. In all passages of an orchestral type, or in which the pianoforte is to express power or grandeur, the arm is used; and the left hand in particular must study this effect for the execution of forceful bass notes.—

A third and highly important movement of the arm is the turn in a horizontal position, i. e. about an axis to be imagined as passing from the middle of the wrist to the elbow. This sort of movement first appears in the so-called side stroke. That is, if a tone played by the thumb is followed by an accented chord or double-note, which is left to the last fingers, — or by a single tone to be sharply marked by the fifth finger—the entire hand rises upward from the thumb, to execute the stroke with greater precision. The reverse action occurs, when a marked accent is to be thrown over from the fifth finger to the side of the thumb. The hand then rises sideways so high, that the thumb stands high above the fifth finger, and falls with full momentum; it is at least well, at first to practice the movement in this broad style.

The necessary turn of the hand is effected by the arm, in the elbow-joint. Take special care in practicing that the upper arm remains perfectly passive, an oscillation of the same appearing anything but elegant.

There is, besides, a special variety of pianoforte figures, which might, indeed, be executed with pure finger technique, but which, when treated as a continuous series of side strokes dealt alternately to the right and left, admit of far more fire and bravura. To this class belong most tremolos, and broken runs of octaves, sixths, or even thirds; even the trill at times requires this style of execution. The turn of the hand and forearm discussed above then passes into a continuous balancing back and forth. A fully developed technique, which with its pupilage has also left behind the anxious contact with the keys, can widely employ this variety of arm action. Above all, the pupil should study passages like that in the last movement of Beethoven's sonata Op. 26, with quiet hand; an artistic rendering will attain a fine effect just through the free employment of the arm.

The question still remains to be answered, how far an equal result may perhaps be attained with scantier means. For our fundamental principle of technique has always been economy of movement. A side stroke might also be performed without the arm; for even a hand partially fixed does not exclude wrist-play. In like manner as the earlier mechanical training assumed the latter as the rule, the arm-stroke as the exception, we ought at least, for the sake of consistency, to interpolate the side stroke from the wrist as an intermediate step between pure finger technique and the style of playing in question. The superior effect of the arm-turn is our reason for not doing so; for in the first place, the mere lift of the hand nowhere attains more delicate effects; the balancing of the forearm can bring out the tenderest piano; secondly, the latter is comparatively easy to learn. The elbow-joint naturally favors the turn. The roughness otherwise so easily felt in arm playing also disappears, as all the passages of this class are executed in touch with the keyboard. As soon as the pupil has stopped the accompanying motion of the upper arm, nothing further has to be studied but the equal height in the lift of the hand toward the right and left.

By way of a supplement, the stroke from the shoulder-joint may also find mention. True, the forearm, once employed, should derive all its strength purely from itself, from the elbow-joint, and refuse further co-operation, if only for the sake of practice. Still, cases occur in which even the strength of the forearm does not suffice, and the immense volume of tone brought out by the lift of the upper arm is required. To this

13

end flexibility of the shoulder-joint is needed, which is developed along the lines laid down for elbow practice. The explanation of the latter renders details concerning this (in any event) rare case superfluous.

In addition to the above varieties of touch there is another, to which the lifting of the wrist or arm forms, in a measure, the transition. This is the *mezzo staccato*, indicated by a slur over the usual staccato signs (dot or wedge-shaped stroke). It will already have been taken up in the practical course, which could not defer noticing this shade of touch so long as the theoretical, whose progress as here mapped out has till now afforded no fitting opportunity for its introduction.

The mezzo staccato is a union of the legato and staccato. It retains something of the singing touch, and combines with the same one of the liftings, noted in connection with the staccato, of the finger, the hand, the arm, or the combinations of these varieties. The finger presses the key down, catching it close with a singing touch, but holds it during only three-quarters of the indicated note-value, then releasing it with an upward spring. The tone-power may be varied from the merest breath, through all medium grades, up to the most imposing fulness. For rendering a very warm, strongly marked accentuation, this mezzo staccato furnishes the most appropriate means.

The measure of impressiveness in the tone stands, firstly, in a natural ratio to the amount of pressure and the upward spring. The more pregnant the tone, the greater will be the leverage setting it in vibration. For the most powerful tones the arm rises, for the less powerful the hand, for soft tones the finger; for the very softest only the finger-tip will be drawn inward. Usually *the same* leverage, with which the touch was effected, will execute the upward spring. But, as often remarked before, the symbolic movement also develops in a contrary sense, when the very softest finger-touch requires the lifting of the arm or hand. —

In a purely material sense the gesture is meaningless, if the finger-tip only produces the tone desired; for the touch of the hammer is but instantaneous.—Respecting the lift *after* the stroke, this view may be right in a measure; but the lift *before* and *for* the stroke is naturally not affected by this assumption. —A certain degree of gesticulation is justifiable in every sense; an utterly passive mechanism can never be a desirable product of technique; the hand should possess the properties of a passive mechanism only with regard to its *obedience*, which must be guided by the equally innate principles of volition and causation. It must, therefore, likewise be a living, inspired mechanism.

A special variety of the mezzo staccato is the *carezzando*, discussed in detail by Kontski in his Method. This is executed by stroking the keys, and was frequently employed in practice by the above virtuoso.—Kalkbrenner mentions the same under the similar term *caresser*, and Chopin is also said to have employed it, although stroking the key in exactly the contrary direction to that of Kontski's style.—According to Kontski, the finger strokes the key with the inner fleshy face of the tip-joint, touching it nearly in the centre, gliding gently towards the front edge, and in the middle of this path causing, by gradual pressure, the hammer to strike. Such a gentle, gradual approach of the latter to the string necessarily results in a very soft tone. This tone is best adapted for chord-like passages or melodious notes in slow tempo. Amid the many shades of touch, this variety possesses a charm of its own. Here, too, the finger-action attains to psychic symbolism.

Too long employed, this shade of tone grows enervating, and robs the pianoforte of its classic vigor of timbre. As it volatilizes the latter to a zither or harp-like tone, it can claim only transient practical use.

13*

CHAPTER X.

The touch with low finger-lift. Repeated employment of the same finger in advancing series of tones. The glissando. Crossing the hands, and their mutual relation in playing. The combined modes of touch. Polyphonic playing.

The chief technical forms are exhausted with the foregoing chapter. It may be assumed, that the technical ability will have attained, at this stage, the skill necessary for mastering the following forms without further explanation. The matter now added for the sake of completeness will therefore be treated as an appendix.—

For the passage touch, the precise lifting of the fingers was stated to be a *conditio sine quâ non*. In certain passages this is not correct; for cases are found, in which the finger rises only so far, that in its highest lift it still remains in contact with the key, and even exerts the pressure mainly with its tip-joint. A style of playing then arises, having similarity to that recommended by Bach and Hummel. The finger-tip is the chief active agent; it may even glide inward after executing the touch.

This style finds full justification in the following cases: (1) In the trill; (2) in the tremolo; (3) in all passages of extreme velocity, executed either without, or with very little passing over and under; e. g. Mendelssohn's Song without Words in *C*, Part 6; the Études within the compass of five tones, in the Gradus ad Parnassum; and in Czerny's works all those passages which are calculated for effect rather as a whole than in the details of their elements. Such are those having little figuration, but possessing in the close contiguity of their tones a smooth, polished quality, and thus not requiring a carefully chiselled shaping of their separate parts.—Neither can it be denied, that many others having more figuration admit of such execution with the low lift; nor that the pianoforte tone itself receives, through this treatment, a novel nuance of its sensuous diversity of tone. Examples of this case might be found in the final passages in sixteenth-notes, in Mendelssohn's Op. 14, and in numerous passages with harmonic roulades.

It is enough to call attention to the delicacy of the resultant shades of tone, if all be played distinctly; the artist striving after universality will have to study them in passages whose delicacy and extreme velocity allow this touch to be used.—It must, however, be added, that the pearling touch resulting from the higher lift is also beautiful even in the most delicate passages, always affords greater assurance of precision, and never spoils anything. Play one of the passages named above in both styles, and compare them.

Everywhere, however, that much figuration and frequent passing over and under is found, the pearling touch can hardly be dispensed with; firstly, the scale itself, and then in passages within a distinct range of keys, where the thumb is not turned under, when their figuration renders them more noticeable. For instance, the second Étude in the Gradus ad Parnassum would by no means bear the low touch, like Études 16 and 17.

Trill and tremolo figures, and arpeggios, form a special exception, as in them velocity is attainable only by keeping the fingers close to the keys set in vibration. (Compare, besides, the suggestions in the previous chapter concerning the joggling of the arm).

We now proceed to other forms, founded on an apparent exception to the foregoing rules.

The legato, together with the precise lift, have been looked upon as the most important points. Now, cases occur in the closest legato style, where one and the same finger must play connectedly several successive different tones.

This finger, like the hand in the case of the wrist-stroke, must now depend wholly upon itself, without support from or relation to twinned members. It therefore needs more strength than in a flowing legato, and these changed conditions render it difficult to sustain equality in all those cases, where such isolated strokes occur amid the easier conditions of the connected legato.

Example:

Beeth. Op. 10.

The ear must be sharply critical, tone and touch must everywhere be equal, and the fingers regulate their powers in true proportion to attain this end. The case mentioned occurs most frequently in polyphonic playing. In slow tempo the mechanical action must see to it that the legato is sustained as long as possible, and the forms discussed for the singing touch then find their application; in rapid tempo a deep-reaching touch of the tone in question suffices.

Such a slide often facilitates the fingering by bringing about a regular succession of the fingers, and is then preferable to the legato; e. g.

As regards staccato playing with this repetition of fingers, nothing need be added; for it may be classed with one of the earlier forms. The repeated stroke of different fingers on one key was likewise included in the earlier elementary training. Here we should observe, that modern compositions, to show off the elasticity of the fingers, often contain long passages for this kind of finger vibration. Single finger-strokes occur no less frequently than doubled notes or chords. Thalberg's two Don Juan fantasias contain examples. — The pupil should practice simple staccato scales with the finger-stroke from the knuckle-joint.

This touch combines with the wrist to form a style of stroke divided between finger and wrist; — when one of the outer fingers is fixed, and the others repeatedly strike the same tones, e. g.

A method frequently mentioned of effecting a legato is the sliding of the fingers from a black key to a white. A similar kind of movement has called into being a certain purely ornamental variety of the passage, which about Weber's time was greatly in vogue, but is now as good as laid on the shelf, — partly because it requires different instruments from the present ones, and partly from its (musically speaking) quite valueless and furthermore very cheap effect. We refer to the *glissati*.

In these the key is pressed down by skimming over it; the touch thus has no free stroke from above downward, but is linked with the key preceding. The finger glides along in close touch with the keys from one to the other; it bends over toward its narrow edge, and in this inconvenient posture must exert force enough to produce a distinct series of tones. The thumb, too, lies on its narrow edge, and must cross the successive keys in advancing.

For simple *glissandi* the hand is inclined somewhat in the direction of the movement, especially on black keys.

With octaves the direction towards the thumb is the easier, towards the fifth finger more difficult. In the latter the tip of the last-named finger is set perpendicularly, its nail gliding over each new key. All *glissati* with doubled notes are, in fact, best made with the nail; for as it usually occurs in long scales, thin-skinned fingers might come to grief.

In special cases the following distinctions are to be noted:

(1) *The glissando on white keys only.* The almost perpendicular finger glides, with the broad side of the nail turned

in the direction of the movement, and with a pressure sufficient to sound the tones distinctly, to the last tone of the passage in hand.

All these passages are practicable only in *C*-major, though they may occur with a slight deception of the ear in *F*-major as well (Liszt, Faust Waltz). Quite similar in sound to such *glissandi* are series of tones played without passing under, with the common instinct of the finger-tips and without lifting the first finger-joints, either by one hand alone, or by crossing and combining both hands. To this class, therefore, belong short figures of from 3 to 5 tones (perhaps up to 6, or at most 8), which, as in Liszt's "Regatta veneziana", are executed with close, rapid slurring, intended to resemble in effect the Papageno pipe. If the hands are set side by side, and continue the run by crossing, runs equalling the *glissando* in velocity can be performed in any key; e. g.

(2) *The glissando on black keys.* The position of fingers and hand is just the opposite of the foregoing, the finger gliding on its inner fleshy face. Several fingers may execute the glide together. Distinctness and smoothness are here far less easy than in the previous variety, and require longer practice. If the thumb has to glide towards its own side, it must touch the key lightly, turn its tip inward, away from the direction of the run, and slide over the keys on its edge. It is more difficult, when the thumb-tip retains the normal direction.

(3) Chords, doubled notes, and octaves.

―――――

The mechanical function of the hands having been treated in detail, (the left hand, as remarked, in all cases transposing

the examples given for the right to suit its own constitution),
we must now consider the mutual relation of the hands in
playing.

The hands are two mutually equivalent organisms. In
them the player possesses a duality, wherein each member
must be in itself a thoroughly trained, artificial mechanism in
little. As each finger has its determinate scope, and represents
an individuality of definite character, in like manner each hand,
as a unity of five organisms striving after one and the same
end, must be an individuality of more comprehensive intention
and higher significance. The fingers, in supplementing and
supporting each other, exhibit their intended purpose. With
few exceptions, the action of the individual finger attains
meaning only in the light of its connection with the rest. Not
so with the hands. Each commands at least half of the total
range of tones, and is in itself a complete whole. The right
hand exercises control over the fluent elements of the light-
soaring, higher regions of tone, and the element of melody in
all its forms. To its share falls the full abundance of all
shades and charms of tone dwelling in the pianoforte, which,
in itself barren, yields so rich a variety of tone to artistic
treatment. The left hand does not so exclusively embrace
the domain of the more delicate outlining and plastic moulding of tone-elements; its primary designation is rather to re-
establish the ethereally sweeping outlines of the shriller tones
upon the firm base of the deeper accompaniment. Its function
then, however, extends beyond these bounds; in works of
broader scope it has to co-operate in the figuration and polyphonic interweaving of the whole, and to develop in its share a
delicacy of delineation fully on a par with that of the right
hand. Finally, modernism has overstepped even these wide
limits, and developed in the left hand an individuality capable
of undertaking the entire rendering and the work of the
right in certain cases, becoming a player of independent
ability, who executes melody, passages, and accompaniment
together. Nevertheless it must be admitted, that this last

phenomenon is an isolated one, and suffers, despite apparent opulence of material, from one-sidedness of form; consequently, the general function of either hand may be stated thus: — That the left hand, though it must possess equal abilities with the right, has on the whole less to do with the fluency and brilliant elaboration of the latter, but has for its element mainly fulness of tone and the mastery of wide stretches and leaps.

Hence it follows, that while each hand possesses characteristic and independent individuality, each must act in most intimate accord with the other to carry out its share of the total design. Externally, the requirements of technique shape the action of either hand as follows.

Each finds its most natural sphere of activity on its own side of the keyboard, and may thus regard its half of the latter as its peculiar province. But the delight felt in technical mastery expands these limits in equal measure with musical necessities. The left hand trespasses on the ground of the right, and *vice versâ*. Amid the manifold forms of this changeful scene, the exactest rhythmical unity and kinship must prevail. In particular, the strictest simultaneity of all coincident beats must be maintained, and an anticipation by the left hand, which so easily becomes a habit in accompanying, resolutely suppressed. As in a drawing the line must be sharp, not blurred, the rhythmic entrance, too, must fall on one and the same point, and the clearest accuracy prevail throughout the interweaving threads of tone.

The conditions above noted determine the usual mutual relations of the hands as controlled by the technical laws explained in the foregoing pages.—As an additional technical resource, the crossing and interlacing of the hands has now to be considered. Either is allowed to pass over the other; this crossed position may even obtain for a considerable time.— There are to be distinguished, in all, the following cases:

(1) One hand follows up the other in executing *one* series of tones; to this class belong, for example, nearly all scales

in works of the Bach period. This style was necessary at that time, because the art of passing over and under was not universally accepted; and modernism has adopted it on account of its easy brilliancy.

Its indispensable requirements are, a smooth, skilful connection of the hand passing over with that playing—a leap of unerring precision, the length of whose arch is exactly timed for accurate striking. Each hand must execute its allotted portions of the passage while gracefully aiding and avoiding the other. The hand crossing must either swoop freely down upon the one playing, or glide over it, as the case requires, and the latter must skilfully withdraw from beneath the other, in order to assume its new position. All appearance of forced evasion must be avoided; the movement of either hand should preserve independent freedom. It is a matter of gymnastic training to exhibit the latter under the most trying conditions.

(2) The series of tones played by either hand may be of various length. In briefest form, each hand has but one note (stroke). The mechanical action derives its swing and power from the technique of the hand and wrist previously discussed; for wider intervals the flexibility of the shoulder-joint comes into play. Aim and touch must equal in precision and distinctness the smoothness of the movement; e. g.

The touch is primarily conceived as powerful. The length of the sweep and of the striking-lever naturally support this idea. The accentuation, in particular, can attain to a power at the alternate entrance of the hands unattainable in the execution by a single hand; for this reason simple passages are often divided between the two hands. And contrariwise, the very breadth of the sweep symbolizes, in soft passages, the most volatile, ethereal sigh of the pianoforte touch, and must be conscientiously practiced in this latter nuance. The finest examples are found in Bach, e. g. in the *C*-minor Fantasia, and the Gigue in the *B♭*-major Partita.

(3) While the hands, in the preceding cases, supplemented each other, so that a Whole could be presented only through their constant alternation, each is capable of complete and independent expression; and two such parts may take possession of the pianoforte to such an extent, that the hands shall cross in mid-career. This form is found even in classic works, e. g. in the second movement of Beethoven's *D*-minor Sonata; but was not fully developed until the actual virtuoso period.

Of higher importance is the conclusion of the theory of touch, still left for presentation. True, the chief forms have been set forth, but the combined varieties have not all been mentioned.—A review of the same would take up much time, if all shades of touch were again to be enumerated, together with those having reference to the intensity of tone-power, which are to be treated later in detail. Not that it would be difficult to exhibit this theory in such detail; but the prospective profit affords no sufficient justification for so burdening the student. In no event can a method of technique enter into all possible details of form; it must suffice, to give suggestions respecting the same, and to dwell principally on the elementary forms.—We shall enumerate merely the four varieties of touch classifiable according to combinations of the joints. That is, the stroke with the finger-tip may combine with the knuckle-joint, the wrist, or the elbow-joint: — that with the knuckle-joint may combine with the wrist or the elbow-joint; — finally, the two last-named joints may combine.

Several of these combinations have already been discussed. The combination of the finger-tip touch with the wrist has still to be examined, it being one much used and of very fluent effect. It yields a touch of great elasticity — of the greatest, perhaps, when short, bell-like tones are required. The suppleness of touch thus attained, which exceeds in looseness that of the pearling touch, yields, especially in *mezzo forte* or *piano* passages, a timbre of equally soft and elastic charm, which is adapted for moderately rapid passages, and even for singing tones.

The remaining combinations of touch, particularly those employing three joints, and finally those with all four, afford no characteristics of eminent importance; *one* joint will usually predominate, as chiefly instrumental in producing the effect.

As regards power of tone, however, distinctions of touch are found, requiring further mention.—All exercises have begun with a solid, substantial tone-color. This is the normal power of tone to be observed, inclining rather to *forte* than *piano*.— We will term this the medium grade, and recommend besides only two others as most urgently needed for practice, namely, the very powerful, and the very soft. Although the shading is far more diversified, the necessary instructions for the same cannot be exhaustively given before reaching the treatment of the rendering. A hand capable of executing these three shades with proper firmness, clearness, and distinctiveness, has acquired the ability needed for all further refinements. True, the *crescendo* and *decrescendo* also require most careful study; but complete mastery of the above-named shades render them almost native to the hand.

The very powerful touch will prove in all cases an excellent preparation for the medium and soft grades, and, when practiced to this end, will confer elasticity upon the entire technique. Inexpert fingers—*not* stiff ones (this distinction is important)—have often acquired brilliant velocity through this means alone.

The very soft touch is the most difficult matter in all technique. The first attempts of soft playing degenerate too easily into indistinctness; blanks and obscurities occur, and its too early employment cannot be too earnestly deprecated.— But it is all the more evident that this task must be achieved, and that it is the highest aim of all technical study, from the mere fact of its extreme difficulty, aside from its indispensableness for a fine rendering. When the touch does not possess in high measure the general characteristics enumerated in Chapter IV, and more especially those of looseness and the most soft and clinging contact of the finger-tip to the key, it is not yet ripe to solve this problem, and the medium grade must still be chiefly cultivated in connection with the most powerful.

A normally trained hand, however, should undertake the practice of all Studies in the three grades named, and even such a hand will be obliged to devote most painful attention to the last.—There are a softly pearling and a softly slurring, but distinct, style; one with a high and one with a very low lift of the fingers, some hints concerning which were given at the beginning of this chapter. The player may decide which color is to be taken, and which is practicable in any given passage.

The employment of the pedals also demands attention. When, with the idea of touch, that of the *production of tone* and its *differences* is combined, the pedal cannot be refused a place in any method. Nevertheless, its discussion is still deferred to a later part, because mechanical training is here the guiding principle in systematization, and from the purely technical standpoint the management of the pedals admits only of hints whose nature is too simple and self-evident. They would touch nothing further than the placing of the feet, precision of releasing, and a certain dexterity in treading;— points which can be thoroughly explained only in connection with the rules of rendering, and are therefore put off till then.

The foregoing method of technique has exhibited the fundamental forms of all those movements, which can be developed by all the elementary tone-forms within the compass of pianoforte music; and has thereby fulfilled its main purpose.—

It can no more be its aim, to bring forward the endless variety of combinations capable of evolution from these forms, than it could be expected of a science of the Beautiful to detail the endless variety of art-works already existing or to be created.

The diversity of technical forms depends, as we have seen, not upon the distinctions into which a *single* principle may separate, but upon several fundamental ideas, each of which evolves from itself a great diversity of phenomena. These are: The Figuration, the varieties of Touch, and the grades of Power. A merely approximate estimate of all the possibilities in combination issuing herefrom suffices, to show the source of technical forms to be inexhaustible; and nothing is so well adapted, as this reflection, to set the final goal of technique in its proper light.

No single form, in its exclusiveness, is the object in training the hand, but only the combination of all. Each in itself is but an intermediate link, a transition period on the path to the end, which consists in the perfectly easy, smooth suppleness of the playing members and joints, and in their precise, instinctive adoption of the prescribed form; and must attain, in every situation, distinctness and beauty in all elements of tone.

At the close of the method a species of technical performance remains for discussion, which sets forth the last requirement in its most concise and stringent form. This is Polyphony. True, it generally eschews the more brilliant side of modern acquirements, and confines itself chiefly to a style which dispenses with gallopping up and down the keyboard. But that it requires precisely that training of the hand, which, after conquering the separate elements, possesses the above-mentioned precision of general mechanical suppleness and smoothness in the highest degree, will be apparent from the following.

In polyphony, especially fugue-playing, none of the simple mechanical forms demands such exclusive attention, that technical study is obliged to begin again with elementary gymnastics. The parallelism of the parts, and the interweaving of regular figuration in the complicated structure of independent series of tones mutually superposed, very seldom allows the technical interest to disport itself in étude-like gambollings. The many-sidedness of simultaneous claims constantly forces the purely mechanical element to assume a very peculiar standpoint. The mind, even in purely technical observation, becomes far more actively engaged. Eye and finger require an entirely new training, such as is not demanded even by the most brilliant lustre of homophonic bravura. The interest, too, is drawn closer to the musical spirit by the concentration of the mind, and the figuration ceases to make effect in the showy, arabesque-like style.—It is apprehended only in the sense of a deeper meaning. The hand must therefore have conquered the mechanical elements in detail, and have attained to that higher unity mentioned previously.—As soon as the technique awakens interest not for its own sake, but for a higher aim which it serves, that standpoint must have been left behind on which the attention was anxiously directed to material preconditions.

To be sure, it lies in the nature of the polyphonic intertwining, that the figuration cannot exhibit the same motley diversity as in music of a more homophonic character—Études and the like. Polyphony limits the figuration to smaller forms, which alone are adapted for interweaving in several parallel parts. Yet brilliancy is not excluded; in Händel's and Bach's fugues a lively, bold figuration often prevails, and in Liszt's transcriptions of the organ fugues even the wrist is called into requisition for thundering octave passages. But the singing touch is mainly employed in all forms. It is the original conception of polyphony to symbolize living dialogues, and this lends to the expression of each individual part a character rather of vocal declamation than of instrumental brilliancy.

Consequently each tone-atom must be lovingly considered by the player, and the finger-tip has to apply the art of the singing tone at every instant and in every nuance.

Another reason that the most many-sided and final result of mechanical training is a precondition for polyphonic playing is found in the fact, that the rules of fingering hitherto learned in detail now cease to control, and the fingering is derived from the most universal laws.

The fingerings given in the foregoing flowed spontaneously from the fundamental forms of technique, and were discussed in their places. —

In order to devise a theory of the fingering, it will be indispensable to go back to the fundamental forms. The universal law was found to be the natural succession of fingers on corresponding series of keys, the passing over or under with the suitable fingers, and above all things the groundwork of the legato style, the easiest and most natural consequence of the parallel series of fingers and keys. Türk said, the most convenient fingering is the best; Clementi, that the simplest is the best; which means much the same. — For the simpler successions of tones this principle develops all rules in detail, both those already discussed, and others as well, having reference to the regularity of the fingering with figuration correspondingly regular, to the practicality of retaining a given position of the hand as long as possible, to the distinctions between the third and fourth fingers in chord-passages, etc., and which might be added here and there by way of supplement, although they naturally result from the foregoing.

In polyphonic playing precisely the same law obtains; but it is harder to carry out, and the mind being thus more intently engaged than in the simpler forms, the expression, that in fugue-playing the rules for the fingering come to an end, is in a measure explainable. More exactly, the remark would read: No fingering current in the simple forms can be developed in fugue-playing with similar regularity, because the

14

idea of polyphony includes a continual shifting of the relations of the tones. —

The chief concern in polyphonic playing is the skilful distribution of the middle parts. The hands must co-operate as if they were one — an organic unity of the mutually equivalent playing-levers which, more especially in the execution of the middle parts, must aid and support each other in complete reciprocity. Eye and fingers must live in most immediate unity with the will.

Cases of course occur in which the regular fingerings run on for a time in the easier track; but they must be prepared at every moment to sacrifice the habit of rule to the requirements of polyphony. Here, too, the strictest legato remains the decisive principle for all fingerings; but must oftener employ extraordinary means, like the side-motion, the silent change on one key, or the slide from a black key to a white one.

Respecting the distribution of power, too, the polyphonic style differs from the other modes of playing. Each tone-series (part) must be executed as if played by itself with a single hand. This rule calls forth the energy of finger-action in its purest form, and as never employed till now. The playing of doubled notes discussed earlier is only a reinforced homophony, which requires, to be sure, increased exertion, but is guided to the convenience of a fixed track by the feature of regularity. This is wanting in polyphony; besides, part-playing is developed therein in a broader and more comprehensive manner than is possible in third or sixth-playing. The stroke from the knuckle-joint and the singing pressure of the finger-tip are more continually exerted than in any other style, so that the old-time view, that in fugue-playing the *non plus ultra* of finger technique is exhibited, is right in a degree.

However, it must not be overlooked that in the rapidity of homophony the strength of the fingers is called out in another way, which is on a level with the above. Each is important in its way, and perfection is found only in the union of all forms.

CHAPTER XI.

The Beautiful in Technique.

All pianoforte technique has primarily the one aim of producing a tone fine in itself and felicitous in expression. A touch at all times responsive to the artistic aim is the highest ideal of technique. Viewed from another and by no means irrational standpoint, it consists simply in a series of movements of the fingers, the hand, and the arm, of which the eye can take account quite as well as can the ear of the tones. The ideal demands perfection in all parts; then why should it not require of these movements, wherever practicable, here finished beauty, there expressive symbolism? Let us attempt to define the limits of such an expression more closely; we shall best succeed through a comparison of pianoforte technique with that art, which has its being in motion alone — the art of dancing.

In every art both substance and form are determined by the nature of its material means of expression. This is, in dancing, the movement of the entire body. Gesture and play of feature are meant to exhibit, in part events, in part psychic conditions; and this they really can do, in a certain degree. Yet their symbolism retains a too outward character to follow the finest impulses of the soul. Now, in the same measure as the art of dancing thus falls short in positive meaning, will it push the deference to beauty of form and grace of movement into the foreground, and consequently appeal to the eye rather than the emotions.

The action to which it animates the limbs does far less violence to their natural inclination, and requires a much less considerable augmentation of their native faculties, than the

14*

technique of pianoforte-playing. To the latter innumerable difficulties are opposed in the conquest of the crude material, and in carrying out a consistent conception by means of an extraordinarily complicated system of movements. But the more diversified the field, the loftier too is the loveliness of that perfection which exhibits therein the thought of unity.

But the technique of the pianoforte is unfree. Above all, it is restricted to limited space, the compass of the keyboard, which in certain circumstances cuts off every possibility of endowing the movements with special grace. Often enough, the claims on the latter are stifled in their inception by considerations of distinctness and tone-color. The claims of beauty must give way to the practical ends of technique.—

Or again, the requirements of both may be parallel. The artistic hand unites within itself perfect lightness and extreme strength. Each joint is so subjected to the will that it exhibits, according to the instant necessity, now absolute firmness, and now absolute yieldingness. Of no less moment is the outward repose which characterizes every performance technically ripe. All mechanical action is based on economy of movement. All haste, all involuntary jerks of any member, are excluded; otherwise the precision of play is endangered. This absolute mastery of the will is certainly a feature essential to beauty; for that same technical practicality, which was a hindrance to the free development of grace, will exclude, on the other hand, all unpleasing movements.

In no case can pianoforte-technique, viewed from the standpoint of beauty to the exclusion of the idea of practicality, satisfy the eye for long. For its range, despite all diversity, has too great sameness, and its details of form are too transient, to make an impression by themselves. However, a consideration of this external point need not be disdained, so long as no weightier interests are sacrificed.

Let us now pass from the question of beauty in the form to a discussion concerning the possibility of lending expression to an ideal conception through the symbolism of movements.

Gestures, as the material of dancing, are symbols, quite as much as the tone, the material of music, is a symbol. But the latter, in its capability of swelling and subsiding, has at the outset such a sensible kinship to the impulses and surging of emotion, not to speak of the artificial resources of melody, rhythm, harmony, and polyphony, that the symbolization of psychic processes by music often resembles a copy—even surpasses, indeed, in refinement of inner elaboration, the emotions aroused by ordinary life. The mimic art, on the contrary, is restricted by the outwardness of its resources. Its wealth of nuance does not equal that of music. While the latter follows the life-stream of emotion into its inmost depths, the former shows only the changes on its surface. It symbolizes, not the entire course of a psychic situation, but only its most salient features. In comparison with music, and with pianoforte playing as well, the dance is therefore limited in meaning.

What, therefore, may be the possible symbolism of the technical movements of pianoforte playing, in so far as they appeal to the eye alone? In it, gestures are also the sole means of producing an effect. But their variety is small, and their definiteness not equal to that of the mimic art. On the other hand, a symbolism undeniably resides in the movements of the fingers. Animation, lassitude, repose, unrest, tenderness, harshness, all find expression with a certain distinctness. But the means of presentation remain primitive. Besides, the symbolism of gesture not seldom conflicts with that of tone. Take, for example, the chorale in Mendelssohn's 'Cello Sonata in *D*. The spirit of the same is dignified and lofty; but the technique of the left hand, viewed by itself, has rather the appearance of haste than devotional calm.

Slight as may be the capacity of our technique for symbolical movements, and however they be fettered by the superior law of musical practicality, the less would we urge neglect of their consideration. Our gestures possess one invaluable advantage over those of the mimic art, which is, that they find exemplification in the tones. The symbolism of the visible touch is inseparable from that of the tone. The softer a *cantilena* is to sound, the more supply will it be followed by the movements of the hand and arm. The more abrupt and unrestful the intention of a passage, the more vehement and hasty will be the style of playing developed. Leaving quite out of consideration its effect upon the eye, we must concede the symbolical character of the technical movements, if only because they not unessentially contribute to urge upon the player the intensest absorption in the emotional life.

But under all circumstances we must not lose sight of the fact, that beauty and symbolism are always secondary considerations in technique. The fundamental principle is practical tone-production. The claims of the eye always defer to those of the ear. Moreover, we should not forget, that the slight opportunity of diversifying the gestures always brings danger of a certain mannerism, as they easily lose their meaning through becoming a habit.

Section II.

On the Rendering.

CHAPTER XII.

On the share of Technique in the Rendering.

The second part of our course of instruction treats of pianoforte playing from the side of its ideal conception. The first presented the material preconditions—the elements of the entire art.

In this connection—as previously in the fourth chapter—attention is again called to the insufficient precision of the terminology. The meditative intellect, dealing with conceptions, always finds itself at a loss to clothe with words distinctions, which result only from the need of presentation. In reality, the matter here grouped in two parts and divided under various headings is an inseparable Whole. The Beautiful is in general, no less than pianoforte playing in its modest individual sphere, an organic entirety possessing simultaneously all the properties belonging to it. The analytic understanding actually perpetrates an act contrary to truth, when it presents in succession things consubstantial and coexistant. Their separation is necessary only for the sake of precise apprehension, the human faculty of apprehension being adapted for successiveness.

In view of this prologue, the heading of this Section will appear at once justifiable and unjustifiable; the former, because technique alone does not solve the problem of pianoforte-playing, ideal elements having still to be added; the latter, because technique is always a factor of prime importance. — The relation between technique and rendering is, in general terms, the following.

Firstly, technique is the material with which the player works—without finished material no finished work of art is possible. Secondly, it is in itself a work of art, and holds a far higher place in the art of the pianoforte than marble, for instance, in the art of sculpture. It is a material prepared with great toil and special insight, for whose mastery no *foreign* instrumentality is employed, but the artist's uninterrupted individual energy, so that it must become an integral constituent of the physical and psychical faculties of the practitioner. It is a lustrous treasure, whose arduously acquired polish must be protected with anxious care from the slightest dimness of tarnish. Furthermore, this mechanical material floats midway between concrete materiality and ideality. Its parts are not contiguous in space, so that the imagination could make selection, from among them; they reside in the ability of the artistic hand. Its nervous and muscular sensibility must coalesce so completely with the mental consciousness, that it performs each action aiming at a definite manifestation of energy in exact accord with the intent of the will. The forms, therefore, do not lie in concrete contiguity, but in ideal conjunction in the mental sphere of memory and in physical skilfulness.

Further, technique is distinguished from any other material, in that it yieldingly accompanies all outward manifestations of pianoforte-playing, with unflagging animation, from the very outset up to the loftiest regions. Every other material of art, once obtained, relieves the artist of such care, and permits him to live in the idea alone. The question of the pianoforte mechanism thrusts itself forward on each and every standpoint. Inexorably it bars the way to any higher development, where it has not received its full due. The artist can never depend upon it so entirely as the painter, for instance, on canvass and colors, or the architect on building materials; but must devote, in the most ideal flights, a portion of his full energy to the notice of this material. Now-a-days one often meets, in many circles, with an undervaluation of technique as a special branch of art. To be sure, the number of those pianists who from the purely mechanical standpoint make naught of all difficulties presenting, has increased so rapidly in the last decades, that any player, whose sole merit lies in brilliancy of execution, is doomed from the beginning to failure before the public. But it does not follow in the least, that technique does not remain all the same a *conditio sine quâ non* for every artistic performance; for the ideal should and must show no deficiencies in any part. At most the question might be raised, whether at the present time, when the laurel no longer wreathes for virtuosity as such, a study of that great mass of compositions is profitable, which owe their being to this virtuosity alone. And this question must be answered affirmatively; for firstly, the player controls with far easier mastery the technique of those works which follow solely the noblest tendency, after having conquered the difficulties herein presented in a higher degree; and secondly, the sense of the beautiful, despite all inclination to the sublime, should also lovingly enfold the less significant elements. The technical difficulties are of a threefold nature. The first step to be taken is to learn and practice the simple joint movements until the utmost precision and velocity are acquired; then the same are to be applied in the passages occurring in practical literature. These are the two aspects of the material of study which might be classed under the heads, previously distinguished in theory, of Mechanics and Technics in their pregnant sense. Admitting, that these two elements are always united in practice, we may still be permitted to uphold the antithesis for the sake of precision at least — the more so, as the course of every pianist's training proves, how greatly the proportion varies in which now the one, and now the other, receives the preference.

In contrast to these, a third aspect of technical difficulty cannot be sufficiently dwelt upon, which on the one hand embraces both of the above varieties, and on the other aims directly at that point, where the mental and mechanical meet; — I mean, the quality and quantity of touch. The most thoroughly trained technique, which controls, in the most difficult passages, all gradations of power and every nuance of tone, is not in itself that factor which alone gives assurance of a spirited and soulful rendering; though it is considerably nearer its goal, providing that the player is possessed of true musicianly feeling, than the clearest understanding of an ideal style of rendering whose expression is frustrated by imperfect finger-training. Just in pianoforte playing mere feeling can do but little, for the pianoforte has not even the advantage of a continued tone, which most nearly answers the immediate psychic requirement; and the exactest possible copy of an interpretation suited for the violin, by no means yields a fine pianoforte rendering. But even if all ideal conditions of a thoroughly artistic rendering be really assumed, the mere refinement of the tone to a *ppp* of perfect clearness, and to a *ff* of purest beauty of tone, requires a study, particularly for the singing tone, whose end is hardly calculable. The cultivation of technical bravura has its limits. The development of the passage is so grouped, under the main forms discussed in the foregoing Section, that the pianist who has mastered them may be called technically ripe. Compared with these, the refinements of touch are as innumerable, as the capabilities of musical characterization in general.

Thus, a fine *piano* is one of the most arduous acquisitions of technique; and only with it is the possibility of a further refinement of the tone attained, and each new *decrescendo*, each throwing into relief of single tones, must be studied afresh. Every composition of importance has its peculiar physiognomy and requires individual conception; herefrom arises the necessity of a technical study devoted specially to this individuality, which in the case of a well-trained player will be concerned very far more with nuances than with passage-technique. A mere mental elaboration will not suffice. The clear understanding of any given nuance does not insure its execution. Neglect in the study of touch always leaves room for the possibility, that a single unintentional pressure may give the rendering of an entire *cantilena* a different stamp. A celebrated singing master once answered a question as to the secret of rendering by saying, that ninety-nine hundredths of the same lie in the training of the voice. In pianoforte playing the training of the touch plays the same rôle; therefore nothing is more trivial, than to lay a cold rendering entirely to mental vacuity. From feeling to its technical expression is a long step.

After these disquisitions, which aimed at exhibiting the importance of technique in the rendering, we now turn to the actual task.

All technique, both in its simple and complex forms, and in the meaning and outline of movements, presses in its inmost thought toward tone-production. As the next step in our course, we proceed to examine successively the distinctions found in this material now occupying the foreground. Though itself a condition of technical action, its consideration had to be deferred. The relations are now reversed; technique is the condition, and our attention is absorbed in the meaning of the tones. The present standpoint has the advantage, over that of the first Section, that the presumption on which it is based appears justifiable, whereas the former one was assumed like an undischarged debt payable in the future. While, in the first Section, the glance strays beyond its nearest object to a scene yet unexplored, whose present mystery lends to the whole situation a feeling of suspense, it now rather looks down as from a height, and surveys the presumption in question with the superiority of higher powers now acquired.

The essence of the beautiful in music is the idea of form, expressed in tones, and, moreover, a certain sum of elements, which extend symbolically to phenomena poetically connected with life. Thus it falls to the share of pianoforte-playing to present as clearly as possible, within its sphere, the features resulting from both sides, and to this end these features must be examined in turn.

But before directly entering upon this task, an intermediate link must be considered, which holds a position between this and the technical part, and which, despite this position, possesses an importance no less than that of the mechanical preconditions, and permeates the entire idea of pianoforte-playing as an integral, indispensable element.

That is, before the material can be examined in detail, it must have been actually acquired; the intermediate link is, therefore, clearness and conscientiousness of execution. The whole technique must exhibit in all its parts the highest practicality, the most intimate connection between cause and effect; no movement must fail of its influence, in its characteristic symbolism, on the tone, and distinctness must characterize all elements even in the dizziest rapidity. After his physical training, the player must also be developed psychologically. He should educate his conscience to be a strict judge, so that

in everything which he performs he may be guilty of no neglect, not even the very least. What the conception demands,
must be executed; the ear must, so to speak, give its receipt
for each tone. The finger must neither give more, than the
intent of the will requires, nor fall short of this requirement.
The purpose of the technique must be at one with the tone
into the minutest detail.—Gymnastic exercises on dumb key-
boards are not forbidden hereby; for rendering stubborn joints
flexible they are often an indispensable resource, if only out
of consideration for the sensibility of the ear. Only the results
thus attained must be retested in connection with the living
tone, corrected, and revivified.

The first rule runs thus: In playing, no tone must ever
be dropped. Whatever notes are written must be made clearly
and distinctly audible. So long as this distinctness forms the
chief aim, it is clear that no other attempt will at present be
made to enliven or shade the tones, each atom standing on
an equality with the rest. This is a second and equally important point, commonly comprehended under the requirement
of Equality.

Equal power and precision, however, must animate all
tones not only objectively, but the feeling of confidence must
likewise extend subjectively to all elements. It was mentioned
before, that confidence is best developed by the rule of frequent repetitions, all of which must finally exhibit equal perfection. To this end rather a strong touch and powerful tone
must be evenly maintained, all parts participating equally.

Connected with these rules is the strict requirement, of a
thorough familiarity with all signs of notation. These latter
embrace no inconsiderable part of the science of the pianoforte, and are usually and wrongly taught incidentally. For
learning them in detail the student is referred to the first
chapter in Vol. 2 of Köhler's "Systematic Method for Pianoforte Playing and Music".

When the pupil does not understand a sign, he must immediately ask for information. A strict comparison of the

visible with the audible is a most stringent requirement, and carelessness on the pupil's part cannot be too watchfully suppressed. The latter's knowledge frequently does not even include the notes and rests in their entire range; and how many signs there are besides these. For the interpretation of earlier music familiarity with the so-called *agréments* is absolutely indispensable, and to this end we refer to the extracts from Türk's School in Chap. V of this work, or still better, to the above School itself. Though the æsthetic value of the embellishments is not to be estimated very highly, their historical interest gives them importance. Their at times excessively frequent employment, with its tinge of monotony and trivial affectation, can often not be brought into accord with the lofty spirit of the old musicians. It may be explainable in part from the incapacity of the ancient instruments to emphasize leading notes sufficiently. Of late most embellishments are written out in notes; only the turn, inverted mordent, and trill, retain their signs.

CHAPTER XIII.
On Rhythm in general, and the art of keeping Time.

The picture, which arises from a clear and conscientious performance of the characters on the sheet of music, is still unformed material. The technique alone is by no means capable of reproducing musical forms in an outline approximately corresponding to their inner meaning, unless guided by an essentially mental faculty. This essential addition, which could be approached only tentatively in the first Section, is Rhythm. The mere distinctness of tone-production affords, it is true, a material of sterling worth in its inmost essence; but the same entirely lacks form, and in this condition is incapable of presenting a work of art. That, which from the outset had to be presupposed, must now be discussed more in detail.

Rhythmical beauty springs from the idea of order, of law, of unity in diversity. There are two arts, in particular, whose rhythmic life-spring is rhythmic proportion:—Architecture, and Music. The former unfolds it in simultaneously visible dimensions: the latter in the succession of tones. Firmly crystallized and rigidly moulded, tectonic rhythm is hardly capable of psychic significance; whereas that of music is the better adapted for symbolizing emotional life, as this latter itself exists in the very flow of time. Further, architecture can display in its rhythmic disposition far less minute delicacy than music. From their size, its monumental works can be admired only from a distance, for a survey close at hand admits of no total impression; hence, a subtility of dimensional relations aiming to approach the refinement of musical proportions would fail of its effect. Musical feeling, on the contrary, allows a subdividing of the time-values up to the limits of sensual perception. This point finds detailed consideration in the author's work "On the Beautiful in Music", Chap. 3.

Among all instruments, the pianoforte is that which most fully develops musical rhythm. Even the organ, powerful and orchestral as may be the rhythm unfolded by its mighty effects in the sweep of most marvelous polyphony, ranks herein below the pianoforte; firstly as lacking the accent, and secondly because its serious character does not admit of the minuteness and rapidity of brilliancy. The pianoforte embraces the rhythm of organ literature in its own department, and exhibits, besides, velocity in its own characteristic perfection. It is distinguished from the orchestra, too, by the extent and persistency of the minutely divided rhythmical elements in the passage. The former is unable to display nimble rapidity, on account of the numerous parts to be considered, to the same degree as the pianoforte. In coloratura, brilliancy, and splendor of figuration the latter stands unrivalled, and pushes rhythm to its highest development in all forms, especially in the widespread reaches of the simpler successions of tones.

The pianoforte player should be fully capable of exhibiting, with the utmost distinctness, these varieties of rhythmic development under all conditions; while no musician can dispense with a complete grasp of the element of time, it devolves upon the pianist to be the finest practical rhythmist of all. This shows in the very fact that he must execute a whole, or perform his part in its multifarious relations to the voice or other instruments in such a way, as to assert its import as the leading and central feature governing the disposition of the whole. From the start, rhythm is inevitably one of the first requirements of the pianoforte pupil's training, already necessitated by the co-operation of the two hands. This rhythmical groundwork is a condition of all further development, and accompanies the player's entire career. So-called freedom of expression is truly effective only where the firm time-foundation is felt throughout; even under the hands of great masters it is used but in moderation, and with pupils must be energetically discountenanced as long as their feeling for strict time wavers.

The art of rightly displaying the rhythm of a musical work is concisely expressed in popular language by the words: *The player must keep time.* True, rhythm in the full sense of the term is more than mere keeping time — the art of accentuation belongs essentially within its scope, and it is expressed in the widest sense in the disposition of the whole, in the proportionality of the subdivisions. The latter depends upon the player's theoretical insight; timing and accentuation, however, belong to the practical execution.

The two last features, especially timing, form the elementary groundwork; though accentuation already reaches into a deeper spirituality of rhythm. With a knowledge of both, the highest manifestation of rhythm, as expressed in the entirety of the work, practically comes of itself.

As physical volume fills out space, so does tone fill out time. It is distinguished in dimension from visible bodies by the fact, that it is apprehended by our sense in its length, whereas they are seized by the eye in the three dimensions of length, breadth, and height.

The first rhythmic step is the dividing of a tone or time-period of any desired length into equal sections. The most practical form of exercise herein will be, for the pupil to mark the beginning of each division of time by beating time with the hand, and together with this to sing the tone. One may then proceed to a regular repetition of equal tone-values alternating with equally regular interruptions, thus familiarizing the pupil with the idea of the Rest.

The formation of equal time or tone-values is the first knowledge to be acquired. Later troubles in timing, and uncertainty in counting, often arise simply from an insufficient knowledge of this rudiment. One cannot sufficiently insist upon thoroughly drilling the pupil in all possible forms of the function in question. For instance, he may mark the entrance of otherwise silent time-values by tapping, or recite a series of numbers in exactly measured order. The teacher may then set him the task of counting only the first and last number audibly, and to follow in thought the rhythmic progression of the others. When necessary, the teacher will correct the count of the last by saying "too soon" or "too late". Such lessons can be given to several at once; mutual rivalry will enhance the attention to rhythmical precision. The equal rhythmical measurement can also be practiced in other forms, e. g. in marching, evolutions, and gymnastic movements of all descriptions.

The transition to *piano* would be effected by the repeated striking of the *same* tone, the exercise to be continued for some time within this limit, to fix the hearing intently on one element and prevent its distraction by the advent of new ones.

When the formation of equal values is assured, the next task will be to measure unequal proportions. The simplest are found in the relation of $1:2$, $1:3$, $1:4$. Such proportions arise either from the multiplication or the division of the original time-values.

The teacher should first take up the first case. The pupil

should mark, either by simply tapping or by touching a key, time-values of twice, thrice, or four times the length of the original ones. When able to perform this, he may be taught the kinds of notes which most simply express these proportions. If the quarter-note is taken as the unit of measure, the longer values will be expressed by the half, three-quarter (𝅗𝅥.), and whole notes. The idea of the Measure as the sum of several units of measure, (measure-notes), must also be explained, together with the various kinds of rests. Then let the pupil familiarize himself with rhythmical forms like the following:

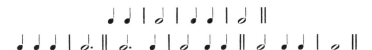

Conversely, this task is now to be supplemented by division. The unit of measure originally adopted is to be halved; thus the apprehension will now be sharpened by comparing a double with a single degree of rapidity, as before by comparing a half with the original whole degree of rapidity. Then proceed to the threefold, fourfold degree, etc. Taking the quarter-note as unit of measure, the knowledge of the signs of notation would now have to include eighths, triplet eighths, and sixteenths. The measure-notes, in all rhythmical exercises of this kind, are of course to be marked by counting aloud. The table of exercises would follow the above in form, but practice should be as much more diversified, as the division of the original time-values is more difficult than their multiplication. More especially, let the various degrees of rapidity be intermingled, somewhat as in the following example:

Experience has taught often enough, that, when one hand plays triplets while the other plays simple notes of the same denomination, the difficulty does not lie solely in the simul-

15

taneity of these rhythms. It is rather the transition from the
eighth-note rhythm to the triplets, and *vice versâ*, that gives
the pupil trouble. It often happens, that one who readily
learns Mendelssohn's Song without Words No. 20, cannot get
the 7th measure of Chopin's $C\sharp$-minor Polonaise into his
fingers. Exercises like those noted above will therefore prevent
many subsequent difficulties. In all cases the pupil must
count aloud.

A new point now claims attention. Until now it has been
assumed, that time was beaten to one and the same tone.
This method will naturally show the best results where the
uncertainty in time is considerable, or the pupil began at the
beginning. In most other cases it may be taken for granted
that the teacher will have permitted combinations with other
tones here and there.—For the methodical course in its strictest
sense the present is, however, the proper place to supplement
the foregoing by the addition of several tones. An exact
method admits of no skips, and attention must therefore be
called to the fact, that here a new chapter introduces us to
the element of melody and to the really musical phrase. This
step is of course an essential one.

Its connection with the foregoing may be effected by
filling out the metrical examples in the latter, which were
devised partly by the teacher and partly by the pupil, with
melodious ideas instead of one and the same tone.

From this point the course of the method need be only
briefly indicated.

As soon as the former metrical examples embrace a
greater number of tones, the next step forward will be the
co-operation of the hands in playing, in the divers relations
now arising. Hitherto each hand played first alone, and then
in octaves with the other. Now the simplest proportions will
be combined to compound rhythms of gradually increasing
complexity. For the practical development of the method a
long series of examples must be devised, of which we will
give two:

The first might form the beginning, the second be found among the last.

Now, for the first time, the *entire* classification of *all* the notes and rests, of the various kinds of measure (time), is to be taught in a new chapter. This is a subject which, however easy it may seem to a good arithmetician, often gives pianoforte pupils much difficulty, particularly when their arithmetical training has been insufficiently attended to, as is frequently the case with children.—Under such circumstances, arithmetic lessons should be taken between the music lessons, which plan might be beneficial to many an advanced pupil. For it is not only necessary to be able to form fluently the fractions arising from simple halving up to 1/128, but to determine quickly the proportionate value of any given note or rest to any other. To this end the pupil should himself prepare a series of tables, to be arranged and kept in a separate cover. The first will embrace an exact view of the notes resulting from halving up to 1/128; the second a similar view of the rests; the third, based on tripartition, all forms of triplets, from the whole note up to the 1/128; the fourth, a view of all note-values arising from the addition of a dot to the notes hitherto learned; the fifth, a similar view of the notes with two dots. The two last-named tables might be extended under certain conditions to four, should the pupil have special difficulty with the division into triplets having one or two dots. But it is by no means enough, to know fluently by heart each single

15*

table described above, and the mutual proportions of its
elements; a new requirement demands, that the elements of
each table should also be readily and accurately mastered in
their relations to those of each other table. A question like
the following: "How does the velocity of an eighth-note with
two dots compare with that of triplets of sixteenth-notes?"
might give many a good arithmetician pause for a few seconds.
But the pupil should be perfectly familiar with such proportions,
and it is more practical to gain such familiarity connectedly
and thoroughly in special arithmetic lessons, than to touch
upon the topic incidentally in the music lessons.

I must now call attention to a particular kind of difficulty
in timing. It includes that great number of passages in which
each hand, although dividing the measure-note into parts of
equal length, has a rate of speed differing from that of the
other, so that in the parallel passages simultaneity of touch
occurs only at the entrance of the measure-note itself. The
case most frequently occurring is, that one hand divides the
measure-note into two parts, and the other into three. Where
the tempo is slow enough to emphasize smaller time-values
than the measure-note by counting, this style of playing is
quickly learned. E. g. when triplet eighth-notes run parallel
with simple eighths, one would count three for each quarter-
note; the second simple eighth-note then comes in between 2
and 3 in the same manner as, say, a fourth triplet sixteenth-
note. But whenever the tempo is taken faster, as is required
in nearly all such passages, this manner of counting is no
longer practicable. For pupils lacking a fine sense of time a
line is here drawn, which they can overstep only with extreme
exertion. In all other passages the distinction between a fast
and slow execution is one of degree; here it is specific. In
rapid tempo no one stops to think of an accurate "striking
between" like that above mentioned. The sole point to be considered is, that each hand shall accurately feel its own degree
of rapidity; a very slow study of rapid passages of the kind
in question is therefore the most primitive means of attaining

the end proposed. It often happens, that pupils readily apprehend such figures as long as three can be counted to each quarter; but when the limit of counting in this manner is reached, rhythms like the following begin:

In most cases I have found it most practical to let the two hands practice separately until a positive feeling for the degree of rapidity required of each is developed, and while practicing always to accent energetically each measure-note. These accents will keep the hands together when both are playing at once. If one succeeds in awakening in each hand an unerring and confident feeling for its degree of rapidity, everything is gained; but should one not succeed, the counting of the minutest note-values to be taken into consideration will hardly avail to break down the natural barrier.

When the hands have figures in three und four notes respectively, e. g. in Chopin's Fantaisie-Impromptu, the counting of smaller notes than the quarter becomes utterly useless. For these a correct execution is attained by sharp accentuation, and by the (not enough to be emphasized) positive feeling for the requisite degree of rapidity. The same holds good of all similar figurations,—for instance, when one hand has 5 notes to 7 in the other.

Here we again repeat, that training to steadiness in time is a matter to be continually carried on from the very outset up to the highest acquirements of pianoforte-playing, and if properly comprehended has by no means to occupy the pupil's interest in such exclusiveness as a separate task. When so comprehended, only portions of the theory will here and there require attention. But, where the feeling for time appears unsteady, this theory will have to be taken up by itself in the lessons, in its full extent, together with practical examples; then it may be expected that even the most sluggish apprehension will be roused to some perception of rhythm, though the fact should not be concealed, that the task of training such minds is one of the least profitable. That feeling, which pulses in the breast like an invisible wheelwork, is an advantage of which but few are possessed, and for whose attainment the psychic powers are very variously organized. Some are impressionable for everything within the scope of rhythm, observing and learning by their own instinct. Others must exert themselves to measure off two equal time-values, and often fail despite most earnest endeavors. Such take note of nothing by free instinct, and it is the teacher's most toilsome task, to call into activity during the scattered lessons that faculty whose perfection requires so great individual exercise. Unhappily, the further abilities of such pupils are often in no much better condition, and unintelligent or indigent parents would hardly make up their minds to expend three times as much for music lessons as custom prescribes; though in this case the expectation of awakening the feeling for rhythm would be proportionately greater.

At the close of this chapter let me once more emphasize the old saying: "Time is the soul of music", and characterize all pianoforte playing as a misconception of its artistic intention, in which this most important of all elements is not most firmly grounded.

Finally we should not neglect to mention, that counting aloud, aside from its influence on the time, also brings other technical and psychical advantages. With pupils experience proves, that everything practiced to loud counting sounds evener, stronger, more finished, and that the player clearly obtains a more confident command over his piece than without such counting.—His powers are stirred to intenser exertion, and if the loud counting ceases in the last stage of development, the technical sense will feel confidence even when confronted by the most difficult tasks, in consequence of the resulting ease and freedom. This comes from the methodical principle so often applied, that every task seems easy when led up to by increased and exaggerated requirements. The dividing of the attention by two—despite all unity—so sharply contrasted tendencies, gives to the technical sense a firm *point d'appui*, a trellice, as it were, for the support of the winding threads of tone.—Spoken rhythms are more material than imagined ones, but nothing is so desired by the inner consciousness, particularly in the midst of so vague an element, as a hold on something external.—

CHAPTER XIV.

On Accentuation.

The player who fulfils the requirements laid down in the foregoing, adds to definiteness and nicety of touch and tone, the elements earlier spoken of, that characteristic which lends *form* to the material. The work of art which is to arise under his fingers obtained its material in technique, and its form in time; it now needs the finer strokes, which shall endow its visage with *expression*.

The analysis to which the art-work has been subjected by no means exhausts the ideal fulness which it is capable of assuming.—The imagination steeps its work with ever fresh ideas, until the material has absorbed to the full that phase of life for which it was organized. It must display not merely its material *(sensuous)* beauty, but bear the soul beyond into a loftier, more ideal region. *Diversity* in unity is the life, the soul of the work.

Mere time-keeping amidst the motley whirl of the note-values is simply an unfolding of the musical life in numbers, in one aspect of its quantitative characteristics. The same likewise pulses in its power, in dynamic relations; these are the complement of the former. Their meaning has, however, a more ideal nature; it passes over from the purely quantitative into the qualitative.

The dynamic assertion of rhythm lies in the accent. Mere numerical proportions are too monotonous. — As the barren silence of time was before interrupted and bounded by tones, and thereafter the monotony of equal measure-notes gave way to sections and divisions amid the maze of tones, the tone-weft even in this condition still seems too uniform. Only during a few moments is the hearing arrested by the charms of the tones and their arrangement; it soon relaxes, as the thinking powers are not enough engaged.

It is the aim of the accent, to give the ear a clew to the disposition of the tone-forms and their kinship with the uttered meaning; and furthermore, to exhibit clearly the simplest rhythmical divisions mentioned before. As these latter were previously given, they manifested themselves only to abstract reflection, or to the eye by bars on the sheet of music. If they are to be perceived by the actual musical faculty, they must be emphasized by a stronger stress on single notes; and this is the function of the accent.

This function devolving on the accent therefore splits into two distinct ones. The one last named, which has clearly to exhibit to the ear the simple rhythmical divisions, is the concern of the so-called metrical or mensural accent. The other, to be considered later, which articulates the tone-weft after the analogy of oratorical forms, devolves upon the declamatory accent.

The metrical accent strikes most sharply on the first note of each measure, as the thesis of the uniform rhythm upon which the whole is based naturally calls for the clearest presentation. In a measure consisting of but two half-notes, a preponderance of tone-power, however slight it may be, will therefore fall on the first. In simple ternary measure the first note is likewise accented, the other two being unaccented.

When many notes occur in a measure, sub-accents arise. These are not so strong as those described above, and fall on the subdivisions which naturally result from the arithmetical constitution of the measure. Thus sub-accents are found in $^4/_4$ time in the middle of the measure, on the third quarter; in $^6/_8$ time on the fourth eighth-note; in $^9/_8$ time on the fourth and seventh eighth-notes; in $^{12}/_8$ time on the fourth, seventh, and tenth eighth-notes. The more notes a measure is divided into, the more is felt the necessity of multiplying the sub-accents, which latter also take rank according to their stronger or weaker accentuation. Thus, in a $^4/_4$ measure divided into sixteenths, an accent will fall on the first note of each group of four. But the strongest accent falls on the first quarter, the next strongest on the third, because the former marks the beginning of the measure, the latter the middle. The second and fourth take weaker accents. If a distinction be drawn between these, the accent of the second quarter will be found stronger than that of the fourth. In $^6/_8$ time, with rapid and crowded successions of notes, there will fall, to speak exactly, an accent on each eighth-note, the strongest on the first and fourth. In $^9/_8$ and $^{12}/_8$ time similar conditions will produce the same result.

This kind of accentuation is logical and natural. Concerning its observance in practice only one remark is to be added. In general, the distinct audibleness of each accent must be insisted upon. The player often feels the accent in his fingers, while the hearer does not perceive it; in such a case the strength of the fingers must be more energetically exerted. On the other hand it should not be forgotten, that the distinctions accessible to the theorizing intellect in the shading of the sub-accents are at first, in practice as well, the normal requirement, and must, especially in slow practice, be observed and executed in sharp contrast. But the player must not go too far in this, above all when the piece attains fluency and accelerated momentum; he should particularly guard against the idea, that only a very sharp and apparent emphasis fulfils the end of accentuation. While, as above, too gentle accentuation is to be condemned, neither must the effect of the rhythmic accent be sought in glaring colors. It rather lies in the finest sensibility of the finger-tip, often more in the *idea* of sensation than in the material expression.

The accentuation has only here and there a claim to vividly emphatic presentation. In general it should no more occupy the foreground than the scansion of the metre in declaiming a poem. This holds good, primarily, of the metrical accent. The declamatory accent has another justification. Exceptions are found, however, in the former case. Even an outspoken metrical rhythm is at times in place, this depending entirely on the character of the piece; not only strains which accompany the dance require a strong and telling accentuation; the grand, the heroic, the fiery, the majestic, are founded essentially upon the same. But the *purely* beautiful, as the general manifestation of music and of all other arts, requires for the metrical accent that measure of reserve which must always accompany the material expression where other and higher characteristics come in question.

In following the gradations of the accentuation, therefore, the finger will need in equal measure both its most telling power and exquisite sensibility of touch, the overstress being often marked only by the slightest shade. Sometimes the player will have rather to think and feel the accent, leaving its expression in fact to the mysterious sympathy of the finger for the key, that his thought may be uttered with the utmost delicacy. The tone is the finest of sensible materials, and a trained ear apprehends its subtlest gradations.

With regard to the practical employment of the metrical accent the following is to be said.

In few compositions is the accent to be equably observed from beginning to end; in most cases unaccented passages are interspersed, for uniformity of accent, as of tone, is apt to grow tiresome and monotonous. There are pieces, it is true, whose contents call for an almost level uniformity of accent—

in which a certain sturdy strength and gaiety of mood find expression within narrow limits. To begin with, we find studies in which a purely technical aim is bound up with the accent. To these may be added, further, the great number of *characteristic* Études, Preludes, and short pieces such as Cramer, Clementi, and others have written. A part of the same, although mainly intended for mechanical training, combine therewith the advantage of a concise, one might say epigrammatic, ideal meaning. In these the accent is kept up from beginning to end with regularity, like the swing of a pendulum, and attains its full effect according as it shades the power of its tone in its position as main or sub-accent. This, to be sure, accompanies the general variations in the tone-power; on this head more will be given below.—The first Étude by Cramer, the second in Clementi's Gradus, and the *C*-minor Prelude by Bach in part I of the "Well-tempered Clavichord", are striking examples of regular, uninterrupted accentuation, which æsthetically as well as technically forms part of the rendering.

Another class of compositions has its essence in the very preponderance of metrical rhythm, the latter attracting all other factors, however ideal their nature, into the pulsing power of uniform metre. I mean the dance. In its character as a composition this is quite similar to the foregoing species. It either cultivates exclusively the external end, though this does not apply to the technique of the fingers, but to that of the feet; or it is prevailingly a lyrical or an ingenious, epigrammatic tone-picture, whose point of departure is the material subject, which it inspires with the spirit of a poetic mood (Chopin). But its fundamental form is still evenness of rhythm, which remains recognizable beneath the most changeful dress. In the dances of the first kind the bass, in particular, marks the entrance of each new measure by a more or less powerful accent. This peculiarity alone often lends to the composition its ideal charm, when its intention is a purely external one. The strength of the accents varies here, too, yet despite this variation they retain a certain regularity, which is recurrent.—A principal rule gives to the metrical accents, where they *begin* or *end* sections, their greatest weight; thus within these groups there prevails even among the main accents a law similar to that governing the relation between main and sub-accent within one measure. This obtains even in compositions of the loftiest description.

A tasteful reading will endow even those dances, whose intention is purely external, with variety in the accentuation; we give one of the best known Galops as an example:

The accentuation may follow with equal propriety either of the 3 series *a*, *b*, or *c*. Series *a* is the simplest; series *b* throws the periods into stronger relief; series *c* is the most animated, as causing most interruption to the general uniformity. At the repeats the player can always choose a different series; at the close of the first double period of 16 measures the main accent falls on the second quarter:

In such dances the accents of the soprano and bass usually correspond, and are also modified alike. But in waltz music many exceptions are found, the melodious style of the better authors, like Strauss, Lanner, and Gungl, often admitting of a declamatory delicacy of accentuation.

When the dance more closely follows the pianoforte style than the orchestral, and a melody (as in Chopin's D♭-major Waltz Op. 64) pearls on in the exquisite undulations of the pianoforte run, minute fineness of accentuation will be chiefly confined to the highest part, the basses alone continuing to mark the dance-movement; *occasionally* the robuster sensuousness breaks out in an isolated *fortissimo* accent, e. g. at the repetition of the first part of the above-named waltz after the trills, but is instantly dissipated in the inspiration of the tenderer grace which permeates the whole. Similar touches will be found in all more ideal pianoforte compositions of this kind. Diversity within the general unity is the cardinal rule of art, and no art is so dependent upon this law as Music. Just because it lacks definite objectivity, the general rules of art require the stricter observance.

Thus even in the metrical accents the principle of diversity, for which the above example was offered as a suggestion, must be carried out with careful calculation. The player should weigh all cases with serious reflection, and lend his reading elaborate variety even in the simple metrical accents.

In common parlance, those divisions of the measure on which the accents spoken of above are to fall are termed *strong* beats, the unaccented divisions *weak* beats. For the original and natural idea gives to those notes which mark the beginning, middle, or any main division of the measure, increased weight and consequently the accent; these are the strong beats. They have the significance of a core, or point of departure, to which the weaker is linked as an offshoot. For in itself a thing is nothing; it requires comparison with others to bring out its own qualities.—Now the case may occur, that the order of the accents is reversed, the weak beats being accented, the strong ones unaccented. This species of accentuation might be styled *negative,* in contrast to the *positive* kind previously treated of.

This species of accentuation is æsthetically quite justifiable. The soul of animation is not the ideally unchangeable normal and regular. It is rather characterized by the subdividing of the norm into the irregularity of the individual, its direct contradiction. The abnormal is true life. Neither the consonance, nor the geometrical ideal, nor the proportionality of the human frame as exhibited in its perpendicular front, is true beauty; they contain only the embryo. All these ideas must diverge into the dissonance of the most intricate developments of form. The unity manifested in all diversity is the more effective, the more its inner meaning is developed.

Thus the normal rhythm, too, is torn asunder, wrought into contrasts and irregularities, its consonant relations turned into dissonances. This is the sense of the negative accent.

The principle of change and diversity is so far-reaching, that hardly a composition can be found having no such irregular or negative accents. The simple Galop, given above as an example, closed with one in the sixteenth measure. And for the practical execution the rule may even be laid down, that greater stress should be laid on the negative than on the positive metrical accents. The latter often appear in themselves sufficiently marked by the natural place which they occupy in the measure. Once introduced by the single or double accentuation of a few measures, their continued flow makes

itself felt in the same sense even without special emphasis.—
But the negative accents, not being apprehended as a matter
of course, require double emphasis.

If we seek to draw distinctions between the various kinds
of accents enumerated, three cases of individual character may
be adduced.

(1) First of all, an isolated tone may stand out amid the
flow of ideas, without being distinguished by peculiar length;
here it is immaterial, whether it interrupts the regularity in
the sense of mere metrical variety, or of declamation, which
will be treated of further on. The composer indicates such
tones by the familiar accent-mark $>$, or *sf*, or *sfz*. A pertinent example is found in the coda of the andante theme, in
the middle movement of Beethoven's Sonata in *G*-major Op. 14,
where the accentuation is shifted throughout to the even (i. e.
the weak) beats. This irregularity is explicable from the rhythmical monotony maintained in the whole course of the theme.

Similar cases are found in the following passages:

Beethoven
Adagio Op. 22.

Beethoven
2nd. Movem. Op. 14.
E-major Sonata.

Beethoven
Adagio Op. 53.

Clementi
Gradus ad Parnassum
I. No. 2.

To this case may be added all those instances, in which a slur starting from the weak beat binds together two notes of different pitch, the second of which is not longer than the first.—According to a well-known rule, the first slurred note takes a comparatively strong accent in this case, while the second is lifted with the gentlest finger-tip staccato.

The classic composers in general possessed the art of introducing an oft-recurring element of delicacy and grace, by means of this style of binding tones, into passage-like or melodious parts. Indeed, the dancing motion of such delicate tone-elements depicts a most gracefully evasive coquetry; even at the present day the interpreter of the earlier classics is free to imagine these slurs in appropriate places, in the sense of the conception just noted, although not indicated by the composer, and to shape his rendering accordingly. For instance, the coda of the first Bagatelle by Beethoven, Op. 33, may be executed with this nuance, and the passage in question will thus fully correspond to the charmingly naïve character, so attractive in its pure innocence, of the entire composition.

The answering bass passage then following must naturally, for the sake of contrast and variety, be executed differently, i. e. with a firm legato.

Now, where such slurs commence on weak beats, the piquancy of the resulting rhythm is further enhanced. Examples of this accentuation are probably quite as numerous as the regular ones just named. The player must take care, amidst the double meaning of such rhythms, to keep the proper regularity of the same continually in mind, and to recall it to the hearer as well in the right place. At times the slightest hint is enough; in other cases a sharper manifestation is needed. This depends on the spirit of the composition. Schumann's works often bear, in their interlocked rhythms, a preponderant part of their poetical essence. Impetuous forces urge the emotion to effusions apparently quite devoid of form; yet here and there a fine touch of the finger must remind the hearer of the unity of regularity. In pianoforte style, at least, the classics held the normal rhythmic thread somewhat better in hand, and in this point the performer need not keep his mind at such feverish tension. Regularity usually quite naturally recurs after irregularity.

One of the finest passages is found in Beethoven's Adagio, in the Pianoforte Concerto Op. 15, wherein the slur with its negative accent is repeated through six measures:

Extremely delicate and piquant is the shading given to the otherwise so sturdy Prelude in *C* by Bach (Selection from Bach's Compositions by Marx, No. I), which the Editor marks as follows:

The passage in Chopin's Nocturne Op. 9, No. 2, is familiar:

Refinement in the execution usually lies in delicacy of accentuation and the still more delicate touch of the second

16

note, which should in general be thrown off by retracting the finger-tip, rather than struck. To what fine individualization of the finger-tip the player must have attained in order to render such passages rightly, cannot be judged of from a purely mechanical standpoint; to inspire the finger with the nuance of touch requisite therefor, an understanding in the widest sense is needed of the graceful and (more especially in rhythm) multiform spirit of the classics.

Of course, the slur just described does not exclude a robust accentuation; by way of example we will only recall passages in the first part of Beethoven's *D*-minor Sonata.

Particularly in polyphonic movements, too, the dramatic relation of the parts is kept in living tension by such nuances, and herein the diversity of rhythm attains its climax.

(2) We proceed to the second class of negative accents. — The first stated, that they *first of all* affect isolated tones amid the flow of equal notes; to this the second adds, that the accented tones may be specially prominent among a series of otherwise equal elements by their *length,* in which case they would take a doubly strong accent. This is the familiar rule of Syncopation, expressed briefly as follows: "That syncopations are long notes on weak beats, and must be sharply accented." The idea of *length* is relative. It depends upon the adjoining notes; an eighth-note will be called long among sixteenths, whereas it is short among quarters. — Under this term are also included such notes as are prolonged, among others equally long, by binding to one of like pitch — a case which occurs most frequently through binding over the end of one measure to the beginning of that following. E. g.

Beethoven, E-minor Sonata Op. 90.

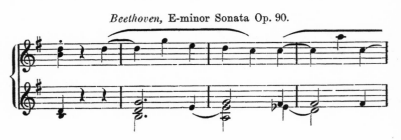

The rule for the accentuation of syncopes is, to be sure, of nearly universally binding significance, but is subject to exceptions where higher laws of art take precedence. The principle of alternation (variety) in purely sensuous rhythm bestowed the accent on the syncopations. But where the latter become so frequent that their consistent accentuation would grow monotonous, the syncopations themselves must give up the accent. The latter must likewise often be reduced to a minimum in soft, unobtrusive passages. — The two cases are combined in Beethoven's Sonata in *G*, Op. 14, where the syncopes in themselves are to be lightly accented, and at their successive repetition through six measures should finally be marked no more than the other notes.

From the fourteenth measure on:

(Notice particularly, that the syncopes exhibit in this case the resolutions of dissonances, and at the same time the end-tones of the short motives of which the phrase is constructed.)

The following passage, from the Adagio of the *D*-minor Sonata, demands appropriate accentuation on account of the urgent declamation:

(3) A special case in irregular accentuation occurs, where it is carried out through entire compositions. True, this is a merely quantitative, rather than an essential distinction as compared with the other two cases, but will be stated separately for the sake of exactness. Until now, the rhythmic form in question occurred only in transient passages, and served by contrast as a foil to the impression of the regular accent. But the case may occur, that a whole part of a composition adopts syncopation (or negative accentuation), to present a contrast to other parts; or even that entire compositions take their character from the same. Of the former case there is a fine example in the Trio (second movement) of Beethoven's *C*-minor Sonata, Op. 27; the latter is found in the Mazurka.

In this dance, elevated by Chopin from its sensuous original into the most exquisitely ethereal poetry, the third quarter-note, or sometimes the second, takes the principal accent. The rhythm, however, discovers a dual aspect, for the normal accent, too, at times rises triumphant over its rival. In fact, throughout this irregular accentuation, the normal groundwork is assumed in the background and felt in advance. On such a basis a second rhythmical idea is built up, which enters on the third quarter and, running parallel to the first, maintains the sense in eager tension by its conflict with the latter. It charms by its very abnormity. Strictly speaking, therefore, we cannot say that the irregular accentuation obtains throughout; on the one hand it shows inconsistency in falling on the second quarter as well; on the other, it is at times ousted by the regular accent. This may be shown in the following example from Chopin:

Chopin, Op. 7.

The observations on the negative accent in the Mazurka are, further, of general application. The strongest accentuation of weak beats, whether isolated, frequent, or occurring throughout a movement, cannot neutralize the positive accent.

From the accents previously under discussion we must pass to that species of accentuation which is usually relegated to the so-called loftier style. It is hard to find an exact term for the same, as neither the word "declamatory" hitherto employed, nor the terms proposed by other theoreticians, precisely cover the conception in question. Johanna Kinkel ("Letters on Pianoforte Teaching") distinguishes between the grammatical and oratorical accents. These terms are unsuitable, because the end of the grammatical does not by any means coincide with the beginning of the oratorical, and this latter is not at all something independent of the grammatical. Köhler contrasts the grammatical and æsthetical accents. He calls the former those native to and constant in the measure—purely legitimate; the latter he considers as a free product of imagination, founded in the sense of beauty. But this view can likewise not be maintained. Æsthetically, the pure metrical or grammatical accent is certainly not inferior to the other; it too is born of imagination. Neither can it well be denied, that the higher, so-called æsthetical accent, is also founded on unchangeable natural laws, provided that the laws of spoken sounds and human utterance be not regarded as something apart.

A strict precision of terminology will therefore be dispensed with here. The chief concern of the method is the presentation of the practical relations; whether the second species be called the higher, the oratorical, or the declamatory accent, its relation to the first kind already considered is no other, than that stated for the transition of the technique to interpretation. The passage of the former into the latter is so imperceptible, that the boundary is not noticed. The metrical accent is the elementary one, and furnishes the first groundwork, as did the technique before; the other embraces a wider field, yet not only silently presupposes the former, but must allow a part of its own conception to find exclusive realization in the same.

The first accent exhibited the *material* foundation of the composition; the second must aid in presenting its *total character*. But as the latter, for the most part, must let the pure sensuousness of the tone-material operate in its specific characteristics, and is by no means *rich* in inner meaning, whose features admit of a clear objective explanations in set terms, the first accent, elementary as it may be, belongs essentially to the accents of performance or declamation; — precisely the same relation as between technique and rendering.

Another classification might contrast the accent of the *cantilena* with that of the passages, distinguishing between two varieties thus more sharply separated. It might assign the metrical accent by preference to the rapid and fluent element, the other to the singing, sustained one. But such a distinction is inadequate; for even in the passages the metrical accent alone is *not* sufficient in the sense of the higher rendering, and the execution of the *cantilena* can by no means be effected without the latter.

The regular metrical accents divided the musical structure into its smallest members; it applied the latter as a measure to the long-reaching contours of the same, that its dimensions might be more readily grasped. — The repetition of this indispensable manifestation of life grows tiresome, however the principle of variety may be followed. True, the receptive mind has already seized, in the chaos of tones, a series of enlightening activities; yet, however each may in turn endow for the moment the monotony of that preceding with a more charmful expression, lasting satisfaction is not attained. The receptivity of the material is not exhausted, and the thinking mind craves greater wealth of ideas.

The regular repetition of the metrical accents still retains too much of the abstract character which geometrical or arithmetical ideals possess. These accents differ but little from the uniformity of the measure by bars, which is one of the elementary characteristics.—

As remarked above, the impression of such elementary forces forms at times one of the most potent agencies of the rendering, and their indispensability is unquestionable. . But this impression or effect must be led up to through the motley variety of special effects, the multiform abundance of individual manifestations of life. In such contrast the effect of simple regularity is set in its proper light. Now, in general, and aside from this connection, the regular accents are only the threads of that canvass, upon which are depicted forms of quite other individuality, and of very different dimensions. They merely bound, with delicate lines, the entire space wherein the actual figures are to be exhibited; they only set the measure of the steps, which are thereafter to be performed by real, living personages.

The abstract accent-forms are filled by the musical ideas in the same way as the verse-rhythms by the periods of the sentence. But this similarity is paired with a distinction. A poetical work of art depends neither on versification nor on the symmetry of its periods in the same degree as music. The less an art can lay claim to absolute clearness in the presentation of a positive meaning, the more does it depend on form. If, even in an entire composition, the emotional phase whence it sprang attains in but the rarest cases to singleness of meaning, one cannot possibly await from a single motive the same definite expression, as from a word.

Logical laws determine the development of a train of thought. A succession of emotions lacks this inner necessity. Even the demand for unity of mood cannot be admitted to have full and unrestricted justification. Hence the limitless freedom which the declamation of the interpreting artist enjoys in such musical works as, renouncing the laws of form, give themselves up to the undefined surges of emotion.—I call to mind Bach's Chromatic Fantasia.—In one feature of expression, however, music has the advantage of speech; namely, polyphony, which not seldom lends greater stability to the mood, even in cases where only one principal part and its accompaniment are given.

Among all the resources for making clear the meaning which in part lies in the composition, and in part is added by the player, none is so important as the accent in its universal significance, both metrical and oratorical.

Musical ideas are divided into the two oft-mentioned classes of the instrumental and vocal, or the styles of the passage and the *cantilena*. To these may be added a third intermediate element, which mingles both forms, i. e. the *cantilena* with interwoven passages, or conversely passages having vocal (melodious) touches; one might also say, singing passages, or conversely passages whose sole effect does not lie in figuration, but in which a nucleus of melody predominates.— This third element therefore has, strictly speaking, two subdivisions, according as vocality predominates and is mingled with an instrumental element, or *vice versâ.*—As final condition we find the simultaneous combination of these features in parts progressing together.—We take up the cases in turn.

(1) The accentuation of the passage is controlled by a higher law than mere metre. The latter, though remaining in force, is often subordinate to that accent which results from the figurate constitution of the passage. Most passage-forms, especially those from earlier periods, are founded on one or more motives, and it is consequently the function of the accent clearly to exhibit their plastic form. The minutest motives (or none at all) are found in scales, and similarly in harmonic passages progressing straight forward. Such figures have consequently no accent, unless their length should render a purely metrical accentuation desirable. At most, the tones forming the beginning and end might be marked. If such passages are a commingling of scales and arpeggios, ascending and descending, the beginnings of the sections may also be marked, but here, too, the rhythm is the prime consideration.

Examples:

In the third movement of Beethoven's Sonata in *E*, Op. 14, the little run in the right hand, wherever and in whatever form it may occur, takes the accent only on the first and last tones:

This passage resembles a short straight line; the two accents given mark the boundaries of its plastic form. This line in certain places forms an angle with another, and their point of meeting is likewise to be marked:

If the passage, on the contrary, is constructed of definite motives, the first question is, whether they correspond to the metre or not. When the first tones of the motive fall on comparatively strong beats, the accentuation exactly follows the concatenations of the passage. Thus the first Étude by Cramer would require throughout the first four measures an accent on each quarter; in the two following, an accent on 1 and 2 would suffice; from then on, however, each quarter must again be marked.

In the first Solo in Mozart's *D*-minor Concerto, the passage

also requires four accents in each measure; whereas that following later

needs only two accents.

On the other hand, when the metre contrasts with the division of the motive, the latter takes an accent only in the rarest cases. In the first movement of his *D*-minor Trio, Mendelssohn directs this style of execution in the following passage:

Weber does the same toward the end of the "Concertstück":

Similar passages must in general be content with the regular metrical accent. Much depends upon the relation of the passage to the entire organism of the piece. The excursive cadenzas of the Liszt school naturally allow many licences in this direction.

Another feature of moment for the phrasing of the passage resides in the pitch. The accentuation of the following, from the *D*-minor Sonata by Beethoven,

results from the fact, that the relatively highest or lowest tones most clearly exhibit the plasticity of the passage to the ear.

For a similar reason the finale-theme of the Appassionata requires the following execution:

With broken octaves, the figuration lies in the melody which the leading finger carries out, and the accent is determined accordingly; e. g. in the first movement of Beethoven's Op. 22:

In these questions of accent, the general tempo must be carefully considered. Where it is not rapid, only the metrical accents need be observed under certain conditions. The player, in settling the accentuation of the passages, must carefully heed this circumstance.

The accent renders the passage brilliant; it animates the flowing current of tone by its pulsations, which break out like impulses of an inspired will from amid the mysterious intertwining of inexplicable powers. Its employment is most pertinent where the passages, in their flying intricacy, have the upper hand and the leading part; e. g. Chopin's C-minor Étude Op. 10, No. 12, admits, together with sharp metrical accents, of yet sharper figurative ones, which for instance on page 2, where the left hand leaps from below to a higher tone — may fall with full weight on this latter, although it is the second note in the measure. Such irregularities in accentual rhythm enhance here, as everywhere else, the animation of the work;

they are always fully justified, where passion and fire find
expression, and this will usually be the case where the leading
part lies in the passage and a rapid tempo obtains. The accentual dissonance will appear somewhat milder when the
passage forms the foundation of a melodious leading part, as
in countless modern compositions; though here, too, the conception will be only strengthened if, together with a soulful
interpretation of the melody, the performer searches out, or
even invents, independent and vivid touches in the accompaniment.

The accent may be quite omitted where the character of
the piece or passage calls for tranquility; e. g. in the runs
after the short movement in $E\flat$-minor, in the first Bagatelle
by Beethoven, which lead back into the theme; or in many
other adagios, in which the passage-figures accomodate their
modest claims to the spirit of the whole. Thus the last variation in the middle movement of the F-minor Sonata Op. 57,
is best entirely without accent, only here and there with the
slightest hint at accentuation, in order that the exhaustion and
resignation may find expression — this conception having the
most justification of all between two movements of such tremendous impetus. Again, a lack of accentuation is characteristic
of a great part of the semi-improvised *pianissimo* passages of
the Liszt school, their effect lying, not in the motive-work, but
in the total impression of the whispering tone.

The force of the accentuation always stands in a natural
relation to the general power of touch and tone; an exception
to this rule could be instanced only in very peculiar cases.
In gentle playing the accent is soft, in loud playing strong;
and in the *crescendo* and *diminuendo* it supports the general
tone-effect by following the same.

The significance of the conception as a whole will finally
decide, how far the accentual life requires individual presentation. An Étude by Czerny, or a Fantasia by Thalberg, will
be content with simple regular accents. The refined rhyth-
mists Chopin and Schumann will elaborate the nuances of the

same to a very high degree of artistic taste; and Beethoven, wherever musical life in its most ideal and — despite its melancholy isolation — most healthy power is involved, will exhibit the loveliest, most opulent, and *truest* meaning of the accent.

(2) To the passage the *cantilena* is diametrically opposed, and its accentuation is determined by similar laws. The player must conceive the melody as a connected, orderly chain of tones, symbolically imitative of the spoken phrase, and hold fast to this, both the originally first and the final impression. Foremostly, therefore, familiarity must be gained with the main features of this form (the melody), and the *aims* of the progressions issuing from the prevailingly subordinate tone-elements must be examined.—But attention must also be paid to the prevailing degree of warmth of the mood expressed by a melody in itself, or more particularly in its position as connected with a work. The singing touch, as taught in the earlier chapters, is the first precondition, and from among its numerous degrees of power and expression the suitable form is to be chosen. Thus in many cases the entire coloring of the melody will require from the outset a kind of accentuation, which makes itself felt, in contrast to the lighter touch of the passage, as an accent. This applies principally to the modern interpretation of melodious pieces. In other cases the melody will avail itself of the softer, or the very softest, shades of touch for a part of its tones — at times even throughout. These are distinctions which have been touched upon before, and will be more carefully explained later; our present concern is merely to explain the main features in the course of the melody, and to indicate their emphasis as the supreme law of musical declamation.

Regarded as a form, the melody is a metrically ordered succession of tones, between which a certain number of distinctions are apparent. The latter result from differences in length, pitch, or harmonic relations (consonance or dissonance). Naturally, the long note has greater weight than the shorter, the high note than the lower, the dissonance than the consonance. Now, in the first place, the *sharper* accentuation will have to fall on notes prominent in the way just described, the weaker comprehending the other notes in varying proportion, graduated so, that the more the tone in question is divested, through its position, of a prominent character, the lighter its accent will be. Further, the course of the whole progression must be noted. The middle of the same usually represents the current of the idea at its full height, and may also lay claim to stronger accents than its beginning or end; always provided, however, that the melody is divided according to complete periods, of which one at least is requisite in any event to exhibit a whole. As we know, several phrases may combine to form a melody; the given rule would not always be pertinent to each of these taken singly.

No melody, whether conceived as a whole in the sense indicated above, or as part of this whole bounded within the same by a comma or any slight punctuation-mark, is without principal notes, or at least *one* principal idea, which is to be regarded as the aim of its progression and accented accordingly.

Where several such phrases separated by commas combine as one melody, one should ask, in which part the chief meaning lies; for in it the accentuation will be most vivid and pronounced. The other phrases are to be accented strongly or lightly in proportion to their importance.— But if the melody consists of several short periods, combining to a song-form in twofold or threefold division, the culminating point of the progression will lie in the middle; and the more emphatic accents, as compared with the other parts, can also be decided on here according to an ascending scale of power likewise to be accurately determined.

At the repetition of the first idea in the third part of the song-form will follow, on the whole, the accentuation of the first; but where often repeated, the accentuation must be varied in accordance with the familiar principle.

Several characteristic signs for the emphasis of a note frequently coincide; the highest tone may also be the longest, and a dissonance besides. In this case the accentuation is the more pronounced; but if the signs are doubtful, and so distributed that the longer tone is near to, though not coincident with, the higher, or the dissonance of the latter is not sharply enough contrasted with other elements near by, the player must consider, which position is the most important. Here the rhythm will often decide, though probably the characteristic of height will ordinarily take precedence of the rest; only when the highest note is markedly shorter than the others will it decline the accent. But in many cases it may well happen, that besides the strongest accent described, other tones, which by reason of length or dissonance also laid claim to it, may receive somewhat less pronounced emphasis.

Where the culminating point of the progression, in a twofold or threefold song-form, does *not* lie in the middle, as sometimes happens, the flow of accentuation will of course follow that of the general expression.

These rules apply to normal conditions, and will suffice in most cases. But some other points call for notice.

First of all, the remark applying to the passages must be repeated, that the regular metrical accent always deserves some attention. Aside from the necessity, that younger players must learn to give the latter its due before studying the refinements of accentuation in the rendering, a sensibility for the regular accentuation, as the primary groundwork, must be continually stimulated.

The same will often make itself felt through the most complicated accentuation; though not always marked by loud emphasis, enough can be suggested by the sustained and tranquil touch of the strong beats to aid the ear in following this pulse, too, in the life-stream of the tones.

But in many other cases the metrical accent will in itself sustain the rendering; and such will be met with, in particular, where the tones of the figuration are monotonous or where the other features appear in such intermingling, that the decided salience of a particular principal tone cannot be discovered.

Syncopated notes usually take, in the melody, the same strong accent given earlier as a general rule for such; but occasionally yield, despite their preponderance in length, to higher tones, as shown in the example from the second movement of the *D*-minor Sonata (comp. above).

The dramatic signification of musical speech renders exceptions possible, it is true, to all rules hitherto laid down; more especially, the sense of the words may be opposed to the above law, that the main power lies in the middle of the tone-current, and may shift the stress to either end of the phrase. — True, the pianoforte has no words; but when it transfers melodies from operas, oratorios, etc. into its sphere, it must likewise retain the suitable declamation. In consequence of this versatility of tone-life, the composition of the melody may imitate symbolically from the outset, without being founded on given words, the diversity in the expression of speech with its own full freedom; — may begin with questions, end with an exclamation, be swayed this way and that by doubts, etc., and thus depart from the normal course of the rhetorical phrases and of its own expression just described. Low tones, even the very lowest, may also attract the principal accent; with reference to these the rule might also read, that notes specially prominent amid the comparatively even flow of the melody either by their height or lowness of pitch, receive the strongest accent.

Examples:

In the following fugue-theme by Bach, the main accent falls on *g*, on account of length and syncopation.

Similar reasons determine the accent of the following theme:

In the following theme the metrical measure-accent alone turns the scale:

The same obtains in the following theme from Beethoven's *C*-major Sonate, Op. 53:

Here all must evidently be sung, and no element should be scanted in accentuation. The high $g\sharp$ at the end, to be sure, will attract a *somewhat* stronger emphasis.

In the following theme the relative height and length, — or, indeed, the regular accent on the strong beat — leave no doubt as to the accentuation:

Beethoven, Op. 53.

In the next example the relative height of the tones decides the accentuation; though all tones are to be played with a singing touch:

17

Beethoven, Op. 14. *G*-major Sonata.

Further, one should carefully note in this case that the boundaries of the motives forming the melody lie between the first and second eighth-notes.

The introduction to the Polonaise by Chopin, Op. 22, (Andante), has passages in point, where the dissonance decides the accentuation of the melody-note. In the second theme of Beethoven's *G*-major Sonata Op. 31 (1st movem.) the *syncope* requires the main accent.

Finally, we add a statement of the accents for a more extended song-form; namely, the theme of Beethoven's *A*♭-major Sonata Op. 26. — The first period embraces 8 measures, forming an opening and closing phrase of four measures each. The climax of intensity is found in the fourth measure, the accent here falling on the melody-note *d*♭, on account of its height and its intention as a suspension. In the sixth measure the melody rises still higher, to *f*, and receives here, too, a sharper accent. From here on the power of tone diminishes, only the chord *f*♭-*b*♭-*d*♭ taking a slighter accent by reason of its dissonant character. — The next group of 8 measures repeats the first with some variations, follows the same closely in accentuation, and requires a novel accent, for metrical reasons, only in the second measure, in order to mark *a*♭ as the most important among 6 equal notes. — The second part of 10 measures rises to a somewhat more unrestful mood, which is not, however, expressed in the tempo, out of consideration for the character of the total impression. Still, it makes itself felt in the accentuation by a more forceful emphasis of the notes *a*♭ in the sixth measure, and *g* in the eighth. The syncopes in the bass, entering at the beginning of this part on the third beat, also require independent melodic emphasis. The last group of 8 measures corresponds to the second, and takes the same accentuation.

Here we must add, that in recitative melodies several successive notes may well demand declamatory accents of equal power; this is frequently necessary, for instance, in Bach's figurate chorale "Wer nur den lieben Gott lässt walten" (Marx, Selection No. 8).

A distinction between the two signs ⌣ and — (or ⌄) must also be noticed. The first sign is an acute accent, preferably brought out by a standing finger, or in many cases even by a blow or unbound (freely entering) touch. The horizontal line is a milder accent, with a more singing tone, and to be executed by finger-pressure or a gentle stroke passing over instantly into a pressure, but generally in legato style. When it enters freely, the dot is commonly added to the line.

Further, I call attention to the fact, that in modern literature, especially with Chopin, a particularly *piano* entering-touch may often be logically equivalent to an accent. E. g. in the $D\flat$-major Nocturne the $b\flat$ in the fourth measure might be taken thus:

The tone then has the same pronounced importance as if one were to use a stronger touch, as Chopin directs. But this style of playing must be employed with caution, as it readily becomes a mannerism. For classical works it can hardly be recommended, on account of its over-refined charm.

(3) We now proceed to the abundant variety of forms which are neither purely *cantilena*-like nor passage-like in their construction, but combine these styles. These include, firstly, sustained, melodious compositions in slow tempo, and ornamented with coloraturas and pianoforte passages.

17*

The best examples may be found in any middle movement of a Hummel Concerto, in the Adagios of Beethoven's Sonatas, and in numerous modern Nocturnes (e. g. Chopin, Op. 9 No. 2, Op. 37 No. 1, Op. 15 No. 2).— The rules for the accentuation here present a combination of those in the two numbers preceding, nothing essentially new having to be added. In these cases the passages, from the very disposition of the composition, will be assigned no such predominant part, that their accentuation could make itself so forcibly felt' as was assumed under No. 1. They must therefore in the main take on a melodious character, only occasionally passing over into brighter figuration, and keeping their accents therein more in the background. The total impression will be *melodious*. At times the substance of such passages is purely figurative, instrumental, without melodious touches. In such cases the straight-line form must be, as before, clearly marked by accentuation, especially at the points where two lines meet; e. g. in the Larghetto by Hummel, Op. 18, ninth measure:

and, further, in the 14th measure, where extreme height and depth are marked:

Or the passage may contain — either throughout, or in isolated points, especially towards the end—melodious thoughts. In this case the same occupy the foreground in expression, and shape their accentual execution quite in *cantilena*-style; e. g. in measure 13:

Here the end takes the main or melodiously marked accent on *e♭*. The other two, on *a* and *g*, are figurative and weaker.

The singing tone is often more deeply hidden, and the player must be habituated to earnest musical reflection in order to discover the melodious point. Thus in the following passage taken from the Finale of the Beethoven Sonata in *B♭* Op. 22, the highest *c* is marked by a singing touch because leading into the theme; whereas the whole passage has otherwise a quite unmelodic, figurative, even *emptily* figurative, character:

Concerning these two passages the remark may be added, anticipating the next Chapter, that the singing tone is at the same time to be held longer, and that the sharpness of the accent may therefore sometimes be mildened.

The second half of the cases to be classed under this number embraces the melodious ideas, usually thematically planned, which, though conceived in the sense of song, are exhibited by the means peculiar to the pianoforte and outrivalling vocal technique. Such are, in particular, the freedom and lightness of the pianoforte passages, which the imagination develops simultaneously with these ideas, and which add to the pianoforte melodies greater fluency of ornamentation as compared with vocal ones. Moreover, the pianoforte uses the wider range of its tones, and does not restrict connected melody within the narrow compass of a single voice-register. It links together tones often lying several octaves apart, and precisely as if they lay within the compass of one voice. The player must transfer these two expansions to the conception of the musical phrases, but order his interpretation in exact accord with the rules discussed before. On the whole, therefore, nothing new need be added; the musical apprehension must either seize upon the ideal, the vocal thought in the flow of the passages, or regard the latter, when their character demands it, as vocal throughout in the sense of pianoforte resources, and accentuate them accordingly.

For instance, the theme of the Beethoven Sonata in *C*, Op. 53, begins with a pure pianoforte passage to be played with the wrist. The *vocal* nucleus lies in the thirteen-times repeated *c* in the soprano, of course not *thought* as a so oft-repeated tone, but as sustained. The same is continued by *f♯*, given, in accordance with the pianoforte conception of the first figure, by a double wrist-stroke, but imagined vocally as one tone. The highest tone *g* is the culmination of the motive, and takes the main accent; this note appears but once in the pianoforte theme. — The sixteenth-notes following are, to be sure, impracticable as genuine melody in the prescribed tempo; yet they contain, issuing and developing from the fluent spirit of the entire beginning, a so natural intensification of expression, that the vocal conception instantly recognizes therein a progression analogous to its own inmost nature — a progression, which it might perhaps exhibit by its own resources with fewer and slower notes, but which it finds natural from the standpoint of the pianoforte, and regarding whose accentuation it is not a moment in doubt. — This point is important, for the themes of many Sonatas, Rondos, and *salon* pieces, are planned in this style, and require a corresponding interpretation. Of course the passage will sometimes prevail in its purely figurate charm, and in such a case the accentuation must be ordered according to the rules explained. — The logic of the rhythmical faculty is subjected to a severer test than in pure *cantilene* or passages; all the more must the careful precision of execution be strengthened and practiced in the interpretation of just such pianoforte themes.— Clearness of phrasing, the intensifying of the elements of movement to their utmost animation, the climaxes of expression, are here as elsewhere the points claiming sharpest observance, and receive, as the cardinal points, the strongest accentuation, just as in the simple *cantilene.*

For example, the theme of the *F*-minor Sonata Op. 57 should be accented as follows:

The highest *f* has the strongest accent; at the end, *e* has a still milder, singing accent.

The Minuet in the Beethoven Sonata Op. 22 has two very lovely intensifications; the one lies in the first half-period, and receives the main accent on *e* in the fourth measure, the other in the seventh measure on *g*; the eighth measure also takes, from sympathy with the fourth, an accent, though a weaker one.

Beethoven, Op. 22.

The theme of the Finale of the *D*-minor Sonata Op. 31 has a melodious tone in the motive itself, and must emphasize the same a little, although it is quite in the style of a piano-forte passage; etc. etc.

The theme of Liszt's *E*-major Polonaise takes an accent on the $c\sharp$ in the first two measures; while the main accent must fall on $g\sharp$ in the fourth measure.

The allegro interlude in Weber's *F*-minor Concerto has three accents:

the first on account of high pitch, the other two from metrical reasons.

A passage like the following from Henselt's Concert, 1st movem., contents itself with metrical, though singing, accents:

In the theme of Chopin's $E\flat$ Polonaise only the first tone requires to be marked in the first measure; in the second measure the accents are irregular, falling on the second and sixth eighths, as guided by syncopation and pitch.

Having now considered, in pianoforte themes, the passage in its purest form, then the *cantilena,* and finally the combinations of both forms, we have analyzed the material in its full extent; and it only remains, briefly to discuss the coincidence of these features in simultaneous combination.

(4) In most cases, rhythmic life unfolds its diversified texture in several series of tones progressing together. Seldom does *one* principle so monotonously control a work or a passage, that the player's attention is wholly concentrated on the fineness of a single line of rhythm. The simplest *cantilena* usually has an accompaniment which, however subordinate it may be, must at moments betray its existence by the soft

pulsation of an accent. True, examples are not wanting, where only the flow of homophonic passages, or a simple melody without a specially figurated accompaniment, occupies the scene of a musical work (one need but recall the Finale of the *Bb*-minor Sonata by Chopin, or the second theme in the *C*-major Sonata by Beethoven, Op. 53); — but in general at least two contrasting rhythmical manifestations animate the musical form; this obtains in the majority even of the simplest compositions, not to speak of the multiform web of polyphony, whose proper interpretation depends chiefly upon the correct accentuation of each individual part.

In these cases it is needful, carefully to weigh the character of the several parts. Where one feature predominates, the accentuation of the others must be restrained. When two or more are equally balanced, the precision of accentuation applies equally to each.— In the *cantilena* style the accompaniment must be held very decidedly in the background: this applies particularly to pieces of a modern character in songform (Liedform). But it is seldom suppressed to nullity, especially where it is brilliant. With increasing warmth and passion it will often unfold the entire fulness of its accentual life — and here no such brilliant accompaniment need be instanced as that in Henselt's "Danklied nach Sturm" Op. 5. The latter stands at least on a level with the melody. The above remark applies even to Mendelssohn's modest Songs without Words, in which the accompaniment is subdued, but still makes its accentuation felt at moments, and sometimes even calls for fiery accentuation throughout.

The greatest variety is naturally found in works of most genuine inspiration. The deeper the meaning of a composition, the richer will be in general the forms of its rhythm. We mention but one example.

The first Solo in Beethoven's *C*-minor Concerto clearly exhibits all these cases. From the 11th measure on

a lower part in triplet-form, which takes a light regular accent, accompanies a higher part having a declamatory accentuation. Following this, purely passage - like pianoforte episodes, which take in part a sharp regular accent falling together with a figurative one, alternate with short orchestral intermezzos, until the twofold accentual element recommences in the measure

and is continued through eight measures. Then pianoforte passages recur, 6 measures with sharp accent, followed by 4 with a milder one. The latter resolve into the second theme

In this theme the accompaniment quite recedes, and the declamation of the soprano alone holds the field. But this lasts only for 6 measures. In the last of these the accompaniment already falls in with an accent on the fourth quarter, with a strong continuation in the seventh measure, but

subsides again in the eighth.—These conditions continue, intermingling or alternating, nearly to the end of this Solo. Here, again, pianoforte passages take exclusive possession, maintaining the sharpest and most brilliant accentuation to the close.

The accentuation characterizes the player, and one may say, that its treatment displays a certain style. One virtuoso will mainly cultivate refinement in the accent, another distinctness and correctness, while the third seeks to draw out its full power. Absolute objectivity, it is true, demands an exact solution of all the problems touching the accent; but individuals differ both psychically and intellectually. The shading of the accents will remain subjective despite all the finish of the school; and one great charm of virtuosity lies in the distinctions between mental and physical personalities. Who has not been forced to note the mighty impetus of accent of the Liszt school, the piquant charm of dancing rhythms in Th. Kullak's playing, the fine declamatory and clearly regular accent of Thalberg, or A. Dreyschock's full, noble tone and exquisitely sensitive accent, distinct in the softest *piano*, as characteristic of the styles of these artists? Rubinstein's manner of accentuation is, like his whole style, ravishing — of most fiery power, tenderest poetry—but not always faithful in details, sometimes even not lovely in form. His creatively inspired reproduction often gives prominent importance to insignificant tones. By contrast, one can imagine no more finely proportioned accents than in Tausig's limpid, reflective style; no greater intellectual energy, than is shown in Bülow's rhythms. — Finally, the bad habit should be mentioned, of multiplying irregular and marked accents for the sake of an effect of virtuosity which must be condemned. Real effect lies in truth, not in striking touches.

CHAPTER XV.

On the crescendo and decrescendo. On the principles, resulting from the combined intent of the realistic and idealistic conceptions of music, and applicable to this and similar styles of execution.

The accent has given the tone-picture animation. Distinctness, intelligibility, perspicuity, are thus bestowed on that material, which, in its specifically sensuous quality, mirrors more faithfully than any other both beauty of form and the vital course of certain psychic conditions. The breathing-process of the feeling consists in two movements, which, aside from any specific meaning, characterize all emotion; an outpouring from the breast, and an in-drawing into the fathomless depths of its life. — The outpouring of the feeling toward its object — whether to the endless heavens, or forth into the boundless world, or toward a definite, limited object — resembles the surging, the pressing onward, of a flood. Reversely, that feeling which draws its object into itself has a more tranquilizing movement, that especially when the possession of the object is assured, appeases itself in equable onward flow to the goal of a normal state of satisfaction. The emotional life is an undulating play of upsurging and subsidence; of pressing forth beyond temporal limitations into eternity, and of resigned self-contentment and yielding to temporal necessities.

Likewise immanent to music is the faculty of following the last-named manifestation of emotional life—its upswelling and subsidence. The *crescendo* and *decrescendo* are the means which the player must employ, for the portrayal of this new element of musical idealism.

It is the part of theory to examine, when and where the conception of the art-work demands and must demand these nuances; and herefrom the practical rule naturally flows, the mechanical conditions being mastered.

But another rule, beside the mere imitation of emotional phases, determines the course of the musical art-work. The idealistic conception of music is by no means the sole justifiable one. In the organism of a composition there resides, besides the symbolism of soul-life, so much that is material, purely formal—yes, plastically formal—that these factors, too, must be taken note of in laying down laws for the aspect of the rendering now under consideration.— The one-sided view called the *realistic*, which occupies this standpoint exclusively, must adduce the idea of diversity as that principle, which sanctions the addition of the *crescendo* and *decrescendo* to the earlier nuances. Though the realistic view denies the emotional intent of music, it must nevertheless recognize therein an exhibition of powers having the innate faculty of manifesting themselves in a sum of forces and shades, among which the one in question affords a superior means for attaining variety.

Our standpoint, occupying a position between the two, must include both principles. All rules for the swelling and subsiding of tone can certainly not be drawn from either alone; neither covers the multiformity of all cases. But they are mutually helpful, and where they do not guide the performer together, the one supplements the other.

The point in which they coincide is the *intensification in the musical expression*, and the subsidence of the same into *tranquility*. There is a sum of characteristics in music, which, aside from any relation to any phenomena of life whatever, express in a natural manner impulses of the originally tranquil embryo to flights of development; and others, which mark the return to repose from these latter. The former naturally take the *crescendo*, the latter the *decrescendo*. These characteristics, with reference to their amplification, exhibit fairly boundless variety. The progression from a consonance to a dissonance may be effected by *two* neighboring tones; this is an intensification of the lowest degree. But a motive may be portrayed page after page, in ever-increasing might and ever-changing illumination. Here a *crescendo* of wide extent would result. The progression from below upward is an *intensification*, the return from above downward is a *relaxation;* all developments in composition, even the tiniest tone-picture, *must* contain the contrasts of repose and motion; and therefore intensifications and relaxations, following its disposition and phrasing, can be pointed out. Such features lie in the harmony, rhythm, melody, and conception of the form of composition. Yes, we may go still further; they are grounded in the contrast between the polyphonic and homophonic styles. Each, in contrast to the other, may mark an intensification or relaxation, to be indicated by the *crescendo* or *decrescendo.*

The idea of the intensifications is superior to the one-sided rules of the idealistic and realistic views, as it includes them both. The idealistic view receives only the feature of *subjective* charm as a new conception in the Beautiful in music; the realistic view terms this arbitrariness, and maintains a more objective and prosaic standpoint.

But cases also occur, in which the intensification has no directly assignable reason, and yet a *crescendo* or *decrescendo* is required. In such the decision must be undertaken by one of the two factors alone. Thus on the one hand, the *crescendo* and *decrescendo* will be demanded by a distinct dramatical idea attributed to the tones, a kind of rhetorical declamation, which brings out a more precise and individual meaning in the tones than they can present in their general character or in themselves. True, such music is originally conceived with words. But, setting aside transcriptions of dramatic music for the pianoforte, which must primarily follow the sense of the words, a music is imaginable — especially in the sense of modern tendencies — which should proceed from special conceptions of dramatic and lyric situations. And here cases might arise, whose rendering could not be determined strictly by the laws of form. Contrarily, music will often vainly seek enlightenment for its rendering in its symbolical connection with the emotional life, and will determine the shadings described only according to the principle of diversity and variety.

If the idealistic view tries to explain the matter in its own way, it will always succeed in doing so if it holds to the most general features of the above-mentioned emotional phase — its upsurging and subsidence. However, such general conceptions, which fit everything in music, tell us too little, and leave too much room for arbitrariness. At the very least, they possess no advantage above the realistic view, whose principle fully meets such cases.

This prefatory excursion into more general questions of æsthetics has been allowed so free scope, in order that, when enumerating the individual cases, we might not appear guilty of inconsistency in regard to their derivation. Further, the above remarks, as of generally binding import, may also serve as an introduction to the explanations following of the remaining nuances of rendering.

(1) Every progression from lower tones to higher is, in its original conception, an intensification, and demands a *crescendo*.

This rule applies both to passages and melodies. The upward steps of the latter, or the ascending figuration of the passages, have a very various extension. The above style of execution is employed, not only in a limited, but in a wide, even the widest, scope. Where the upward impulse is distributed over a long course, the separate sections of the same, which likewise contain momentary intensifications, must also be executed with a *crescendo*. The intensification as a whole must, however, prevail, and therefore the separate *crescendi* must bear a proportion to the general increase. The descending lines are to be executed *decrescendo*.

Examples:

Adagio from Beethoven's Sonata Op. 27 No. 1.

Finale of the same Sonata:

The theme of the first movement of the Sonate pathétique Op. 13 has fine instances of the *crescendi*. The following passage is of course *decrescendo*, from its descent:

In an ensuing passage of the same sonata a long crescendo occurs:

This reaches its climax in the tenth measure, and the player must carefully calculate his strength. In order that no weariness or overexertion may be apparent, one should begin quite *piano* in such passages, and work up the *crescendo* very measuredly. — This obtains in a still higher degree in the Beethoven C-major Sonata Op. 53, 1st movem., 2nd part, in the passage leading over into the theme, where the bass has the following figure:

Here a *crescendo* is to be calculated for 14 measures, though the intensification is not continuous, as the right hand increases the power of its short phrases step by step, beginning each new one *piano*. Still, the intensification desired must on the whole be so expressed, that the separate *crescendi* constantly increase in power.

In movements having a brilliant figurate accompaniment, the latter shares with the melody, and frequently to an even greater degree, in the nuances in question (Chopin, Op. 10 No. 12). But where the theme occupies the foreground in charm of expression, the accompaniment must be more subdued, and break out only now and then with its psychic manifestations. In most cases it closely follows the reading of the theme in all nuances (e. g. Theoder Kullak: "Au bord d'un ruisseau", Op. 73). Where it forms a very faint and foil-like background, it abstains from any forward impulse, and only at the very highest sweep of the melody does it cautiously join in the swell of passion. Otherwise it holds to a uniform *piano*. —

(2) When single tones, figures, motives, even melodious phrases, are repeated several times at the same or an only slightly varied pitch, they are to be executed either *crescendo*, or alternately *crescendo* and *decrescendo*. The expression may often require this in the *original conception* of the composer; otherwise the monotony of such passages is to be relieved in accord with this rule.

Examples:

Beethoven, Op. 14.

Long-sustained trills on one tone are to be treated similarly; e. g. the one at the end of the $C\sharp$-minor Sonata, which may be played with an alternate *crescendo* and *decrescendo*.

A still more instructive example is the Beethoven Dead March Op. 26, in which the melody continues for 6 measures on one tone, but takes a *crescendo* as indicated, in the fifth measure, again passing over to *piano* in the sixth.

18

The passage in the Finale of Beethoven's *D*-minor Sonata demands like treatment, and must be played thus:

Further:

Beethoven, Bagatelle No. 1.

The Finale of Mendelssohn's *F♯*-minor Fantasia contains analogous passages; e. g.

Schumann's *F♯*-major Romance requires the same shades of tone for the repeated *c♯* at the close; the more so, because the tender, dreamy, dying away is thus brought out most effectively.

(3) A leading up to a dissonance, and the expansion of the latter even over a wide space, — but often, too, a mere momentary expression of the dissonance—demand a *crescendo;* and in other cases just the reverse, the *decrescendo.* The latter results, where the tension is sustained by a delicate coloring, by the profound pathos of tender melancholy. The *crescendo* is rather a free, natural impulse in a robuster sense. — This rule bears a resemblance to the accent-rule in the foregoing chapter; in fact, the declamatory accent often requires the mediation of, and preparation by, a *crescendo.*

The introduction to the Chopin Polonaise Op. 22, given before in illustration of the accent, and also the introduction to the song by Schubert, "The Wanderer", (compare Liszt's transcription) contain pertinent examples. In many cases the progression towards a dissonance combines with an upward movement, and the *crescendo* then requires double power of tone. The shortest succession of this kind often demands a *crescendo;* e. g. in the middle movement of the *D*-minor Sonata by Beethoven Op. 31:

For the soft touch of the dissonant harmony an example found at the end of the second piece in Mendelssohn's *œuvre posthume* "Zwei Klavierstücke" (2 Pianoforte Pieces; Leipzig, Barth. Senff); also in the chord before the last in the *F*-minor Sonata Op. 57, middle movement The *pianissimo* of this chord characteristically leads back the mood from its exhausted resignation, as a gentle reminder of pain, to stormy agitation.

(4) In many, particularly more extended and serious compositions, that part which is devoted to the development of an idea in various harmonic situations, or in contrapuntal, fugue-like style, exhibits a general character of unrest and agitation. On account of its length a continuous *crescendo* is hardly practicable, and an alternate *crescendo* and *decrescendo* will obtain. But the former nuance will be the prevailing one, the *decrescendo* not appearing until the close in many cases. A fine instance of a prolonged *crescendo* is contained in the development part of the first movement of Schumann's *G*-minor Sonata.

To this class also belong the cases, in which a *repetition* of the same motive or thought, of *brief* extent, occurs in the more tranquil parts of a composition as a transition to fresh

18*

developments. In these a *decrescendo* — though always keeping the general character of the composition in view — will be quite as justifiable as a *crescendo*. But one of the two *must* be used, for the sake of variety. The *crescendo* excites expectation directly, the *decrescendo* indirectly, by indicating the end of an idea, or a leave-taking, a departure, after which something else may be expected to enter.

In any event, the picturesque effect of either nuance in the proper place must be provided for. The *crescendo* often marks the approach, the irruption, of impulses and powers; the *decrescendo* breathes a mournful note of cessation, expiring, departure — the continuous withdrawal and disappearance of an object from the tone-picture. Music is the romantic kaleidoscope, readily receiving, in its beautiful, mysterious, and darkling mirror-disks, souvenirs of emotion from actual phases of life, and blending with them its own elements.

(5) On the realistic foundation of variety stands the principle, that even those pieces which, having no marked gradation of pitch, might content themselves with an evenly flowing execution, are to be animated by the *crescendo* and *decrescendo* with life and warmth. Recall, for instance, the Bach Prelude:

or various passages in the Finale of the Italian Concerto, or Bach's Bourrées. Similar considerations will decide the style of executing the development part of various sonata movements, and many fugues, whenever neither climaxes in pitch, nor the number of the parts, give a positive clew in some other way. Thus the first part of Mendelssohn's E-minor Fugue, for instance, would be tedious up to the G-major close, if the player were to perform it with the mere stereotyped *crescendo* up to the highest tone; nuances of wider-reaching significance must be added, despite the fact, that no single definite place imperiously calls for them.

(6) The view hitherto followed now requires broadening. — The idea of intensification, it is true, *originally* demands an increase of power directly perceptible by the senses; but this assumption is only the primary conception. Every *development* of an idea is an intensification. This truth, reached by further reflection, modifies the original conception from which we set out, in that the *decrescendo* may just as well be regarded as an intensification as its opposite, it being likewise a necessary transition-point in the development. — This circumstance gives rise to some exceptions to the earlier rules, frequently employed as aids to a more finely developed rendering.

Thus it not infrequently occurs, that ascending progressions must be played *decrescendo*, and descending ones *crescendo*.

This case may readily be explained, if desired, from the proportionate power of the tones, which may quite as well indicate a decrease as an increase when the progression rises into higher regions. The higher, more feminine, tender, is also the weaker; the deeper, more masculine, dæmonic, is the stronger. It therefore depends either upon the total spirit of the composition, or (when it may be variously interpreted) upon the subjectivity of the player, whether the imagination be influenced in one or the other direction. The spirit of the whole, or the principle of variety, will have to decide as to the admissibility of either conception. — We distinguish two principal cases:

(a) Toward the close of a part which progresses in stormy vehemence and violence, and requires a subsidence, even the most decided upward progression of its close will demand a *decrescendo*. A pertinent example is found in the end of the development part of Beethoven's Sonata in *B♭*, Op. 22, first movement:

de - cre - scen - do   *pp*

We find an example of a descending *crescendo* in the development part of Beethoven's *C*-minor Sonata Op. 10, first movement, where the left hand enters with the following notes:

It should be remarked here, that the close of a composition or part of the same never bears a neutral conception, but always requires specialization. Tension (suspense) is invariably present, and is expressed either by *crescendo* or a *decrescendo*.

(b) The style of execution in question may also be employed as a special nuance in various other upward or downward progressions; probably most often in ascending passages played *crescendo* at first and *decrescendo* toward the close. Aside from the principle of variety already mentioned, which sometimes inclines to such conceptions quite as readily as to the normal rule for the execution discussed before in Nos. 1 to 5, there lies in such an interpretation a peculiar meaning. A natural power, whose outbreak is in progress, suddenly curbs its impetuosity. This is a graceful and delicate touch, which can be employed in all cases where the work as a whole breathes elegance and tenderness rather than grandeur and strength, e. g. in Nocturnes, and modern conceptions which display, in the main, refined culture and smoothness. But classical works, too, can sometimes not eschew it, if their sentiment is peculiarly delicate and amiable. Measuredness in the outbreak of a manifestation of strength, whose tendency the hearer can guess, has the advantage of nobility and distinction over natural expression, which may appear vulgar at times in contrast with such a style of rendering.—But one should not carry this too far, and especially not copy too closely the modern fashion, whose rendering sometimes leans more to affectation and over-refinement than to health and truth.

Where an ascending passage leads up to a thought whose interpretation calls for peculiar delicacy, a *decrescendo* is in place in the same.

Examples:

No small portion of the coloraturas in the Larghetto of Op. 18 by Hummel, or in the middle movements of his Concertos, admit of this rendering. Hummel, indeed, is the composer, whose only half-sincere, but by no means shallow ideas permit these touches of delicacy—one might say, effeminacy. We give intentionally the passage earlier quoted, which may now take this nuance in addition:

Hummel, Op. 18.

The following passages, as a transition to softer strains, are performed *decrescendo*.

Beethoven, Op. 10. Adagio molto.

Beethoven, Op. 31. E♭-major Sonata, 1st. movem.

Here we conclude these observations on one of the most important nuances for the rendering. The question can hardly be quite exhausted. But the main reasons given for tasteful variety, and intelligent symbolization of emotional phases, guided by the general spirit and the consistent style of the composition, will probably suffice, even should it not be possible to verify their observance in all details.

CHAPTER XVI.

The Accelerando and Rallentando.

The nuances of rendering discussed in the previous chapter applied to changes in the power. To these correspond, in regard to the tempo, the *rallentando* and *accelerando*, which we shall now take up. It is hardly needful to remark, that terms not differing in general meaning from the above, like *ritardando, stringendo,* etc., require no special discussion, just as in the foregoing the words identical with *crescendo* and *decrescendo* were not enumerated singly. The entire science of rendering turns on the conception of ideas; the direction no longer suffices, that the player must heed the intention of the composer, and shape his rendering accordingly. He should follow the latter in emotion and creative energy; and even if not his equal in productive fancy, he should be his peer in æsthetic judgment. This last is a peculiar right of each individual education, and is to be distinguished from the native power of creative imagination.

The introduction prefixed to the foregoing chapter permits us to treat of the nuances now in hand more briefly. Their employment is likewise determined by form and conception of the piece.

The *accelerando* is in general not so often admissible as the *ritardando*. The reasons for this will be gathered from the following.

The occasions of either are, as remarked, of an outward or inward nature. Either the meaning of a passage expresses phases of emotion, which require an increase or a decrease in rapidity, or the external structure of the composition renders such a deviation from the equable tempo necessary. The principle of variety, simply for the sake of its sensual charm, would also form a part of the outward motives.

Respecting the meaning, we take the liberty of quoting some remarks by Czerny, from his Method (Part III, page 25). As motives for the *rallentando* he enumerates the following peculiarities of passages under consideration:—Gentle entreaty, slight doubt, hesitating indecision, tender complaint, quiet resignation, the transition from a state of excitement to tranquility, meditative or thoughtful repose, sighing and mournfulness, the whispered telling of a secret, leave-taking, etc. For the *accelerando* he mentions:—Sudden vivacity, hasty or inquisitive questions, impatience, moodiness or the outbreak of anger, sturdy decision, indignant reproach, audacity and gaiety, fearful flight, sudden surprise, the transition from a state of tranquility to excitement, etc.

For the sake of exactness we must add, that the enumeration of such phases of life as mirrored in tones cannot be exhaustive. Czerny gives but a few examples. It can only be stated, in sum, that the symbolizing power of tone suggests phases of feeling and actual events, which permit and render desirable, on the one hand, a relaxing in rapidity, and on the other an acceleration of the same.—But, as the material is not free from very considerable sensuous claims, the *uniformity* of rhythm must not, *on the whole,* be subjected to overmuch alteration. — Together with all its poetic meaning, the tone-material must retain its rhythmic plasticity. In general, therefore, uniformity of measure must obtain, and the nuances under present consideration must be employed somewhat more sparingly than those previously treated of. But this does not mean that they, in their narrower field, are not a feature essential to the beauty of musical expression. The *rallentando,* in particular, has so expressive a meaning that it is wanting in scarcely any work.—We now proceed to the principal cases in which, to begin with, the *rallentando* is employed.

(1) Each note, which is rendered in the declamation of melodious phrases with individual expression, and by reason of its place (as explained in the two chapters preceding) has a claim to special significance, takes a *rallentando*. The rhythmic course of the whole determines the breadth of the latter. Where a certain regularity and precision of metre prevails—if the tempo is not too slow—the retardation will be moderate, in proportion to the rest. In sustained movements, whose tempo in itself expresses a certain dissolving of the metre in the element of expressive recitation, greater freedom obtains for the *rallentando*. The total character is therefore decisive. Where coloraturas are frequent, and interfere in their scope with the precision of the metre, the nuance in question will find greatest liberty of development. Thus the *rallentando* must in general be accomodated exactly to the tempo, character, and the metrical conditions of the piece.— Often its duration is only momentary.—A single tone in the *crescendo* or *decrescendo*, with which latter it is most frequently combined, is checked. Among all its applications, this is probably the most important and reasonable. No theme, no *cantilena*, no Song without Words, can be effectively rendered without such support from the *rallentando*. The tone held back becomes more suggestive, more pregnant; it more strongly impresses itself upon the ear, it sinks into the inmost depths of the feeling. This manner of holding back symbolizes the intensity, the impressiveness, the warmth of declamation.

In sustained *cantilene* the *rallentando* can be most frequently introduced on a tone toward the end. Where passages intervene, the player must discover the tone which forms either the climax of the vocal phrases, or which is, amid empty, purely decorative roulades, the sole melodious atom which lends to the material charm of the passage a touch of expression. A single sustained tone often elevates an otherwise meaningless mass into the sphere of expression, in which the passage must also maintain itself, for the sake of unity with the other elements.

In employing the *rallentando,* the style of the composition must also be considered. Some little sentimentality is always combined with retardation, but in varying degrees. Beethoven's sentimentality, even in its tenderest form, is instinct with strength, and in general requires neither many nor very extravagant retardations. The same holds good of Seb. Bach. The soft dreaminess of many Schumann *cantilene* would lose, on the contrary, its most essential means of expression with the *ritardando.* Chopin likewise bears this deviation from the tempo in a high degree.

An allegro usually leaves the *ritardando* less scope than an adagio. In aid of the *expression,* a place will be found for the same in the second theme of sonatas and concertos, or in passages leading up to such *cantilene.*

Examples:

The theme of Mendelssohn's *Variations sérieuses* takes no *rallentando* on account of its firm rhythmical character and uniform metre. The theme of the Beethoven Sonata in *A♭,* Op. 26, also has a too precisely regulated pace to admit of a considerable *rallentando;* the latter would form a cheap addition to the idealized sentimentality of this melody. At the very most, the passage in the middle part

might be suited to it, and even here only the *a♭* could be slightly prolonged.

Somewhat more sentimental is the Adagio in the *C*-minor Sonata Op. 10, in which the principal tones can be more frequently prolonged, though still very little; indeed, it would be hard to distinguish between the *hardly* and the *more* perceptible *rallentandi*. Such an imperceptible pause may be made at the very beginning of this adagio:

In the first Song without Words Mendelssohn uses a declamatory phrase in which, on account of its imitation of vocality, the points of retardation may be more marked; e. g.

The same is true of the highest tone of the following passage, from the first piece in the fifth part of the Songs without Words. The bass note *d* coinciding with *g* pauses *with* the latter.

The following mainly ornamental passage from the Adagio in Beethoven's *D*-minor Sonata takes a *rallentando* on the *e♭*

(last note but one), and with the same the expressive significance which it requires as the transition to the theme:

The passage from Hummel's Op. 18 has its rendering indicated here for the third time, and at last in its complete form:

If a *crescendo* is combined with the *rallentando*, the impressiveness of its expression is doubled; in particular, features of grandeur and sublimity are thus effectively rendered, e. g. the introduction to the Sonate pathétique towards the end:

In the Finale movement of the Sonata in *B♭* Op. 22 by Beethoven the highest tone *c*, in the following otherwise emptily ornamental passage, is held long, on account of the transition to the theme:

(2) The *rallentando* is employed, further, where an idea is nearing its end; i. e. either at the close of a composition, or at such divisions as mark decided turning-points in the same. It is most effective, when such a winding-up of an idea serves at the same time as a transition to a new thought (e. g. the second theme), or even as a return to an earlier theme. But also when a different tempo, or any other feature of importance, supervenes in the flow of the composition, attention is very often drawn to it by means of a previous retardation.

Such causes of the *rallentando* lie, for the most part, in the form, but are likewise transferred by the psyche to the sphere of emotion. A sorrowful leave-taking — that phase of feeling which so readily gains access to the breast — is always suggested by the winding-up of an idea.

The law thus generally expressed embraces the separate rules given by Czerny, which were not ideally arranged; therefore no special enumeration is needful. The retardation of a single tone often suffices, duly to announce the following thought. This will obtain more particularly in works whose rhythmic structure is firmly knit; the last example given in the foregoing number, from the B♭-major Sonata, contains an instance in point. In other compositions, whose freer nature is expressed in their looser texture, and whose rhythmic character is less strict, such as Concertos, Fantasias, Adagios, etc., the announcement of the new theme will often call for a very wide-spread *rallentando*. Here only Hummel's *A*-minor Concerto (1st movem.) need be mentioned, in which the second theme is introduced in this manner. But in such cases the player must take care not to begin the retardation too soon, otherwise its effect may be fatiguing.—Short movements, too, having a very free rhythm and a recitative style, can quite frequently employ the prolonged *rallentando;* e. g. the Fantasia Chromatica by Bach. Long trills and cadenzas will also bear it, as a rule, towards the end.—The effect of clear phrasing and contrasting is always so agreeable, that even long passages in an otherwise concise rhythmical structure, when they lead over into a new figure or to a more tranquil close, may be retarded a little shortly before at some appropriate cæsura, even though most minutely.

Besides the examples already given it must suffice to cite but few others, the majority being too extended for our space. We offer but one further observation. It is not at all necessary, that a *rallentando* should in *every* case accompany the winding-up of a thought or the transition to a new one. The Sonate pathétique in the first part, and the *C♯*-minor Sonata in the third movement, would forfeit their strength and precision by the in any event somewhat sentimental nuance of the *rallentando.* The total character is always the highest court of appeal, which decides the rendering of each individual case.

As remarked in No. 1, the theme of the *A♭*-major Sonata Op. 26 has but scanty *rallentandi* for the expression, *one only* being pointed out as properly admissible. With regard to the phrasing, however, a second will have to be added; indeed, we chose this example intentionally, to present the distinctions in the *rallentando* side by side. — The second occurs in the measure, which leads back from the middle part into the repetition of the first:

The entire close of the theme in the *E*-minor Sonata
Op. 90, first movement, is retarded throughout 3 to 4 measures.
—This sonata has altogether such a poetico-declamatory intention, that it makes more frequent use of this nuance than,
for instance, the *C*-minor Sonata Op. 10 in the first movement;
the form of the latter is so firmly moulded, that it admits of
a slight retardation, at the utmost, in the two last measures
of the first and second parts.

Sometimes motives for expression and phrasing coincide,
allowing a retardation of notes even in movements which
might else remain free from any sentimental addition. This
case occurs several times in the Finale of the *D*-minor Sonata
by Beethoven, e. g. at the end of the first part, where the
development part leads into the theme in *B♭*-minor; at the
return to the same theme in *D*-minor; etc.

The close of pieces is by no means always *rallentando*.
On the contrary, in larger works the power often takes, precisely here, a flight of the highest energy. All depends here,
too, upon the general character. — But in compositions of so
tranquil intent as the first movement of the *G*-major Sonata
Op. 14 by Beethoven, a slight retardation will be proper:

Here should follow a discussion of the *rallentando* immediately preceding or succeeding an *accelerando*. But the
latter style of execution must first be explained.

As with the *rallentando*, the motives for the *accelerando* may be of an inward or outward nature. The former consist in the living impetus of the psychic movement expressed in the composition; in an intensification of the emotional activity, or of that phase of life which is portrayed by the music. The outward motives are derived from the charm of variety or the brilliancy of sensuous effects. One cause founded on the form, which rendered the *rallentando* a desirable agency in the phrasing of a composition, is not applicable to the *accelerando*. The winding-up of an idea is more appropriately indicated by holding back than by hastening. Metrical regularity also seconds this decision; it is more in unison with the feeling that the fundamental unit of measure should be gradually transformed, than that it should be crowded together. The latter style may suit the closes of whole movements, but not the transition from one thought to another. In such a case the conceptive subjectivity would be apt to take the inclination to an *accelerando* for unsteadiness in time, as it demands, above all, coolness and presence of mind in the exposition of the several parts. Further, the meaning symbolically suggested by the *rallentando* — emotion, warmth, mournfulness, yearning—is more readily and easily understood by the feeling than the unrest of the *accelerando*, which invokes an element altogether less sympathetic to music than the former. —

Nevertheless, the *accelerando* is perfectly justifiable here and there even in good compositions, as a psychic expression; we will mention only Chopin's Scherzo in *B*-minor (toward the end). The close of Beethoven's *F*-minor Sonata Op. 57 will also bear it. But Beethoven usually prefers to relegate the last intensification to an independent movement in *più presto*. This must not be confounded with the accelerations at present under consideration.

A slight *accelerando* for the sake of expression is fairly suggested, for instance, in the *cantilena* of Schumann's Novelette in *F*,

19

whose impressiveness is thereby rendered far more intense. Further, recall the second movement of Schumann's *G*-minor Sonata:

On the other hand, the *accelerando* finds its motive in the alternation of the brilliant with the tranquil. For this case numerous examples might be given; any passage entering after *cantilene,* as happens frequently in Concertos and the like, may display somewhat greater animation. Of course, the general character of the work must be examined attentively, and the charm of repose and clearness not too lightly passed over for mere brilliant effect. In most cases such an ebullition in the tempo subsides further on; it seldom plunges headlong into the formless swirl of ever-increasing rapidity. If greater intensification is necessary, the composer provides for its expression by special *presto* movements or divisions.—A slight *accelerando* touch is also appropriate where comparatively empty passages occur between more pregnant ones;—a case found not only in accompaniments which meaninglessly bridge over pauses in the principal part, but meriting attention even in the flow of passages pure and simple, in those phrases which can lay less claim to interest than the others.

Examples:

Mendelssohn, Prelude in *E*-minor, Op. 35.

etc.

and further, from Schumann's *G*-minor Sonata (1st movem.), the 8 measures before the entrance of the bass theme:

This also applies to most of the free Cadenzas in set time by Liszt, Raff, and others.

When an idea is repeated several times, it is often performed in changing tempo, the first time *accelerando*, the second *rallentando*. Here, too, the choice of the nuance depends upon the total character. — The second Bagatelle by Beethoven, Op. 33, repeats in the last part the fundamental motive of the first theme

14 times, in varying pitch and width of intervals, with interpolated measures of different form. The monotony of this passage is entirely obviated by an accelerated rendering, and is transformed into roguish humor. — But the *acceleration* must not be carried out in continuous progression; that would also be monotonous; where an 8-measure phrase ends, a *rallentando* of the same figures sets in toward the close. The passage is therefore played thus:

The following rhythm then continues in similar wise, until the two last figures close in still greater; almost headlong, acceleration; after them the chords before introduced as intermediate thoughts rush to a close in like haste; only toward the end they grow tranquil, and go out like little sparks.

The very first theme of this Bagatelle will bear an *accelerando* in the middle. Altogether, when a piece is worked up out of one figure, the *accelerando* and *rallentando* can hardly be dispensed with; this is true even of many Bach Preludes, finds very obvious support in Mendelssohn's songs (e. g. Part. 5, Song 1), and also includes a large number of modern compositions which spin out any figure of no special meaning. In these last the mere sensuous variety of charm, in the others the expression of feeling, demands the rendering in question. In good compositions the middle, again, is by preference the point where emotion is intensified, and requires a more impetuous surging of the tone-masses.

We now arrive at the discussion of that point, deferred when treating of the *rallentando,* which refers to the rapid succession of changing nuances in hastening and delaying. The same are not unessential means of expression in all music, whose character lies in free declamatory rhythm or in song-like intensity. Hastening and delaying contrast like *crescendo* and *decrescendo;* in their first and most natural sense, the idea of intensification counts the *crescendo* and *accelerando* among its resources; that of tranquilization the *decrescendo* and *rallentando;* and the two are frequently combined. The outpouring of emotion from the breast, the vehemence of its impulse, finds expression in the former; its tranquil expiration in the latter. In any music of deeply moving import, both may blend in the interpretation; nor can the principle of variety, as remarked before, by any means be rejected as a motive for this style of rendering, even in the most ideal sense.

Hardly an Adagio is imaginable, in which the same is not indispensable. Here we shall cite only a passage from

Beethoven's Adagio (Op. 10, *C*-minor Sonata), to be played as follows:

The 4 measures preceding the same also take a gently urgent crescendo.

But this style of rendering finds true transfiguration in the Chromatic Fantasia by Bach, which without such change of tempo could not attain to its lyrical expression; no less indispensable is the same in movements like the Finale of the Schumann *C*-major Fantasia. While the passage

requires this reading on ideal grounds, the two following measures may be treated according to the former principle, of somewhat hastening comparatively meaningless parts.

The literature of musical salon-coquetry likewise often employs this variety of style. For emotion inevitably moves —whatever be its subject—in pulsations of varying rapidity.

In closing there remains to be mentioned the combination, which is not self-evidently natural, of the nuances just examined with the *crescendo* and *decrescendo*. The *accelerando* may even combine with the *decrescendo*, the *rallentando* with the *crescendo*. The latter case was discussed above; consequently only the first-named combination demands attention.

This, like so many of the pianoforte charms earlier enumerated, will instantly make the impression of a nuance
challenging the intellectual faculty; because, unheedful of what
is self-evidently natural, it finds its *raison d'être* in other,
more complicated relations. A breathless haste, a repressed
vehemence of emotional impulse, a self-contained glow of living
energy, are expressed therein. Setting aside these psychic and
dramatic motives of the subject, there also resides in it a sensuous tone-color, which possesses the charm of the piquant
above that of the common, and can be often employed, more
particularly, in brilliant modernisms.

Touching loftier compositions, the grand natural power of
Beethoven's thoughts will assuredly but seldom require this
nuance of style. Mainly those composers who think dramati-
cally, or who have seized upon the more exquisite refinements
of execution, will furnish examples of the same. Mendelssohn
admits here and there of such nuances. — Brilliant passages,
continually growing faster and softer, have a charm of a
peculiar kind, which obtains value from the mere fact, that
it is based on a finished technique.

CHAPTER XVII.

Colors of tone and touch. The use of the pedals. Deter- mination of the tempo. On unity amid the diversity of the nuances of rendering. Conception of the rendering.

From the varieties of touch many different charms of
tone arise. Their employment, like everything having reference
to nuances in the rendering, is determined partly by the subject, partly according to the principle of sensuous variety.
To the nuances of tone enumerated in the first Part must,
however, be added the alterations in sound resulting from the
use of the pedals; and the rules to be laid down for this will

form a supplement to the hints then following on the employment of the various touches.

The legato passage, together with the pearling knuckle-joint touch, form the broadest and most natural foundation of all pianoforte music. As the entire technique was developed from this embryo, the ideal aspect of the rendering will also have to concern itself chiefly with its cultivation.—The highest perfection of the pearling passage-style persists throughout all pianoforte literature as a condition, without which no subject can be presented. Beethoven's Sonata Op. 111 needs this charm no less than a Fantasia by Thalberg.—After the pearling touch, the singing touch is most important.

The singing touch must lend its inspiration to many elements, which apparently lack all song-like qualities. Often there is *one* tone amid the brilliant interweaving of the passages that awakens a songful response, and elevates the outwardly merely Charmful into the sphere of real feeling. This touch shows its purest color in song-like compositions imitating vocality. For a truly *idealized* tone-color the rules given in the technical Part will, after all, not suffice. True, the nature of the finger-pressure therein described is a characteristic feature of all pianoforte melody; but it must be paired with a soulfelt insight into the nature of the *cantilene.* — Marx is right in saying, that the mechanical training alone cannot solve such problems. He who is not moved and fired at heart by the melody which he plays will not, despite all power and delicacy of the finger-tip, acquire the idealized tone-color which must characterize a truly artistic performance. Whoever would play, for instance, the Finale of the *E*-minor Sonata Op. 90 by Beethoven correctly, must be so inspired by its tenderness and intensity as was the soul of the creative artist. The thoroughness of a good technical training first shows its usefulness, when the subjectivity is fired by ideal life. Melody is the most important element after the pearling charm of the passages. But mere technique satisfies the requirements of the latter in all stages better than those of melody. — Melody is the soul within the sensuously beautiful body of tone; and all the brilliancy, or all the cool intellect, which may illuminate its eye, cannot endow the performance with the magic, with which it is inspired by the soulful spirit of song. —

But, as we see, it is not always the pressure of the finger-tip alone that sings; a gentle, imperceptible *rallentando* can lend to the most delicate tone the charm mentioned. In the majority of cases, to be sure, the predominance of the finger-pressure will prove the decisive factor, especially where, for metrical reasons, no *rallentando* is admissible.

In practicing melodious movements, each tone must be well weighed; the pupil must often make countless attempts to adjust the pressure, before hitting the right degree for a single decisive tone. The singing g in the Finale of the *C*-major Sonata (Op. 53) can, to be sure, be made to carry in modern style by a firm pressure. But only through the inspiration of the finger-nerve does it gain that softly buoyant, tenderly ethereal tinge unattainable through mechanical means alone. The realistic view may, indeed, trace everything, even such nuances, to mechanical action; yet this view does not render superfluous the unremitting care and precision of detail in studying individual shades of tone, which we state as an indispensable rule.

The same might be said of the middle movement in the *F*-minor Sonata Op. 57 by Beethoven. The melody should sing, but as if half exhausted, in a monochromatic tone-color partly devotional, partly lifeweary; and the bass must also furnish a sonorous, song-like foundation thereto. The whole should be held in a dim half-light, and *singing* throughout, however softly. To find the right relation between bass and soprano, and in this again the true proportion of each single tone, requires countless trials, an insight penetrating ever deeper into the inmost spirit of the spell woven by the tones — an insight not only of a musical, but of a poetic nature.— Technique is not the sole desideratum, but only the *first* step;

the *spiritual* tone-color is the higher, the more distant goal, often unattainable to many a virtuoso.

Where pearling coloraturas are intermingled with a singing movement, the two fairest charms of pianoforte playing are combined. They issue, it is true, from different mechanical principles, but must none the less combine, for the sake of the higher unity, in one and the same ideal tone-color. The singing quality will be less strongly marked when it passes over into the flowing ornamentation of the runs. The magic of tenderness, flowing grace, delicacy, and warm feeling, must inspire both the loftiest and the tenderest expression.

Modern melody requires the stronger lights of intenser muscular action. Something of the finer sense of tone is to be sacrificed to brilliancy; marked accentuation at times prevails. But we must not neglect to notice, that the more idealistic player will make many distinctions of rendering felt in this case, as well, which are overlooked by the merely brilliant virtuoso. One often hears players who fancy that by striking or stabbing the key they satisfy all requirements. — But this will be the case only at occasional points, where the full strength must be put forth.

When a melodious part is accompanied in the same hand by another, Thalberg gives the rule that the doubled notes thus formed should be arpeggio'd, in order to give the melody the necessary emphasis. It cannot be denied, that the melody can be more easily marked in this way. But in no case should one neglect to practice emphasizing the melody-note when striking two or more notes simultaneously. Aside from the utility of such practice, the monotony caused by the continuous arpeggios during a long movement is mitigated by the change. This monotony would be unavoidable, for instance, in the first part of Beethoven's $C\sharp$-minor Sonata, should the player constantly strike the melody-note after the accompaniment. Here it is best to save the arpeggio for the most pregnant passages. The middle movement of the Sonate pathétique would be an excellent practice-piece in the sense intended. To give the fingers the necessary independence for the purpose in question, both hands might play the following exercise:

The large notes are to be accented more strongly than the others.

Furthermore, the expression of melody need by no means be confined to legato notes. There are very many most delicate staccato passages, whose intention is intrinsically melodious. Together with the otherwise essential characteristics of the usual staccato technique, finger-pressure must then also be employed, which calls for a sensitive finger-tip in soft passages. The middle movement of the Beethoven Sonata in *G*-major Op. 14 has the first part of the theme staccato, and this with a most delicate and soft tone. But, however *piano* be the effect of the touch on the whole, the highest tone of each chord must be melodiously marked above the other intervals. — Passages in light staccato also require a melodious touch here and there.

Now, with reference to the staccato styles in their individuality, no universally binding rules can be given to determine, in each individual case, which of these subtle nuances the player should employ. Only this is beyond a doubt; — that for the grandest effects of tone the staccato with the arm will be most suitable, for the softest that with the finger-tip. But the more delicate staccato passages may very well be performed in many cases with the wrist, with the finger-joint, or with combinations of these joints, or may even be better executed thus in passages of the more rapid kind than with the finger-tip alone. A peculiarly happy combination is that of the wrist with the finger-tip staccato, or the free stroke of the whole finger with the finger-tip. Octave staccato is taken by the wrist. In all these kinds, the main thing is the perfect yieldingness of the technique, which must retain its elasticity in all grades of power. Should the one kind pass over into the other in passages of otherwise flowing uniformity, the evenness of tone must be preserved.—In the following passage from Beethoven's Op. 31 (*E*-major Sonata) the staccato will be executed chiefly by the finger-tip with the entire finger; while for the repeated *e♭* the wrist will be employed. But, aside from the *crescendo,* no unevenness of tone must be perceptible.

Regarding the other styles of touch, the mechanical part gives the necessary data. The *carrezzando,* the stroking of the key, is best adapted to tender, sentimental passages; in Beethoven's works a suitable example for this touch can hardly be found. It has too much of sensuous charm. Among good composers, Mendelssohn and Chopin might both employ it; the former in many a delicate, ethereal Song without Words, e. g. the Spring Song, the latter in the melody of certain Nocturnes, which seem to recede from the material, and soar up into space. It would mainly appear only transiently. Used throughout, it suits the super-sentimental ideas of *blasé* and empty modernity; although, as remarked, its sensuous charm cannot be denied.

The sustained *mezzo staccato* is a style of touch of marked effect. Both in softest piano and strongest power it lends to the tones a peculiar impressiveness, and declamatory emphasis. We give two examples together. The first, from Mendelssohn's third Song without Words (Part II), employs this touch in the sense of most exquisite grace; the second, from Beethoven's Sonata in *E♭*-major, Op. 31, for impressive effect.

Regarding all nuances of touch, the following general principles may be stated. Merely *for their own sake* they can be used only (1) in Études practiced for special training; or (2) in that species of music, whose end is not psychic, but sensuous, expression. Where the ear craves less intellectual delight, the player must give fuller scope to purely mechanical refinements. The salon literature introduced by Thalberg, in particular his own works, exhibit the alternate nuances of tone for the sake of sensuous variety. To the earlier salon music this fulness of charm was unknown; the later must be prized in contrast.

Existence *for the sake of a higher meaning* is, in any event, the nobler destination of the nuances of touch. The student is urgently warned against occupying his fancy mainly with their sensuous beauty. The attention must be engaged with the significance of the tones, true musical thought; and the flexibility of the modern training of the hand, with all its advantages, may be held at disposal as a factor of secondary rank. Sensuous charm will be brought out in fullest abundance;—but when the interpretation is not inspired by a glowing conception, such mechanical aids may do positive harm.

Whoever, in playing Beethoven's *G*-major Sonata Op. 14, takes note only of the wrist-stroke for the soprano in the following passage:

but does not feel the tender, maidenly fervor of these five entreating tones (the repeated *d*), will not give the right nuance to the phrase. The spirit must lead the way; in its service modern training is a boon indeed; but where it has perished through over-devotion to the latter, harm has come of it.

Let the reader call to mind the two last chords in the first passage of the Finale of the *C♯*-minor Sonata. Whoever should take note therein of the arm-stroke only — not conceiving a poetical picture, as of upheaving billows rushing on with gathering fury toward a rock, against which they must dash in vain—knows nothing of the part borne by the artistic conception.—

Music is not a pure, transcendental ideal—its materiality cannot be denied — but it makes a difference, whether the lustre of this materiality merely shines out in its formal contours, or discovers in its bright halo shapes belonging to higher spheres. Only the primary pupil or the primary virtuoso (for there are such) views, in all, the mechanical training as the final end and aim. This standpoint is characteristic of pupilage in the true sense of the term; to rise superior to this must be the learner's chief endeavor.

The use of the Pedal remains for discussion. Through the same, the nuances of touch undergo further considerable modifications. Their theory is at present, their number being limited to 2, simpler than formerly, when there were from 4 to 6.

The damper-pedal, commonly called "the pedal", lifts the dampers from the strings; the "soft pedal" slightly shifts the keyboard to one side, so that the hammer strikes only two strings, or, in many instruments, only one. (This is the German "Verschiebung", or *shifting* pedal; other styles of the soft pedal introduce a muffler between the hammers and the strings, or lessen the distance from which the hammers strike.)—The damper (or *loud*) pedal reinforces the tone; the *soft* pedal softens it.

The former is usually regarded as the more important. This is a mistaken view; and the custom of many pianoforte makers, to furnish with but one pedal upright and square pianos (in which, to be sure, a shifting pedal is not so readily adjustable), is to be censured. The soft pedal has equal value, for on it a great many refinements depend; these the pupil must renounce, when he has but one pedal at his disposal.—

We shall first take up the Pedal commonly so called. It is employed in four cases: (1) To connect tones; (2) to augment the number of sounding notes; (3) to reinforce the power of the tone; (4) to enhance the poetry of the shading throughout.

(1) It often happens, that the hand cannot bind tones belonging to the same part, being occupied with others. This case occurs most frequently with the wide stretches and full harmonies of the modern pianoforte style, but may likewise be found in earlier compositions, even in Bach. A great deal naturally depends upon the stretch of the hand. One can dispense with the pedal, where a smaller hand would require it. The foot also needs a certain technique for precision in pressing and releasing the pedal. The duration of the tone sustained by the pedal must be measured off with the utmost nicety. Often only an instantaneous pressure is needed. This

is peculiarly applicable to bass notes, which frequently call for stretches in the left hand forbidden by its size. In the modern style, where the ear should follow a *cantilena* amid interweaving passages, the connection of the melody would often be impracticable except by the continual use of the pedal. In this regard, the literature of Paraphrases and Fantasias on given melodies furnishes the most striking examples. The rule requires an exact release of the pedal at the entrance of each new harmony, and the binding of the melody-notes is generally so arranged, that the pedal needed therefore has a double task; namely, besides the binding here in question, the multiplication of sounding tones; which last case will be taken up by itself under No. 2.

Examples:

Bach.

Henselt, Op. 1.

A. Kullak, La parade des voltigeurs. Op. 17.

Excellent practice is afforded by the binding of successive chords with the pedal, which would often present unconquerable difficulties to the unassisted finger-technique. Take the pedal just after striking the harmony, and hold it exactly to the entrance of the following chord:

by this means a clean and perfect legato is obtained, which can, it is true, be accelerated to only moderate rapidity. Attention is called in this connection to the little monograph by Louis Köhler on the Pianoforte Pedal ("Ueber den Klavierpedalzug"), in which the treading of the pedal is indicated by notes and rests with the greatest rhythmical exactitude.

(2) The second case applies to those harmonic figures which form in the bass, in greater or less breadth, an accompaniment to a melody written above. Here, as in the foregoing number, it is the function of the pedal to bind the tones; but this binding is now not required, because they belong to each other as forming a melodious or declamatory series, but because it enriches the harmony by completing the same. Thus the pedal now furthers an external, sensuous charm rather than the clearness and intelligibility of the idea. It is the deep bass tone, in particular, whose sounding-on enhances the harmonic charm, and at whose change the pedal

must be taken anew. — Where passing notes, scale-like passages, etc., are interposed between the harmonic figures, the pedal is interrupted. If the number of such notes is not so great as to disturb the harmony, the pedal may be retained. Here the ear must decide. The higher the accompaniment lies, the more readily will it bear foreign tones.

Examples are scarcely needful. The modern school has an overabundance of such. — But passages *not* in the accompaniment may be played, when their harmony admits, with the pedal for the sake of brilliancy; e. g. the following passage from Hummel's *A*-minor Concerto, page 11:

(3) The reinforcement of the sound is an essential motive for the employment of the pedal. It is peculiarly promotive of brilliancy; indeed, the example from Hummel given above already belongs to this number. Passing notes and foreign tones may also occur in profusion. The tangling confusion of the tones has at moments a stimulating or exciting effect which finds justification, whether in external, sensuous causes, or picturesque, poetic ones.—For the first case Liszt gives an example in his "Galop chromatique":

20

For the second case storms, thunder, bell-tones and sea-sounds, or scenes of dreamy, confused murmuring, humming, buzzing, afford manifold examples. Dreamy confusion often recurs in Robert Schumann's poetic pictures, and requires the pedal.

(4) In the above we already approach the fourth case.— The pedal has the peculiarity of lending to the tone a buoyantly vanishing tinge. Even an isolated tone, played with the pedal, differs from the same without. This impression is decidedly heightened, when the pedal is held through a continuous succession of tones. The confusedly blended, vanishing character of tone thus produced possesses an undeniable poetic charm; but such effects must be cautiously introduced, as their abuse easily tends to triviality, and mars the clearness of the style. High-pitched passages, especially in *piano*, are best suited for a frequent pedal. But the same is at times also indispensable in deeper passages—if continually retaken—as for instance in the Finale of the last Sonata:

From a sombre background, melancholy in its monotony, flitting tones emerge abruptly like unreal visions; the whole is so hazy, so fantastical, so far removed from material stability, that the sense is drawn involuntarily into supernatural spheres. On these eight measures follows, in the treble, a murmuring and whispering, as if in answer from the spirit-world.—In such passages the pedal is in place, as an aid to poetic picturesqueness. A similar example is found in Bagatelle No. 4, in Part 3 of Op. 126 by Beethoven, towards the close of the middle part in *B*-major. The last 13 measures take the pedal;

one and the same bass continues throughout these measures; the right hand plays a figure of constantly decreasing power. The whole must dissolve away — it resembles a dream-scene, wherein the soul floats onward over heath and forest of an idyllic landscape, whence rise reminiscences of the bagpipe and shepherd's flute — all vanishes — it was a memory of youth — the following part, in *B*-minor, breathes a wayward humor.

In general it may be said of the pedal, that it is at present — and rightly — more sparingly employed than at that time of Thalbergianism, when entire compositions depended thereon for their effect. Chopin unquestionably uses it too often. Beethoven is said to have had a great liking for it; his *C*-major Sonata Op. 53, in the last part, is essentially calculated for the pedal and written for the same. — But æsthetical considerations take precedence of historical ones, and for Beethoven's compositions, too, a sparing use of the pedal is on the whole to be recommended. One should bear in mind, that at the beginning of the century the thinner tone of the pianoforte made a cautious employment of the damper pedal less urgently necessary than the full tone of modern instruments.

We proceed to the second, or soft, pedal. — Its chief aim is the production of the softest *piano*. True, the quality of the ordinary pianoforte tone is thus changed, in most instruments, to a milder, more harplike timbre; still, this is not always the case, and the said change is not the principle aim. Czerny, indeed, rightly says, that a soft tone without aid from the soft pedal does the player more honor; and the development of such a tone must be insisted on above all in this connection — as was done earlier. However, in performing, the advantage of the soft pedal is beyond a doubt; in the very softest tone of the best action the same liquid tenderness can never be attained without the soft pedal as with its aid.

This pedal is employed in two ways; either together with the other, or by itself.

Taken alone, it makes the tone peculiarly piquant, tender — a trifle dry — but combines with these qualities, as remarked,

20*

a quality softer than that of the ordinary pianoforte tone. Thus the mere sensuous charm of variety will, for its share, admit of rendering certain passages, in contrast to stronger ones, in this tone-color. Where the same or similar figures are repeated once or oftener, or in the gentlest expiring sigh of the *decrescendo* and *rallentando*, the soft pedal may be taken either in aid of variety, or still further to soften the ordinary *pianissimo*. The merely material is almost always turned into the ideal thereby; for a *piano* produced in this manner inevitably urges the fancy to excursions into an immaterial sphere. Delicate appreciation will, however, draw a distinction between external and internal effect.

When the soft pedal is combined with the other, its fine and piquant effect is veiled by the haziness which lightly blurs the sharp contours of musical form. There appears a new timbre, slightly more romantically sentimental than the foregoing. The fine lines waver and blend. This style, as well, is possessed of poetical and material value. It will usually be in place in just those situations, where the foregoing was admitted; all depends upon the total character of the work, and upon the conception, which, provided that it does not lack unity, may often employ either style with equal correctness. — The combination of the two pedals most frequently occurs with accompaniment figures in the bass, to which the highest part supplies the melody. Here sensuous euphony is to be enhanced; such basses have, in their softness and tenderness, a strong tinge of voluptuous revelry. Neither are genuinely poetic, picturesque motives wanting. The soft, hazy character —united with the tender timbre—always adds an airy touch, renders the melancholy yet more brooding and intense, the gay more amiable, the tender more ethereal. —The charm of the soft pedal alone, however, will on the whole have the larger number of reasons for its employment.

The combination of the two pedals is one of the cheaper resources of rendering, as by the frequency of the abovementioned case in modern compositions thoughtfulness on the player's part is thus nearly dispensed with, and the effect becomes almost trivial. If the soft pedal *alone* is to produce the right effect, the player must think more carefully.—He must always be on his guard against monotony, and wherever he finds it, have a resource at hand for relieving it. Thus it often occurs, that the soft pedal is to be touched only instantaneously, precisely like the other. A gentle, brief pressure of the same frequently lends a delicate tinge of variety to an evenly flowing passage; at times it need affect the timbre of but two or three tones. Of this, two examples follow immediately.

In the first Bagatelle by Beethoven, already so often cited in the matter of rendering, the following passage occurs:

The passage is monotonous with the mere repetition of the same figure. If the second figure takes the soft pedal, it obtains the charm of variety. Fancy directly conjures up, from among its teeming conceptions, an echo, or an answer —a dialectic relation of two conferring parts—as the meaning of this passage.

Another example is found at the end of the first theme in the *C*-major Sonata Op. 10. Here one figure is thrice repeated; Beethoven, it is true, would have it given strongly each time. According to laws earlier mentioned, a *decrescendo* might also enter. Should we incline to this yet more delicate style of rendering, we should play the passage as follows:

At the *decrescendo*, the transition to the soft pedal must be skilfully managed; i. e. the last tones of the passage without soft pedal are to be played *piano*, whereas the first tones with the latter are taken a little stronger, so as to sound very nearly equal to those of the preceding register, then gradually decreasing to the softest tone. —

Poetic tone-pictures, like the "Abendwind" (Evening Breeze) by Th. Kullak, or the introduction to the eleventh Hungarian Rhapsody by Liszt, bear the combined pedals, as does also the whispering treble passage entering after the above-cited passage from Beethoven, Op. 111.— A luminous spirit-sphere replies to a darkened one.

In other cases the employment of the soft pedal, though not exactly necessary, cannot be condemned; to these belong many tender, pearling passages by Liszt (e. g. in *Au bord d'une source)*; the following passage from Beethoven's *E♭* Sonata Op. 31 may also be played in this manner:

Compositions, which are wrought from one figure, may occasionally use the soft pedal by way of variety; sometimes even an abrupt transition to the softest piano has a fine and picturesque effect, e. g. on the third staff, page 6, of the author's Étude "Lore-Ley", Op. 2.

The investigations concerning the soft pedal led up to the modifications in the power of touch. Among these, the softest piano was mentioned. — In the mechanical part, a three-fold proportion of power was assumed as a point of departure, the pedal then naturally being excluded. — Now, in the theory of the rendering, the earlier observations bearing upon practical study must be supplemented by the statement, that the number of gradations is far greater, especially when the pedals are called into requisition. Each grade of power has a distinct character. The motives variously pointed out in the foregoing need not be repeated here; and the method, having reached this point, may be permitted to assume, that the additional remarks on the grades of power may be brief.

The countless varieties of gradation in power are derivable from five *primary conceptions* or *colors;* the rest are to be regarded as intermediate shades formed by transition from one of these to another.

The starting-point is the medium tone-color *(mezzo forte),* which in regard to evenness and distinctness is not alike in all hands, but must be determined by each hand conformably to its natural degree of power. From the mere differences in the strength of the hands it is apparent, that the grades of power admit of no absolute standard, but are relative conceptions taking, as their point of departure, the average strength of the varying individual hands. — This tone-color is the most chaste and simply beautiful. — It must everywhere form the grounding, and where it is carried out in finished purity, the essential point is gained. The co-operation of accentuation and other means of expression is, to be sure, taken for granted. True, this tone-color cannot everywhere bring out the fullest depth of meaning, but it will at least spoil nothing, and is, indeed, the only correct style for many aphoristically conceived works of the briefer kind. — Wherever the term "passage" applies, it is the fundamental condition, and often deserves preference over the turgid and frequently indistinct *piano.*

This color admits of two gradations toward strong or light, i. e. four in all.

The first reinforcement produces the *forte*. An intensified *inward* or *outward* (sensuous) significance is the motive of the same. The accentuation is founded upon a momentary employment of this grade of power; the phrasing of whole movements, their *crescendi* and the features of the declamation, as the motives applied more in detail, have already been discussed, and we refer the student to these earlier remarks.

The second reinforcement, the *fortissimo* (*ff*, sometimes *fff*) is based on a still more potent exhibition of the motives mentioned above. —

Intensity of meaning will in general outweigh external considerations of material charm. The simply Beautiful treated of in the above will now pass over into all those nuances, which are related to the factor of *greatness* contained in the Beautiful; into the grand, the magnificent, sublime, both in a glad and a tragic sense; in joy and pain, in exultation or fury.

Aside from such psychic motives, sensuous brilliancy, or even formal relations, may guide the choice of the *fortissimo*. Accents that bound entire movements, closing phrases of compositions, which yield merely sensuous delight, have a claim to it. The *fortissimo* has the effect of strong light. Compositions which do not disdain pyrotechnic display, will save the most brilliant effect for the close. — But in a certain sense one cannot refuse, to the chastest compositions, the aid afforded by such resources. As a symbolical art, suggesting absolute ideas by roundabout methods, music dare not hold itself quite aloof from the claims of materiality. Beethoven's *F*-minor Sonata could not close otherwise than in a stormy *fortissimo*. — Neither can orchestral effects be otherwise attained on the pianoforte. The art of tone-painting, which depicts storms, uproar, thunder, the crash of falling, and the like, must needs make use of it.

The simple *piano* shades the purely beautiful, through a
sensuously delightful element of charm, into the amiable, gentle,
graceful, tender, elegant. To the latter it is indispensable, as
it neutralizes the ponderous weight of the broader masses of
tone, and replaces it by lightness. The simple *piano* can
therefore be applied most frequently, in entire movements, to
compositions by Mozart and Mendelssohn. — By its contrast to
the *forte* it has, as a means of variety, like importance with
the *decrescendo* and *crescendo*, the *rallentando* and *accelerando.*
Two like or similar passages will be played, in the majority
of cases, *forte* the first time and *piano* the second, or often
vice versâ, where the conception is highly dramatic; several
similar figures take these shades in alternation. — With works
whose spirit is of medium intensity, inclining prevalently neither
to *forte* nor to *piano*, the player should distribute these colors
with a delicate sense of proportion; it may even happen, that
he deviates from the prescribed interpretation, without doing
violence to the work. — Whoever were to play, for instance,
the two passages toward of the first part of the first movement in the *F*-minor Sonata by Beethoven forcibly, and to
give the end of the second:

in particular strong expression, would do perfectly right to
render the following thought:

delicately, (although the composer wrote the direction *con espressione*), in order to intensify the expression of this idea in its two subsequent repetitions. — According to the principle of variety, of the uncompromising avoidance of monotony, several such readings are often equally justifiable in one and the same work. The receptive sense of hearing is gratified when it notes, in the distribution of the grades of power, a well-balanced variety. Thus in the last example it would also not be incorrect to play the second passage preceding the closing idea *piano,* and to play the last, following Beethoven's directions, in *forte.* But then its repetition would have to be treated in the reverse sense, i. e. *decrescendo.*

We need not add, that works of more definite meaning are not touched by the rule just given, or at least remain unaffected by it to the extent in which their expression is defined. The last movement of the *F*-minor Sonata Op. 57 admits, in any case, of but *one* conception.

The *pianissimo* was disposed of, in part, when discussing the soft pedal. Herewith is not meant, of course, that this tone-color can not also be produced without the help of this pedal. On the contrary, a good player should prove his technical mastership by an ethereal touch with no aid whatever from the pedal. The alternation of *p* and *pp* is the highest triumph of delicacy in pianoforte technique.

Nearly all directions for the rendering have reference to degrees of power or tempo. The former have been examined in the foregoing; therefore the general tempo suited to each individual composition still remains for consideration.

The rules on this latter point must appeal directly to the musical feeling. Until now the method has striven to treat its subject with all objective freedom, leaving as little as might be to the subjective conception. In establishing the tempo it trenches, if proceeding without this assumption, upon philosophical objects of wide scope, which lie beyond

the limits of this special treatise on æsthetics. It can venture
only the following brief observations.

Immediate musical feeling measures according to the expression given in *song*, and judges every musical idea primarily by the grades of movement familiar to it in this sphere.
According to the analyses of the first chapter, however, the
pianoforte differs in function from song as regards expression,
in that it leaves the idea of form-growth, the spirit of development, in the foreground, and has therefore to influence feeling
and fancy, not from the side of the natural charm of the tones
and their individual effect, but from the side of reflection. It
is certain, that all pianoforte tempi are somewhat more rapid,
than the pianoforte ideas would be taken by one singing the
same (thinking them as sung). Dilettanti often take pianoforte
cantilene too slowly, because they do not think instrumentally,
but in one-sided vocal style.—The above is of general application. In individual cases, movements vocally conceived, like
Adagios and slow, sustained pieces, are to be distinguished
correspondingly from livelier ones of a more instrumental character, and the former kind will more closely follow vocal
style. Within melodious pianoforte works, too, the specifically
cantilena-like phrases are to be taken more slowly than the
others, in accordance with their original conception; between
these will flash out brilliantly winding passages, whose melodious points must, however, as remarked earlier, be brought
out by retardation. Uniformity of measure must be maintained
as far as possible, despite all deviations. — The movement of
the various kinds of allegro is often determined by externals,
where neither musical feeling and conception, nor experience,
can afford a certain clew. For the most rapid passages, the
degree of technique will usually decide the degree of rapidity.
As compositions are not *abstract* conceptions, but *planned for*
the human faculties of interpretation at their disposal, this
suggestion will suffice in most cases. Musical feeling is, indeed, a safer guide. The fine impressionability of the latter
must strike a general average between the instrumental and

vocal spirit permeating the composition, and fix the tempo accordingly. The Finale of the *D*-minor Sonata Op. 31 retains a songful nuance, and is therefore not so fast as that of the *F*-minor Sonata, whose conception is purely instrumental. In this latter, velocity and bravura of technique are quite in place. Nearly the same obtains of the Finale of the *C♯*-minor Sonata; but the last movement of the *B♭*-major Sonata has a more tranquil course, by reason of its melodious character. — Experience and musical science likewise come to the aid of such inward and outward indications; the whole meaning of music does not issue from vocality, or from the transmutation of this element into instrumental style. Actual phases of life employ music as an integral element of their existence, and the progression of the tones becomes independent of the externalities of rhythm controlling them. We refer to the March and the Dance. The fixing of the tempo of these compositions depends upon the idea of the physical movements, which, given up in part to pure enjoyment, in part filled with characteristic ideality, serve as a suggestion.

Such practical perception determines the tempo of a minuet, of a dead march, a festival march, the various national dances, even of the earlier dance-airs idealized in Bach's music, as the gigue, sarabande, gavotte, etc.

We have now reached the end of the part on the Rendering. The method had to content itself with discussing the chief forms, which were treated of under Accentuation, the Cresendo and Decrescendo, the Accelerando and Rallentando, Measure and Tempo in general, together with the colors of Touch and Tone. A knowledge of these chief forms furnishes a basis for the interpretation of all the numerous art-terms which refer to the subject of a piece, or to any passage in the same; e. g. *pomposo, grandioso, con affetto, con passione, flebile, inconsolabile, leggermente (leggieramente), estinto, amabile,* etc. Thoughtful reflection reduces all these terms to the chief forms spoken of in the foregoing; e. g. *pomposo* to *forte* and under certain conditions, a not too rapid march-movement;

flebile to unrestful movement with an expression now gentle, now vehement; *leggermente* to *piano* with a somewhat high, pearling touch, etc. True, such terms are not fully explained by this translation; for their essential element is an inner, lyrical distinction.—But the method cannot explain these terms in detail, in order to satisfy all the claims of poetical inspiration; this would lead to unnecessary excursiveness and repetition. It feels constrained, notwithstanding, to satisfy these claims to a certain extent; holding fast to its principle, which in many cases has been obliged to concede to subjects, otherwise non-teachable, the aid of the same spiritualization. This can, however, be done only in general terms; which prevents, on the one hand, needless breadth, and directs, on the other, the reflection to those fundamental ideas, which are more stimulative and useful than mnemonic acquirements. At the same time it fulfils the task proposed in the fourth chapter in that measure, to which the same is entitled by the form of this special course in æsthetics.

Before proceeding to this closing chapter, which follows the preceding investigations in the sense of an appendix, one other conception demands examination, which, though variously anticipated in the foregoing pages, could not be treated of in full till now. We mean that idea, in its singleness of unity, from which the great number of nuances in rendering received, each in and for itself, purpose and meaning.

Hitherto we have considered *diversity;* the Beautiful is, however, *unity* in diversity. The method must in closing examine this idea of universality, as the first cause, which unites within itself the various resources of detailed expression in the harmony of the Beautiful.—

Mere diversity of expression does not suffice to render the interpretation *beautiful.* The most manifold variety in the distinctions of tone, power, and movement must bear a fitting relation to the unity of meaning of the individual composition. It is the latter which must first be recognized and understood; starting from this only, as the poetical essence, should the player calculate the proportions in which the multifarious shades are to be laid on.—Herein a most apparent parallelism subsists between music and painting. As in the latter the general scheme of color harmoniously combines the different local notes, in the presentation on the pianoforte, too, unisonity must form the fundamental idea, which must be recognizable as the original and guiding thought amid all opulence of separate shades. It is *determined* by the musical meaning of the composition.

Thus the player has to present the gradations of power, movement, and tone in greater or less fulness, in more rapid or slower alternation, in sharper or milder accentuation, according to the exigencies of oneness in the conception; and he should study not only each separate movement of a large work in this manner, but seek out the bond of unity subsisting between the several movements. — Great compositions will frequently bear the fullest abundance of color even in contrasting passages in closest succession; in miniature sketches the fundamental idea is easier of observance, as in them gracefulness, attractiveness, and neatness of form usually impose the obligation to keep the display of the powers within bounds. Melancholy often directly enjoins monotony; gay vivacity will call for the most charmful, brilliant variety in a more outward sense; depth of meaning, the mightier intensification of the tone-colors in a psychico-dramatical intention.— Thus throughout Beethoven's $A\flat$-major Sonata Op. 110 there breathes a spirit of gentle mournfulness. This is the fundamental idea, imposing moderation on the display of power, and requiring a prevailingly songful, lyrically resigned spiritualization of the harmonies. Contrasts are found, to be sure, as everywhere else. Quaint humor breaks out once in the second movement; and in the Finale, even glowing energy emerges in the midst of these elegiac scenes; but the fundamental idea is that given.—The F-minor Sonata is a sublime picture of titanic greatness of soul — here the most striking contrasts are justified. The tremendous impetuosity of the first part may properly call forth the monotonous weariedness of the second. While in the first the mightiest *fortissimi* raged, in the second the dreamiest *piani* may prevail throughout, and the third may follow in the train of the first.— Similar relations subsist between the third and first movements of the $C\sharp$-minor Sonata; likewise between the two movements of the *E*-minor Sonata Op. 90, and the two first of the *pathétique*, though not so saliently.—As remarked, smaller tone-scenes more easily preserve unity of meaning, and have, from logical reasons, greater need of the latter. Broad canvasses include a greater diversity of objects, and have an opportunity of employing all imaginable nuances; their unity dwells in impalpable spirit-regions. Small pictures usually represent the pretty, the graceful, the delicate—all parts of the Beautiful, of a mainly sensuous nature. Here a *mezzo-forte* touch will form the grounding, and all shades toward *forte* or *piano* will have to be understood in a *relative* sense only. Dilettanti very wrongly take the *forte* in such compositions with the same force as in a widely extended scene full of grand passion.

One cannot sufficiently emphasize the rule, that the power of the nuances of tone has in most cases a relative intent. The player should always first look at the Whole, and arrange the balance of his *crescendi* and *diminuendi* accordingly. Of course, these latter have the larger freedom in small pieces. Prettiness (neatness) bears the melting, ethereal glimmering of color yielded by a soft-sighing *piano* as its ground-tone, in most cases. Good examples are yielded by the Scherzo No. 2, in Gade's Albumblätter, and Mendelssohn's Spring Song. Whoever were to develop the *forte* as strongly here as in a long sonata, would be guilty of a bad blunder. The *piano*, on the contrary, may overstep its mean.

It must, however, be observed, that the entire development of the technique forms a preparation in but an elementary sense for the unity of tone-production. Elasticity, looseness, prompt energy in the action of the playing muscle directly engaged, and a certain brilliancy of tone-production flowing therefrom, were characteristics lying at the root of both the gentlest and most powerful manifestations in the whole field of technique; and he who is thoroughly trained in these, will always be able to maintain a sort of unity in the sense above mentioned. But the harmony of the fundamental idea intended in this chapter is of an ideal kind; it orders according to the principle of thoughtful, well-weighed expression the material, which mechanical art ranged in unconnected successions.

Unity having thus fully asserted itself, and diversity having displayed itself in a tasteful and rational manner under its influence, the *rendering* will be an artistically finished one. Herewith we naturally arrive at the end of the method, which, from the first elements and through all intermediate links, necessarily kept the rendering in view as its sole end and aim. None of its elements can be dispensed with;—but, great as was the stress which the mechanical art laid upon its share, it now becomes needful, on the basis herewith established, to insure full acceptance of the precept: "The Rendering, not the Technique, is the chief matter."

To return at length to the consideration of the question already broached in Chap. 2, concerning the justification, or even necessity, of subjective influences on musical reproduction, we call attention to the following main features; (1) that music does not, in any event, define its meaning with absolute precision, but assumes greater imaginative activity than other arts; (2) that the truth of the Beautiful admits of a various commingling of its constituent parts, though the outlines of a work be otherwise firmly defined; and (3) that the very art of rendering consists in divining, among the different possibilities, that form of unity which corresponds either to the inclination or to the conviction of the interpreting subjectivity.

As the thought can by no means be termed too presumptuous, that, despite fullest recognition of the intellectual superiority of the classics and some post-classics in the point of *production*, artistic training and taste for *reproduction* occupy at the present day a more advanced standpoint even as compared with a Beethoven, it must be considered as a positive duty, in the case of the great majority of minor compositions, to show *more* in their interpretation than they contain.

CHAPTER XVIII.
Suggestions on the general conception.

Deep within the human soul there dwells a sense of discontentment with life — a yearning for a resolution of its dissonances. What reality denies, fancy strives to make. good, and in response to that sense of yearning has constructed two worlds for herself — Religion, and Art. In religion she has built up a system of metaphysical conceptions, which reconcile with life by leading above and beyond it, and promising to temporal imperfection eternal perfection. In art, on the contrary, fancy takes possession of reality, to re-form it, i. e. to idealize it, in accordance with that psychic impulse. She impresses the stamp of ideality on the least material existence, on tone, color, form — on flower and animal; she impresses it on all the manifold affinities between things and living beings; yes, she mounts the rounds of her endless ladder to such a height, as to act efficiently in the sense of religious and metaphysical needs, being on the one hand in touch with dogma, and on the other with the innermost depths of the human subject.

With external objectivity, architecture excepted, music is comparatively least in touch. The emotional life forms its chief material. The nature of tone gives it this bent; for the changing relations of the pitch, power, and harmony are adaptable to the symbolism of emotional phases. This native charm fills the whole realm of tones to such an extent, that the fundamental ideas of the science of the rendering previously developed are based essentially upon the same.

But herewith the musical art-work has not yet attained to its full spiritualization. This charm must be supplemented

21

by a threefold conception: (1) of *form*, (2) of *picturesqueness*, (3) of *poetry*. The first, or formal conception, exhibits the ideality of structure possible within the range of specifically musical combination, and controlled by order, by unity in diversity. The idea of Form presenting itself as one restricted by no very great number of distinctions, the music resulting herefrom will have at its disposal, in particular, the charm of tone-effects, and the art of alternately exciting and relieving suspense of a sensuous nature — the material of so-called effect. Hence arises beauty of the sensuously charmful and plastic order. — The charm of the second kind is limited to imitations, to chords responsive to the phenomena of life. The secret of the tone's picturesque power is studied, and a meaning of another kind thus given to it. The work of art attains to picture-like significance; scenes and sounds of Nature, the motions and actions of living creatures, are imaged in its course. Thus it comes, that the tone is enabled to include within the scope of its imagery a great part of the audible, and even of the visible, phenomena of the world. (Compare the fifth chapter in the author's work "Das musikalisch Schöne" [The Beautiful in Music]).

The last division of the threefold conception, as the most comprehensive and highest, will naturally attract the artist's intensest attention; we have to refer more especially to the interpretation, darkly foreshadowed by the emotion, of beautiful compositions. On this point objective research is still wanting, however, in the field of musical æsthetics. Musical phrase-mongery, flowery poetical periods of ineffable cheapness, everywhere prevail; objective affinities and subjective peculiarities are foisted upon art-works, as if it were the chief concern of music to appropriate by force that which is utterly denied to its own resources. In truth, there lies a meaning in the tones; but of a more universal kind, whose interpretation must not go too far in this direction.

Two composers stand at the head of musical literature, and the pianoforte may pride itself in possessing, in the works

of both, a very large part of their most important creations:
—these are Bach and Beethoven. They differ one from the
other in the same way, as the poetry of dogma differs from
that of the soul itself rising above the terrestrial sphere. Bach
is the poet inspired by the former, and therefore he is characterized by a firm-knit, plastically moulding style — sublimity
and intensity, piety, undivided inner unity. Beethoven creates
within his own breast the spheres of eternity, a supernal world
in the deeps of his profoundly moved heart. The attendant
mood is sublimity, melancholy, sadness. With psychologic consistency, humor follows in their train — the vastness of the
pain, the intenseness of his introspective, world-embracing
mood, would consume itself, did it not laugh at itself and at
the nothingness of all things earthly. —

It is the task of the interpreting artist to penetrate into
all these moods, to understand each in turn, and to feel,
throughout all details, the unity of meaning in the psychic
imagery — warm enthusiasm for the whole. Only where the
inner comprehension has been gained *receptively*, can the *reproductive* interpretation be satisfactory. It is the most delightful — and most serious — duty of the player, to strive upward
to these two pinnacles.

Enthusiastic for the highest ideals, he must not refuse
loving and thoughtful study to the other spheres of literature.
Sensuous beauty is also a justifiable factor. The pearling
element of tone is a charm possessed by the pianoforte alone;
though the numerous other tone-colors never attain to the effect of orchestral diversity, they make amends in no small
measure through charmful delicacy, and by the ideal vein of
skilful virtuosity — a kind of ideality to which the orchestra
does not rise.

The warmth of enthusiasm will always appear in this;—
that the player feels himself stimulated to an apperception of
poetical motives taken from real life. By way of illustration,
we here adduce the manifold interpretations which have been
suggested for Beethoven's $C\sharp$-minor Sonata Op. 27:

21*

(1) *Czerny* dwells only upon the first movement, and calls it a Night-piece, wherein are heard the utterances of a spirit-voice.

(2) *Ulibischeff* finds in the Adagio the moving plaint of a love that knows no realization, and feeds upon itself, like a flame lacking fuel. As the melody sounds more brokenly, the moon discovers her pale, corpse-like face, and veils herself again in a moment behind the gloomy cloud-rack hastening past. One seems to view an immense grave on a wild, barren plain. Melodies rise from this grave, like the responses of a complaining shade, bemoaning its impotence. — In the Presto, Beethoven has given vent to his fury and despair, cursing Destiny, that crushes the human race under the load of its curse — and then weeps again like a child begging its mother's forgiveness.

(3) *Liszt* styled the Allegretto of this Sonata a flower betwixt two abysms (a comparison, which Ubilischeff finds unapt).

(4) *Marx* terms the Adagio the soft song of renouncing love. It is the farewell to all hope of the thirsting soul, when speech fails, when the fearful sigh from the faithful breast can hardly breathe its lay, when the pulse of rhythm, scarce awakened, falters and delays like the last lingering gaze of a sad parting. The life, too, glides downward with ghostly calm into depths, wherein no balm is found for these pains. And in such chaste tranquility, untroubled by all disturbing storms of passion, this mournful song flows on! etc.

Renouncement is followed by the parting in the second movement: "O think on me, I think on thee! Farewell, farewell for ever." — And now life must be lived through — the lover storms abroad and storms aloft, and fumes and complains — and all the stripes and thunder-bolts of Fate shall not bow the noble head of the devoted one.

(5) *Louis Köhler* finds, in a churchyard beneath weeping willows in the pale moonlight on funeral urns, a picture in keeping with the mood of the Adagio. The Allegretto in $D\flat$ leads into a mood smiling through tears, which transforms the earlier

agony of grief into tender consolation. In the Presto agitato, accents of fear and terror, and delirious rapture in the play of unfettered feeling, alternate with moments of sublime resignation teeming with lofty, soulfelt dignity; until, after the fearful career of passion, it falls in deathly lassitude, to break off in a last violent effort of strength.

(6) *Elterlein* regards unspeakable pain, cutting agony of soul, as the key-note of the entire Sonata. In the Adagio the inner suffering appears restrained, repressed; measured sighs escape the tormented heart, but combined, as yet, with a feeling of resignation to the inevitable. The *colorit* of the whole is magical — a twilight, a night-zephir. In the Allegretto we fall as from heaven into an easy, careless, light-living world, and this movement does not agree with the fundamental mood of the others (?!). In the last movement the pain-racked soul upsurges in agonized passion. The repressed feelings find vent; a whirlwind of emotion rages in the heart. As out of the rumbling depths of a volcano, the grewsome demons rise from the crater of the heart with convulsive contortions. The soul struggles fiercely with powers of darkness. But she does not succumb — disenthralling humor glances out in a few passages. The composer's spirit has given free way to its tears, and thus thrown off the spell.

(7) In the eleventh annual volume of the "Neue Berliner Musikzeitung" there is an article by *F. F. Weber* on this Sonata. We quote; — Beethoven, in this sonata, represents dream-scenes which take place amid external, visible Nature. Were we to stand in the hush of night amidst luxuriant vegetation, and did there then approach us, step by step, the natural essences which fill the cells wellnigh to bursting, and in which the vegetable world surrounds us with its living embrace, so that our sense should be finally quite absorbed in the noiseless, yet unremitting activity of the busy vegetable life round about us, that shows in the least leaflet the full intensity of its power: — and should the spirits of this process of Nature continually obtrude themselves upon us, neither withheld nor to

be driven away by any means whatsoever, only occasionally betraying their sublime spirituality by a shy starting back at some sound—no actual sound, but a dream-sound imagined in the shell of our own ear;—were we to experience this, we should then stand as Beethoven fancied himself standing, when writing the last movement of his Sonata in $C\sharp$-minor.

(8) In the fourth annual volume of the Berlin music-journal "Echo", No. 43, is an article by *Peter Cornelius* on the $C\sharp$-minor Sonata, in which he compares the first movement to a majestic Gothic cathedral, whose inviting chimes guide seeking believers on their path through the wilderness to its sacred inclosure. All pain floats upward therein in pious prayer, and is resolved in the harmony of a blessed spirit-world.—In the second movement earthly love holds sway, and would fain drown those sacred chimes with the tones of her harp. To this love is issued the mandate, rather to turn to-wards yon holy refuge, whence she has enticed the devotional throng with irresistible might. In the third movement the dim forest is again sought out. Evil spirits have closed the doors, the holy chimes are mute—yet their echo still sounds; belief is dead in the heart—disconsolate wandering. But the heart is haughty and bold—onward! it must anew soar aloft to the sacred pile, that shines yonder before the tearless eye.

The author has not spared himself the trouble of collecting these eight examples of the interpretation of one and the same work. Should the realist ask: "Is it then really true, that even *one* of the pictures described here lies hidden in the tones? Where is the churchyard, the pale moon, the Gothic cathedral, or nighttime Nature?"—the reply would be, that no proof can really be given of the one or the other, and that the conception by Weber (No. 7) exhibits many incongruities. —Such poetical interpretations derive support solely from the symbolic significance, which forms the subject of other ob-jective combinations as well—from the meaning of gestures, the play of the features, bodily movements; from the intention of landscape notes in painting and poetry; from the peculiar bent of the human soul to reveal its most secret, truest ideal, not in the cool, clear-cut word, but in the picture, the allegory —in that which suggests its own life through similar combination and formation in the objective sphere.—

Any poetical interpretation is lame, even that of an Ulibischeff or a Marx; the fine phrases of such oratorical artists make far too many concessions to their own enjoyment, to do the work and its meaning even approximate justice.

But it is not the concern of the pianoforte player to write out the intent of a Sonata as a poetical exercise before practicing the same; in view of the boundless abundance of affinities between tone and life, he should only begin with the idea, that every noble composition of lyric expression is of such wonderful, innately profound depth, that the soul can translate the most rapturous emotion of its life through *it* alone.— Would he undertake an interpretation, let him bear in mind that *each* is but *one* example of that, which dwells within the tones in far fuller abundance. Beethoven's $C\sharp$-minor Sonata is neither the picture of a churchyard, nor of a temple, nor of renouncing love, nor of an inner struggle; it is more than this —it is the picture of the primal source of the emotions, which are experienced in these several situations. And thus it is with every mood that finds expression in tones. The musical meaning is a degree less developed than that, which the poetical orator can expound from the work before him; he constructs with the tone-material—from this wilderness, this chaos of a still unfinished, unseparated world, a single scene, but loses in so doing the abundant material which refused to be thus wrought up, and which bears a wealth of meaning.

The player must and ought to imagine living affinities. The composition is, withal, a poem—its moods may best be suggested by poetical comparisons—well for the virtuoso, who has ever-present consciousness of musical ideas in allegorical phrase!—but he should never forget, that the latter can be only a suggestion, and that the real meaning is a far broader one.

May this brief exposition of the subject-matter of general musical æsthetics stimulate the student to penetrate in *thought* no less than in *feeling* into the essence of pianoforte compositions. Feeling will be the lovelier, the more it is spiritualized by thought.—Let the player not be content, to leave everything to his blind emotional instinct; in all there dwells a law of beauty, which would be discovered by meditation. In many works the sensuous power of a fine technique may exhaust the meaning—the beauty of the mechanical art, as discussed in the preceding part, is then the intention of the work—but the player must be able to distinguish. The lofty creations of a Beethoven, Bach, Schubert, Schumann, Chopin, Mendelssohn, Brahms, assume beauty of this nature as a precondition; their real essence lies deeper.

Meditation and research—the study of the work in its least detail—the establishment of all elements of beauty on intelligent, scientific knowledge — this is the task. Although pianoforte playing is primarily a *reproductive* art only, the exposition of its subject-matter requires the highest degree of education on the part of the interpreter. The player should draw his inspiration from the spirit of the whole. That he should grasp this, constantly keeping in view, beside the study of the pianoforte, the entire domain of music, and glancing over and beyond the latter to as many sciences as possible, above all to Æsthetics and Psychology, and imbuing his whole conception of life with thoughtful poetry, with a lofty ideality of purpose, of desire, of striving — is the parting injunction wherewith the Æsthetics of Pianoforte Playing ends its task.

THE END.